The *Otter*

James Williams

MERLIN UNWIN BOOKS

First published in Great Britain by Merlin Unwin Books Ltd, 2010

ISBN 978-1-906122-22-5

Published by:
    Merlin Unwin Books Ltd
    Palmers House
    7 Corve Street, Ludlow
    Shropshire SY8 1DB, U.K.

The author asserts his moral right to be identified as the author of this work.
British Library Cataloguing-in-Publication Data:
A catalogue record for this book is available from the British Library.
Designed and typeset in Bembo by Merlin Unwin.
Printed by Leo Paper Products.

DEDICATION

For Jodey Peyton and Hannah Watts, who appreciate otters, and who have given me much encouragement.

THANKS

Thanks are due to my patient wife Elizabeth, for all her support; to Andrew Crawford, Simon Reece and Michelle Werrett, who have advised on parts of the text, and above all to Lucy Mead for so much practical help with all matters ottery.

PHOTOGRAPHIC ACKNOWLEDGEMENTS

The following photographers have generously allowed me to include their fine photos in this book: Ian Anderson, John Crispin, Charlie Hamilton-James, Alison Hickman, Karen Jack, Mary-Rose Lane, David Mason, John McMinn, Arthur Richards, Anne Roslin-Williams, Peter Stronach and the Environment Agency. *(See also page 223)*

CONTENTS

CHAPTER ONE

AN INTRODUCTION TO THE OTTER

Even in the days when otters were plentiful, their surreptitious lifestyle meant that they were seldom seen. People often tell me that despite living on the farm all their lives, they have never seen an otter. What they really mean is that they think I am mistaken and wasting my time looking for signs there.

I find frequent signs of an otter using the stream that runs through my garden, but in 21 years at this house I have seen one only twice. And even those who do get to see one usually have only a fleeting glimpse of a disturbed and secretive animal making itself scarce in poor light at dusk. So it is understandable that less is generally known about the otter than other species. This accounts for some of the myths, misconceptions and downright rubbish that is put about as information on the otter.

An otherwise sane countryman recently assured one of my friends that the otter he saw must have been a bitch, "as a dog otter will never swim under a bridge". How can anybody with a wired-up brain consider that possible?

More plausible is the assertion in the BBC Wildlife magazine for April 2009 that the European Otter has a mating season from February to July, but I know of no information on which this "fact" can be based. However, the recommendation in another magazine that February is a good time to look for cubs, as they emerge from hibernation then, was totally implausible. None of the 13 species of otter hibernates, not even in the high north.

Description of the otter

So it may be as well to start this book with a brief and entirely factual introduction to the animal I am writing about, the Eurasian otter, *Lutra lutra*.

The first point to stress is its size. The otter is Britain's largest predatory animal. It is about a metre long, or even more in the case of a full grown dog otter. Most people expect to see a much smaller animal, because they are accustomed to seeing the smaller species that is commonly kept in zoos and wildlife parks, the Asian short-clawed otter. The most prominent feature of an otter is its long tail, which is almost half the total length, and as thick as a cricket bat handle. Very often it is the only part of the otter that one sees, arcing out of the water as the otter dives, in a manner similar to the flukes of a whale. So distinctive a feature is it that such a glimpse is diagnostic; nothing else has such a fine rudder.

One of the best places for a daytime sighting of the Eurasian otter is on the seashore. This one is foraging among the kelp in Scotland. It is not a 'sea otter' – no such species distinction exists in Europe.

The other end is unmistakable too. Otters have a broad skull, which is in many ways similar in size and shape to the head of a Border terrier. They have short faces; the mouth is surprisingly narrow for so big an animal. The main difference between them and the terrier is the very small ears of the otter, resembling merely two inverted commas: 'O'. This seems to emphasise the width of the flat skull. The only other creature likely to be peering at you from the water is the mink, which is much smaller, with an inconsiderable and narrow head, and a pointy face. It looks like a ferret that has been in a pencil sharpener. A mink is smaller and slimmer than a cat, and has a tail no longer than a pen, though of course fluffy.

The body of the otter is large. Adults weigh more than foxes, sometimes nearly twice as much; I often give the average weight as "a fox and a half", although, as they are not as leggy, nor as furry, they do not give the same impression of size. Despite relying on their coat to keep warm in the water, as they do not carry a layer of blubber for insulation, their fur is surprisingly short, and it follows the outline of the skin closely at all points. Mink have more luxuriant and fluffy pelts, which is good for an animal which has to tolerate winter in the Canadian Arctic.

A dry otter is a rich chocolate brown in colour, all over. When wet they can seem black. There may be a paleness on the throat, or even some small creamy spots under the chin, but

Undoubtedly an otter – the large thick tail, often seen breaking the surface when the otter dives, is a key distinguishing feature of the species and a useful clue when watching from dry land with binoculars.

basically what you see is a uniformly brown, cylindrical animal, low to the ground, with a very long tail. Like most members of their family, (mustelids, or weasels), they have a humped back above their hind legs, and when they run, they bound, almost jump, along. Their backs are too long for trotting, left–right, left–right, to be comfortable or efficient, so they bound. As befits a swimmer, they have very large feet, especially the hind feet. One does not often see their feet clearly, but the size of their five-toed padding in the riverside sand is surprising: 5 centimetres' width is normal, but I measured one recently which left an 8 centimetre impression in the mud.

Otters are always associated with water, although perversely, many of the ones that get spotted are ones that are taking a short cut, or moving to another stream, and are thus temporarily away from the water which hides them from us so often. Many more otters see people than people see otters.

Should an intruder appear, the otter will just submerge, and then either swim to some nearby cover, from which it can keep an eye, a nose, and an ear on the danger, without exposing more than a hand-sized portion of its body above the surface, or it will clear off out of it, by swimming for more than 50 metres without showing at all. If it does not want you to see it, you won't. I was in a tall bird hide at Shapwick Heath when an otter swam unconcernedly right in front of it. Suddenly, she became aware of me looking down on her through the observation slot. No panic, but after a short pause, she just sank. Not a crash dive, with a defiant wave of the rudder; she just sank. I was only 20 yards from her, and had binoculars, but I could not see her. There was no movement in the reeds, so at first I thought she must still be there.

After about quarter of an hour, I decided that she must have gone, and was marvelling at her ability to slip away so inconspicuously without rippling the reeds, when very gently they moved, as she quietly edged away underwater. She had been there all the time, and must have been breathing, at least, if not keeping an eye on me, but I could not see her.

The swimming otter

They have two styles of swimming when they are going unconcernedly about their lives. When they swim on the surface, they have a

very low profile in the water, which deceives people into underestimating their size. Very often most of the body is submerged, so the profile of the head is followed at a distance of a couple of feet by the top of the hump of its hind quarters, and then by the tip of the rudder some distance behind; three separate bits, with the rest submerged: unless one gets a clear view, it does not look like a big animal at all. That is when the otter is in cruise mode.

If it is being more purposeful, travelling, or feeding, it adopts the more efficient 'porpoising' method of swimming, progressing rapidly, at times completely under water, and then regularly jumping clear in a rolling forward dive.

The reason otters are linked to water is that their main food is fish, of all kinds. The small mouth and sharp teeth are an adaptation for catching and holding small fish and eels. For so large a predator it is at first surprising how much of their habitual diet is made up of very small items like sticklebacks and minnows.

I know of four instances of an otter taking lambs, so they could easily cope with larger victims, but they generally keep to fish. Two

An otter cuts a snakey line through a freshwater pond, its low position in the water makes the animal appear smaller than it really is.

of the four rogue otters were debilitated, and desperate, so in their cases it was something enforced on them by circumstance. Until then, they had been fish eaters, too. Otters are happy to take large fish when they can, but there are many more tiddlers than specimen fish in a river, and the bigger the fish the faster and more elusive it is, so the otters take any and every chance that presents itself; that results in a diet of small items, mainly.

To get an adequate meal regularly, an otter must cover a considerable length of river. Dog otters in Somerset, where I live, seem to need more than 10 kms; in Scotland over 50 kms has been recorded. Whereas a fox or badger is never far from any part of its home range, and is well placed all the time to deal with any incursion by rivals, an otter, whose territory is linear, has to be many miles away from some part or other of it all the time. To protect its supply of fish, it has to mark its patch with 'keep out' notices, and it must patrol it regularly.

Marking is done by means of its droppings, called spraints, which it deliberately deposits onto prominent rocks and tree roots, as an easily-found and recognised scent marker, to inform any other otter that may happen along.

The patrolling otter

The other result of an otter requiring so much space, so long a length of river, is that they are wanderers. To defend it, they must patrol it, so an otter seldom spends long in any one place. It has a whole series of resting places, or "holts" where it can sleep away the day, and it moves frequently from one to another, renewing the spraint warnings as it goes. Otter researchers argue whether they have a regular pattern of patrol or not. I say not: there are too many other factors involved, like seasonal foods, disturbance or flooding. But if they do not patrol to a regular rhythm, they regularly patrol: here today, somewhere else tomorrow, back next week, perhaps.

For such a way of life, it is obviously better to be solitary. If otters regularly went about as a pair, they would require more territory to provide the extra fish they would need. As they live on a river, more territory always means longer, which also means longer in time to patrol. A longer territory might take so much time to cover that it would cut down on the feeding time, which is a bad idea for an animal which has to make so many little kills in a night. And anyway, if the items they are eating are so small, they cannot share them, any more than they can co-operate in catching them. Lions and wolves hunt as a team, and share the plentiful meat of the deer or zebra. If you are trying to catch nippy little sticklebacks, the only tactic is, grab it and scoff it: no opportunity for teamwork there.

The socialising otter

Being solitary poses a social problem. How does a solitary, defensive, territory-holding animal meet others of its kind without fusing the system of feeding on which it depends. Otters are both exceptionally playful, and aggressive. This is one of the reasons why they are not found in zoos very often: they can be dangerous without warning. I watched a man doing some minor repairs to one of the pens at the Otter Trust place in Cornwall. He was the regular keeper and feeder of what appeared to be a very chummy

An otter makes a dash for the water. Note the powerful muscular development and the arched lower back, typical of mustelids.

otter, but he had another keeper in the pen with him all the time, just in case, vigilantly carrying a substantial broom with which to ward off any attack from the territory-owner of the pen.

In the wild, they fight frequently. On other occasions they will be seen to greet another otter, and to play energetically and affectionately. It seems probable that these are otters that know each other, probably relations, cubs from a former litter, or siblings. But it is hard to be

sure with a species which is without distinguishing markings, and perpetually mobile.
Especially as any sightings are usually made at
dusk, in a fading light.

The exceptions are often a bitch with her
cubs. The overactive and always hungry cubs
tend to be out and about in daytime more
than solitary adults, so they are noticed more.
Unpredictable and dangerous changes in river
level mean that an otter cub cannot become
independent until it is fully grown and has
reached full strength. So they have to stay with
the bitch for a full year or more.

During the latter part of their adoles-
cence they seem as big as mama, especially the
lummocking gurt dog cubs, who will soon
outgrow their mother. So people see a family
group of three or four otters, and assume that
this is how they normally live, but the norm
for this species is a solitary, independent hunter,
which emerges only at dusk, and so is seldom
seen.

Night sightings

That is another reason why they are poor
animals for a zoo that is open to the public; they
are by instinct nocturnal. This is an adaptation
to the lifestyle of their prey. Many more fish
are available to them after dark, especially their
favourite and staple item, the eel.

As otters catch most of their food by feel
rather than sight, the darkness does not impede
them. But it makes them much less accessible
to our investigations, much harder to study
than other species, as this book will show. And
it explains why there is so much myth about
them, myth that needs dispelling if we their
well-wishers are to offer them the same degree
of conservation that we afford to other, often
less vulnerable, species.

A patrolling otter emerges fleetingly from the river – quite possibly to leave its spraint as a territorial marker on the rock. This unusual photo, taken by wildlife photographer Charlie Hamilton-James, captures the time of day when river otters become most active and it demonstrates why they are so difficult to see at dusk.

How to distinguish an otter's pad mark from that of the badger, dog, fox and mink

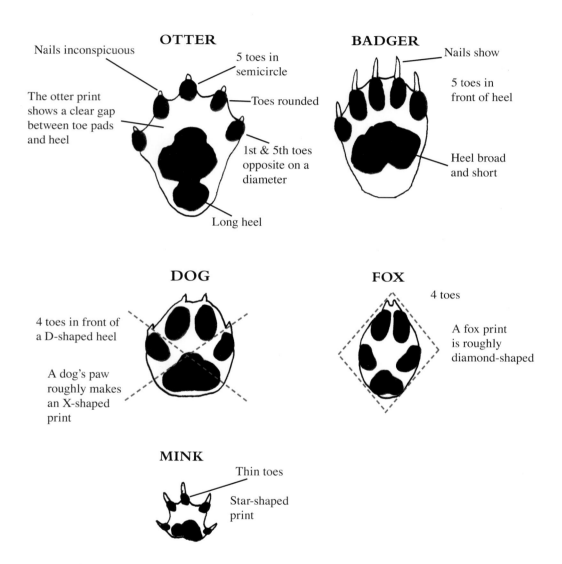

OTTER

Nails inconspicuous

5 toes in semicircle

The otter print shows a clear gap between toe pads and heel

Toes rounded

1st & 5th toes opposite on a diameter

Long heel

BADGER

Nails show

5 toes in front of heel

Heel broad and short

DOG

4 toes in front of a D-shaped heel

A dog's paw roughly makes an X-shaped print

FOX

4 toes

A fox print is roughly diamond-shaped

MINK

Thin toes

Star-shaped print

NB. If the mud is hard an otter's print may show only 4 toes but you can still tell it apart from a dog because the 4 toes will be off centre to the heel mark.

CHAPTER TWO

A PIVOTAL EVENT

The pivotal event I want to describe to you was such an ordinary scene that you would have scarcely considered it an 'event'. It will be as hard for you to appreciate the full significance of that cold morning as it will be for me to convey it to you. What happened? I took my dogs for a walk, and returned in a very good mood. Why? Well, I found some footprints in the riverside mud. Significant? Pivotal? Yes, for us all. Let me explain.

Sunday 1 February 1987 was a drab, unfriendly sort of day; the sky was grey and textureless, merging with an enveloping cold haze which was draining all life and colour out of the countryside. The air was raw and penetrating. It was a day without attraction, a day to enjoy the snugness of our thatched cottage, a day to open the doors of the woodburner and enjoy the flames. But as it was a Sunday, the dogs were entitled to a decent walk. On my working days they had to make do with a brisk morning walk down the lane, and a very scanty outing in the dark after I got back.

So on Sundays I would go farther, frequently to the river. In the green lane I was sheltered by the uncut hedges on the high banks, but when I came out onto the riverside fields, I felt the full chill of the east wind. To give in to my inclination to cut the walk short and turn back would have been to shortchange the dogs, so

reluctantly I hunched on. I set the cattle bridge as my turning point. And when I got there I glanced down out of habit at the mud.

An otter had walked across the mud. There was a set of prints, clearly fixed by the frost, heading upstream. There were no other signs nearby (I searched hard and the dogs got quite an extended morning that day). So we went home for lunch.

We had friends from London staying at the time. They like the things of the countryside, and realise our involvement with it. However, I do not think I succeeded in explaining to them that the excitement, the significance, was of a different order of magnitude from seeing Long-tailed Tits, or a Nuthatch, say, on the bird table. Several orders of magnitude.

The wanderer had returned, after an absence of eight years. But this otter was not a prodigal coming home to its birthplace. It was more an immigrant, an immigrant returning from beyond the grave, and its padding and its spraints brought with them an optimism that quite dispelled the bleakness of the February weather.

The long, sharp toenails show that this youngster lives on the peat moors, not on stony rivers where nails are quickly worn down.

Every journey begins with a step, and those footsteps, which must have been printed on the night of 27/28 January 1987, the only night that the mud was sufficiently frost-free, represented the beginning of the resurgence of the species onto the Tone, a river formerly famous in the annals of the otter hunters for its strong otter population.

To those knowledgeable and otter-supportive old sportsmen it would have been unthinkable that so widespread a species could be completely extirpated from not just one river, nor just one region, but from literally 95% of the entire country. I had watched it happen, and helped record their passing, yet still I found it hard to realise how thorough had been their demise.

Suppose it had been the fox that vanished, not the otter. That too is an animal whose unseen presence one takes for granted. Suppose that a man who said in a pub that he had seen a fox was automatically considered either a liar or a man who cannot tell a ginger cat from a fox.

Suppose that smallholders no longer shut their hens in at night, that there was no barking under the January moon, and that a dead fox by the side of a road made a note in the national papers. It is hard to accept in one's head, even as an example, but that is the extent of what had happened to the otters, the wonderful animals that I have doted on all my life.

And because I feel so strongly that we should not let another such disaster happen again, I wish to recount the story of the decline and resurgence of the otter and my involvement in it.

I cannot remember a time when otters were not a major aspect of my life. My father was deputy Master, and the Huntsman, of the Kendal and District Otterhounds, so otters were often talked about in our house, and we tagged along as nippers to some of the irregularly organised hunts that took place whenever people were available during the war.

Much of that period is a childhood blur in my memory, of course, a sort of composite collage of impressions, but I have very clear recall of one day in particular on the Lupton Beck, at Lupton Mill. It must have been in 1946, as two of the young hounds were called Monty and UNO. (I can remember the hounds more clearly than the people; we children liked them much better.)

The sleek profile of the otter which makes it such an efficient swimmer in water.

Otter traps removed

Although the general rural attitude of those days was much less respectful towards wildlife in general and otters in particular, they were not universally regarded as vermin. The hunting conferred some sort of status on the otter as a beast of the chase, and even those who sought to trap them with gins to sell their skins looked on them as a resource rather than an enemy. So my father spent much time in PR work on behalf of the otters, and in conservation work of various kinds. The hunt maintained a series of

artificial holts, and sought to buy off trappers.

One of my most exciting early memories concerns one gamekeeper who did not want to be bought off. He worked for the widow of a General on an estate where all forms of shooting and sport had lapsed since the old man's death. The widow was keen on her alpine plants, so Christen's main job was to eliminate all the rabbits, a ruthless attitude he freely and unbidden extended to all other forms of wildlife which he could exploit for private gain.

He had got rid of just about everything interesting from his own patch, but still he industriously kept a set of otter traps going, to benefit from the passing of any wanderers crossing from the rivers Bela to the Lune. As both these rivers were good for otters, his efforts were a steady drain on both populations, but from the elevated moorland location of the estate he was not in a position to get to grips with the residents on the main rivers, just the dispersing transients between them. So he extended his activities down onto the main stem of the River Lune, where his well-sited traps became a serious depletion of the breeding stock.

Father got to hear of this, so one evening, towards dusk, he put me on the back of his little autocycle, and we set off through the lanes to Lincoln's Inn Bridge. A real ride, of a dozen miles or so, was adventure enough, but when we got there my role was explained. I was to keep an eye on the bike, and make a noise if anybody came, while he nipped across the meadow and sabotaged the traps. I am not sure how many there were, but it seemed a long wait in the half-light for a solitary small boy, scared but also excited. Subsequently he showed me the site of the main trap as we passed through on a hunt one day. It was put in among the roots of a sycamore tree where erosion had exposed a curtain of tentacle-like roots, behind which was a ledge or small cave. The roots faced onto

a deep pool, and that was part of the effectiveness of the trap; the gin was firmly wired to a strong root with baler wire, but it had a generous length of chain.

The idea was that any passing otter would run along the concealed ledge and get trapped by the foot, whereupon it would dive for the safety of the river. Here the weight of the chain would quickly drown it, before it had damaged the skin by struggling, or had contaminated the ledge with the scent of blood. One good skin to sell, and every chance of getting the next otter to pass that way. As this was on the main river, sooner or later most of the nomads would pass that way. A nice and not-so-little earner. But father said that our secret attentions to his traps had scared him back onto his own (or the widow's) patch, where he had some sort of right to be, and where he could not have been accused of poaching.

The baler wire remained for many years. I took my son to show him the place in the late 1970s, at least 30 years after that dramatic evening. By that time our family was living on the widow's estate, which father had bought in 1948. There was excitement over that, too. Our parents had gone all edgy and mysterious for several weeks, and with a disquieting tension in the air we all set off for Kirkby Lonsdale in the car, in itself an infrequent trip in the days of strict petrol rationing. We were given a penny bun each, and told to sit quiet in the car, while our parents did some business. When they came out of the solicitors, then we were at last told. We had bought a new house, and would be moving to a lovely place with a lake. In fact we were going straight there now, never mind the petrol.

Back up the Old Scotch Road we went, through our village, and on across the moorland and sheep lots, farther than we children had ever been. There was a purpose to our trip. We went straight to the lodge where the keeper lived,

The lovely lake and boathouse where I grew up near Kirkby Lonsdale – scene of my earliest exercises in conservation.

were clogged, but while digging out the banks with my spade I had also to leave sufficient and well-sited overhanging verges for the fish to have shelter from the herons.

The increasing trout population benefited us, as the fishing showed better sport, but it also attracted the otters. The long-gone keeper would have employed an easy and comprehensive elimination of the problem of their increased presence at spawning time, but we eventually hit on a less drastic solution. I would go out and hang a storm lantern with a flickering paraffin flame from the hand rail of the footbridge, in such a way that it could sway in the breeze. As long as the light was a little bit mobile, the otters would not pass under it. If it was more firmly fixed, they could summon enough courage to go past and despoil the spawning grounds.

It may not sound very important when baldly explained in outline like that, but you should try to imagine the whole experience of the important small boy, charged with filling the hurricane lamp, and lighting it correctly so that it would not gutter out in the breeze, nor burn so over-confidently and brightly that it would use up all the fuel before dawn.

And then I had to set off down the winding path through the darkened pinewoods, where most but not all of the noises were familiar and unfrightening. At the bridge there was the fixing of the light, and then the return without it. The following morning it had to be retrieved, and I would walk quietly up the beck, thrilled to see

and father gave him instant notice to go. There would be no more otter traps on that watershed crossing place.

Boyhood otter conservation

And once we moved there it became an ongoing excitement to help my parents restore the wildlife to its right place and levels. One task I learned to help with was clearing and maintaining the spawning beck to try to get the trout population in the lake back to a good standard. I needed to ensure that the spates had not eroded into the peaty soil in such a way that the gravel beds

safe fish darting off the redds (spawning beds) into the shelter of my carefully maintained overhangs, and reassured to find little evidence of a wasteful feast by the otters. Few conservationists can have had such instant rewards for their labours, or such easily ascertainable evidence that what they had done was making a difference. For I could check the nearby lake shores, and find fresh spraint as proof that my lantern had been necessary.

So otters, and their wellbeing have been part of my life since my earliest memories.

Left: big whiskers, big webbed feet, big bottom and big tail – an unmistakeable otter.

Below: Otters are affectionate creatures and seem to enjoy contact with one another.

The otters vanish

Now you must try to imagine what a person with such an early indoctrination felt when all the otters died. And those of you who succeed will start to understand the pivotal significance of the set of tracks in the mud below the cattle bridge on that cold winter's morning.

The thatched cottage we lived in at the time of the miraculous reappearance of the otter had been our home since our marriage in 1968. I was slightly familiar with the nearby river Tone, from following the Culmstock Otter Hounds, and from being a member of the Taunton Flyfishers. So when we moved there I had high hopes of being able to undertake some sort of detailed study of the local otters, and took every opportunity of going down to the river and recording the spraints and padding.

But in 1968, and up to 1970, I could not tell t'other from which: there was too much otter evidence. Although the hunt had started to worry about a bit of a downturn in the population, as far as I could see the river was full; everywhere I looked there was fresh evidence. My plans for a survey came to nothing. I could see little point in recording that there was yet again an otter at the places where there always was.

However, by 1973, I was starting to record gaps. My notes show 9 positive and 17 negative records in the first three weeks of April, and several mink. This was sufficiently worrying that three of us, all hunt followers, made an effort to look at most of the River Tone above Taunton. On 27 April I recorded the results of a concerted effort to check all the main river and its tributaries between Greenham and the town. The stretches where plentiful otter activity had frustrated my attempts at a survey only two years earlier lie in the centre of this. We covered over 35 km of prime otter water, and found only one probable sign at one place. Something drastic was happening. It was perhaps as well that I did not know that the problem was to last 14 years until that cold, grey, auspicious Sunday in February 1987.

LOSS AND RECOVERY OF THE OTTERS

The two charts below show the completeness of the loss of 'my' otters, and their remarkable recovery after that pivotal day in February 1987. I have included the two adjacent rivers, to prove that my otters had really gone, and were not simply hiding round the corner in another part of the catchment. Both graphs show the number of records for a whole year, that is instances of evidence, not a count of otters. That there were five completely blank years is validated by the number of records we at once started to find on their return: it shows, that had they been there, we would have picked them up.

The right-hand chart complements the first. It shows the otters getting steadily more established, right from their return. It also shows that useful information can be deduced from monitoring even one place regularly. The effect of a major pollution in 2002 is obvious, and also, the unknown problem that affected the whole of our area in 2006 shows up clearly. But the overall impression from these two sets of figures is very encouraging, as long as we heed the warning implicit in the first one.

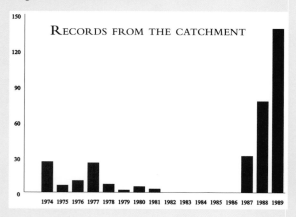

RECORDS FROM THE CATCHMENT

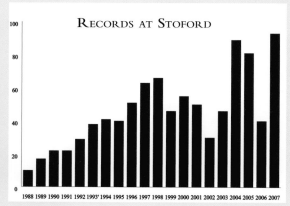

RECORDS AT STOFORD

CHAPTER THREE

THE OTTER ITSELF

For many years I have been trying to poke my inquisitive nose into the private life of the otter, a creature by nature withdrawn and secretive, whose instinctive defensive reaction is just to vanish, and to remove itself to a place of greater solitude and privacy. Despite its aversion to publicity, I think I have pieced together quite a lot of the jigsaw puzzle of its way of life, and it will be instructive to me to try to get as much of it as I can down in one chapter. Rather like a painter stepping back from his easel to peruse the general effect of what he has achieved so far, it will give me an overview of the bits we understand and the bits we do not.

Although there is much we do not yet know about the species, we do know enough to be able to refute some of the more arrant nonsense written about them. I hope an attempt to marshal what I know that I know in one place may be of interest to others, and may help me to direct my future enquiries more purposefully, which may benefit the otters themselves; they do not have an easy time of it, living in the modern world.

The 'British' otter is the species known as *Lutra lutra*. We have only one species, the Common or Eurasian otter. People insist on calling the otters found in the sea off the coast of Scotland 'Sea Otters', but that is wrong; all our otters are the same, the very successful and widespread species, which is the only one found north of the Himalayas and west of Japan, an enormous range. It also occurs further south and east, down through India and South-east Asia, but there it shares the waters with three other species. There are such things as Sea Otters, but they occur only in the Pacific.

Three otter cubs cautiously emerge from a holt. This is the most common number of young to be born in a litter.

When is an otter not an otter? Well, when it is a mink. I have searched in some fairly heavy and joke-free books, but cannot find a definition of an otter. There are considerable descriptions of the features the species have in common, and of the differences between them, but no exact answer to the question of what constitutes being an otter. The books are by contrast very precise as to the definitions of 'dog' and 'fox'. Nor is there agreement as to how many species of otter there are.

You may recollect that Gavin Maxwell (Scottish naturalist and author of *Ring of Bright Water*) thought for a while that he had discovered a new species in the Tigris marshes when he was living with the Marsh Arabs. Most authorities do not accept those otters now as anything more than a sub-species. Chanin in 1985 listed 9 species that Davis (1978) had reduced from Harris' (1968) list of 19. Since then DNA studies have expanded things again, and most people now accept 13 otter species world-wide. I have seen seven of them, and missed out on three which were evidently present where I was. At first glance, an otter is evidently an otter, no matter what the species: a medium-sized, long-bodied, streamlined animal with a broad skull and a major tail, that also has legs, so is not any kind of seal, although it hunts freely and skilfully in water.

Three mammals often mistaken for otters

They are all Carnivores, of the family Mustelidae, the very successful group which includes all the weasels, badgers and skunks as well. The thirteen otters form the Lutrinae sub-family. However, there is no need to go into these technicalities in detail, except to eliminate three animals that sometimes cause confusion. The sea otters of California and Alaska: there are no sea otters anywhere else.

The American mink, a ferret-sized little animal, thousands of which were released into our rivers from fur farms by environmentally illiterate criminals: they became widespread and numerous during the time that otters were very scarce, so many people confused them for otters, but they are much smaller, and have pathetic tails; an otter's rudder is longer than a whole mink, body and tail. I always ask people who are not sure what they have seen, to judge the result of a theoretical fight between the waterside animal and their cat. If it was an otter, they should reply, "Dead cat in under three minutes." Otters are very large, and their tails can be even bigger than cricket bat handles.

The third source of confusion is another species of otter, the Asiatic Short-clawed Otter, *Aonyx cinereus*. This is a gregarious, small otter, and because it is gregarious, it is much less aggressive than our solitary and territorial sort. For this reason they are the ones most frequently kept in zoos and 'wildlife parks.' Therefore most people have come to think that they are the normal otter, and expect something more the size of a mink than the actual size of our otter. When I go to collect dead otters from helpful people, for the post-mortem programme, I am

always assured that it is a surprisingly big one. Often it is only an immature, but the finders are still astonished at what a large creature it is. They formed their expectation at a zoo. From time to time short-claws have escaped into the wild in England, and there was for a while a small population near Oxford. As far as I know, life on our rivers is too demanding for them, and they cannot establish themselves. So I mention them only to prevent confusion.

How sensitive is an otter to disturbance?

When English otters were in decline, people put it about that it is a species particularly demanding in its requirements, and especially susceptible to disturbance or habitat degradation. This became an exaggerated mantra, and otters, by then so scarce as to be pretty-well mythical, became in people's mind a sort of zoological angel, to be found only in circumstances approaching a heavenly, unsullied, environmental perfection.

This is of course nonsense: the species is obviously extremely adaptable, as can be deduced from its success in occupying so wide a range world-wide. I have found sprints in the Anti-Atlas of Morocco, beside rivers that exist as water features only in winter. It occupies the rainforest rivers of S.E.Asia, the snow-fed torrents of the Himalayas, the saline marsh of Spain's Coto Doñana, ice-bound rivers in wintery Sweden, and the benign chalk streams of southern England. They are now to be found in many of our towns and cities. It is perhaps not very surprising that this spring a dead

The invasive American mink is often mistaken for an otter and is fond of watercourses. But it is a much smaller creature with a shorter tail. Culling mink has been important for watervole conservation.

bitch otter was found outside County Hall in Taunton, and one of her cubs was rescued from the grounds of the hospital, but they have also been filmed in Newcastle and Birmingham, places where the rivers are much more degraded and abused. Since we have chosen to build most of our settlements beside rivers, the otters have little choice; that is why I called my first book, *The Otter Among Us*.

If we want to conserve a species with so large a territorial requirement, a species which has to impinge on 'our' space, we cannot do it by setting up a series of discrete reserves, such as we would found to protect birds like nesting terns, or scarce plants like a colony of orchids. But this shows the resilience and adaptability of the species, not its vulnerability.

Requirements of the otter

Although otters have not yet re-colonised all their former range across England, they are already to be found in a wide variety of habitats, so it is difficult for me to address the topic of what their preferred circumstances are. One cannot deduce from the presence of an otter that the circumstances in which it is living are those that it prefers. In a well-established population, some will be forced to occupy places not entirely to their liking; in a situation of scarcity, an otter may have as its priority the need to find other otters, and may be living in a place it would not otherwise choose to settle in.

But their basic requirements are for food, shelter and space. The need for space comes from our species of otter being a basically solitary animal. They do not go about in pairs, nor are they faithful to a mate for life. Yet they are also social, and need, or at least enjoy, the contact of their own kind. Because we cannot readily identify individuals, we are not at all sure how

these apparently contradictory requirements are resolved.

The solitariness stems from the need to feed so large an animal from a river. I think that rivers are the basic natural habitat for which the species has evolved, rather than coasts or swamps, although they adapt so well to these other sorts of place that one cannot be dogmatic about this.

To feed from a river, an animal must either progress along it, or deplete one small area very severely, as a breeding bitch mink will. There is therefore a minimum length that can provide enough food, and a maximum length that a defending animal can afford the time and the energy to protect. Pressure from the neighbour at either end may compromise the full length of the territory. These maximum and minimum distances would have to be expanded if the otters were to go about as a pair, or to form a small clan, as badgers do. That would put strain on the individual animal, in that the longer home range would require more time and more energy to patrol than so large an animal can afford to take away from the important business of feeding.

Otters cannot turn to enormous prey items, as lions do; we do not have such fish in our rivers. Nor can they co-operate for defensive purposes, as badgers do; there are insufficient easily available prey items for a clan. The size of our otter is in balance with the amount of food normally produced by the length of river an animal of that size can readily cover, if it operates alone.

A healthy river

Many, perhaps most of our rivers, are at present in a damaged condition, and carry far fewer fish than they normally used to. There is no doubt that this stresses the otters. It may be the cause of the current increase in fighting, hungry

A fine fish but not a full meal for a large predator like the otter.

otters reacting severely to competitors. It may also be the reason why otters are seen feeding in daytime more often nowadays. It used to be that most otters seen in daylight, in England at least (in Scotland, the nights are so short that otters have to become active before dusk) most otters seen in daytime were travellers passing through, perhaps because they had been disturbed.

As they made their way along the river, they would sometimes snack as they went, although often their speed was too purposeful for much of that. I have several notes of otters moving with an apparent purpose or destination in mind, so steady and determined was their progress.

More recently I have observed prolonged periods of fishing in the daytime, and have commented on the large number of items taken, and the considerable volume of the total meal.

Overtime hunting may be a necessity forced onto the otter by the scarcity of food items.

The otter's diet

Otters mainly eat fish. That is the main form of protein in their chosen aquatic habitat, and what they are adapted for. For so large an animal, otters have very small jaws; their canine teeth are about 21 mm apart, which is a suitable width for piercing and holding a small fish or a narrow eel.

Although they can pursue larger fish in a dramatic chase through open water, their main method of obtaining food is foraging rather than hunting. They fossick around in root systems, weed beds, or the bases of reeds, for whatever is lurking in there. This means that they catch a lot of small specimens, and fish such as sticklebacks, or even bullheads pulled out one at a time

Above: The Helmsdale in Scotland and on the bank lie the remains of a spring salmon.
Below: a close-up of the fish with my flyrod for scale. The otter will often eat only part of a big fish – the heart and the innards are choice parts.

from beneath their stones, form a large part of their diet. This in turn means that they do not usually hunt as a team. It is all this scrabbling about among stones that keeps otters' toenails so short. Unlike badger padding, they seldom show up as a features of a footprint.

But one otter I picked up dead near Glastonbury had long, delicately curved nails, like a shop girl or a bird of prey. It had lived all its life among the peat diggings of the Brue valley, where there are no stones to turn over. There one can see the otters hunting along the base of the reed beds, or diving down into the submerged branches of fallen trees. Much of what they get is fishy, but some of it is invertebrate prey, probably mainly dragonfly larvae.

Recent research into the diet of the otters on the nature reserves in that area has shown that those otters take a larger percentage of birds

than has been found in similar studies in other places. Danny de la Hey demonstrated that the otters take more coots than moorhens, although they took a variety of bird species. This probably backs up the supposition that otters take what they come across; their foraging behaviour is more likely to cause them to encounter roosting coots, which prefer the water margins, than moorhens, which roost higher and farther into the reed beds.

This is further supported by his finding that they take most birds at the time of year when most birds are available, in July, when the newly fledged young water birds must be easy and common targets. Yet Rafael Miranda's study showed that they are apparently not exploiting the prolific food source provided by the recently introduced foreign fish species: the sunbleak, the top-mouth gudgeon, and even the carp. These fish featured far less commonly than their numerical availability would suggest.

This might be for one of three reasons. The otters may be selectively preying on the species their parent introduced them to: their preference may be cultural, or learned, as it is in peregrines. Or they may be exercising a choice from a 'menu'. They take more eels than anything else; this may be a liking, or a recognition that eel is a better source of nourishment. But I think it is probably that the otters encounter more sticklebacks than sunbleak because of the lifestyle of the fish; sticklebacks lurk about weedy water margins, while sunbleak are much more lively, shoal fish from open water. An otter is less likely to encounter a sunbleak, and it would require more energy to catch it. Economy of effort is a vital consideration for a mammal in water, an animal with a long territory to patrol, and a territory that can become a fast-flowing spate.

So one returns to the platitude that otters mainly eat fish, as one would expect. They also eat whatever else is available, crayfish, frogs and toads, small mammals. Dion Warner found in his recent analysis of spraints from the levels in the Parrett catchment that Water Vole featured very regularly, although water voles are much less common than they were. This readiness to expand their habitual diet as occasion arises is what makes them so frequently turn to domesticated fish in garden ponds. Any old fish will do.

So otters, being able to turn their hands to a variety of prey, live anywhere where there is shelter for them. Shelter means shelter from the elements, as well as shelter from intrusion. All mustelids sleep a lot, and they seek a place where they can undertake this necessary, restorative activity. Their metabolisms are set at a faster rate than other animals of a similar size, about 40% higher when at rest. In the water, swimming at up to 5.5km an hour, their 'rev counter' is running at 4.5 times as fast as a dog's.

Not only does this mean that they eat a lot more, by comparison, they also have to eat more frequently, as the whole digestive process has a more rapid throughput. This means that they are very active indeed when they are out and about, but then they need to sleep a lot to balance things out. More than three-quarters of their time is spent in sleep, so the places for this necessary therapy are important.

The river Huntspill in Somerset is an artificial channel built to service an ammunition factory. It runs dead straight for over five miles, and lacked any bankside cover. So, although it was full of fish, it held no otters until Marie White, who was working for the Environment Agency, installed two artificial holts. At once the otters started to use it.

Otter holts

I think more holts are artificial than natural. All the otter requires is a hole of some kind, preferably not too large in diameter, with a dry ledge or space to sleep on. Bedding is not needed, and the animal will cheerfully paddle up a wet drain to reach a dry ledge where part of the stone structure has fallen away.

On our lake in Westmorland they regularly lay up on a flight of bare stone steps leading down from the upstairs room of the boathouse into the water chamber below where the boat was kept. Out of sight and out of the damp are prescriptions easy to find in many man-made drains, culverts and mills.

Otters have many such dwelling places to choose from along a ten-mile stretch of river, and some of them will be favourite places, that have sheltered many generations of otters. Others will be used less frequently, on an opportunistic basis. I think that the otter is going about its business at dawn when it hears an unexpectedly early tractor start up, so instantly decides that it is time for some sleep, and that this handy tree root will do. As otter holts are strictly protected

A pile of flood debris — mainly logs and sticks — on the North Tyne. The perfect home for an otter.

by law, this chancing approach to where they shelter poses an interesting problem of legal definition; almost anything can be a temporary otter holt, even an old scrap car dumped by a hillbilly farmer to try to prevent erosion on a river bend.

But otters do not use holts as often as we think. Like most animals, they enjoy warmth and sunlight, so frequently curl up in a bit of scrub, a bracken patch, or a bramble bush, to sleep the day away above ground. The traditional pattern of activity is for an otter to emerge at dusk, and set about feeding. After food, they are programmed to travel, to go to another part of their range. This can be seen in zoos where the animals roam round and round after they have been fed. In the wild this is when they renew the spraints that delineate their claimed territory. Then comes a sleep. Unless there is some pressing social activity, sprainting, mating or fighting, most otters take a nap in the night.

This intermittent pattern of activity is observable in the otters we watch from the bird hides on the Somerset Levels. They fish, then

they go into the reeds, then they emerge after a while, and fish again. They take naps, which restore their energy, and their warmth. The otters that fish in the night-time do not bother to go to ground in a holt for their naps, but curl up anywhere warm and out of the wind. They very often do the same at dawn, when they settle down for the day.

Natural holts are usually in the holes and narrow tunnels formed in the roots of a waterside tree when the winter floods cause it to tilt towards the stream, and thereby lift some of the roots. Otters will enlarge and adapt such openings, but they seldom dig a complete burrow from scratch in this part of the world. There is little need; they find more than enough tree roots, drains, or rabbit holes.

In the treeless parts of the Scottish coasts they do dig into the peat, which is easier than excavating compacted riverside gravels in this area. So there is seldom a spoil heap to betray the entrance to a holt, and they are often overlooked because they are so small. Otters like a snug dwelling, and can get through a gap of about six inches.

Although bedding is sometimes taken in by an adult this is usually a sign that the holt is being prepared for breeding. Some breeding holts are long established. Others are just rabbit holes up a side stream. I fancy that cubs are, more often than not, born in a natural holt. It may be that most man-made holts, having been designed as drains or part of a water control system, are prone

Her white lip makes this Somerset otter easy to identify, unlike most others. Distinguishing otters one from another is one of the biggest challenges to the field researcher.

to flooding in a downpour. But as bitch otters are even more secretive and circumspect than usual when they have young cubs, we do not know as much as we would like about the early stages of an otter's life.

Breeding

They have been recorded as being born in any month of the year. They do not seem to have a fixed breeding season. In the far north of Scotland, there seems to be some sort of synchronicity that gets most of the young otters above ground at the start of the calmer weather, but here in Somerset we find cubs of different ages at any season. Perhaps we have a peak of breeding between bonfire night and Christmas, but that is an estimate from the discovery of the bodies of lactating females; it may be that mothers manage better at other periods of the year, so we find fewer dead ones.

As cubs remain in the holt until they are much older than puppies or fox cubs would be when first allowed out to play, we seldom know exactly when, or where, they were born. It is thought that a bitch moves her cubs regularly, but we usually only know of this when something goes wrong, perhaps when she is having to evacuate a holt in the face of rapidly rising waters.

We know nothing of the method by which the dispersal of the young is achieved, along a linear habitat among an aggressively territorial set of neighbours. Strictly speaking they are not entirely territorial, in that they do not always, at all times, defend their core area against all-comers. They seem to recognise kin, and to resist strangers, yet our researches by means of DNA in their spraint, which is their territorial marker, disclosed a constant floating population of transient or newcomer otters among the faithful residents. Do all dispersing young have to run the gauntlet of hostile neighbours along the occupied parts of the river they were reared on? That would seem a wasteful evolutionary device.

I incline towards a belief that, at least in some instances, it is the bitch, the mother, that leaves the natal area. I think I saw this happen once on the Taw, when the bitch fled at speed from the pestering oversized cubs that were trying to get the eel she had caught. She swam away at speed, and went clean out of the area. We subsequently saw the cubs, hanging about on the stretch they had been reared in, but we never again saw her with them. Charlie Hamilton-James filmed a similar instance, when the bitch on the Bitton left the two great lummocking cubs, and went off with the dog. And at present, out on the Somerset Levels, there are two semi-independent large cubs which can often be seen from the bird hides, but after a long and dutiful summer of caring motherhood the bitch seems not to be there any more, certainly for most of the time.

Of course, otters are large and developed animals, with intelligence as well as instinct and they undoubtedly have individual differences of behaviour, and varying learnt patterns of behaviour. It is improbable that they all behave in as similar a way as say mice or pheasants invariably do. Although they are all hard-wired for mobility, it is probable that some wander more than others, or more sporadically.

The otter that uses the stream through my garden may at times not show up for over six weeks. It may be that the original animal died, and it took a while for a replacement to find the vacancy, but, more probably, the explanation for the absence is just that my otter was off on a wander somewhere.

In fact there is much about the lifecycle of his species that we are only guessing at, things that we take for granted as part of our body of understanding of other species. We do not know much about their natural sexual cycles, how frequently a bitch will come in season, or how soon after getting rid of her grown-up previous litter. The cubs remain dependent on the bitch until they are at least as big as she is. This is partly a physical dependency, because an adolescent cub may look nearly full grown, yet still lack both the skill and the muscular strength to catch enough food at times of turbulent water. It is also a psychological dependence. That the bitch remains in control of her youngsters even when the dog cubs are bigger than she is was demonstrated on a bit of home video taken by

Years of use as an otter sprainting place have made this grassy mound beside an Exmoor river highly fertile. Vivid green grass identifies it as a sprainting site.

my friend Ian Anderson. A gurt lummock of a dog cub was pestering his mother. She quelled him, without aggression or threat, simply by climbing up onto him and pinning him down; to do anything about this indignity he would have had to start an unpleasantness or a bout of anger. Wisely, he submitted.

We argue about how long they live, how old they are when they first have cubs, and

An otter spraint – full of gritty, undigested remnants of fish and crustaceans.

how frequently they have them. In zoos they sometimes mate on land, but in the wild they have only been seen mating in the water. Is the zoo behaviour a constraint of captivity, or do we see only mating in water in the wild because we mainly watch otters in the water, so the activities they undertake on land are hidden from us?

Most people believe that they do not produce a litter regularly once a year, like a vixen does. Yet one friend has had cubs every year on the small river running past the kitchen window of his mill house, and reckons that some of them were an annual litter from the same bitch. He also found that they used his river according to a predictable pattern, predictable enough to use for the basis of a filming schedule. I have checked the passing of otters through my garden for over twenty years, and can find no system of frequency or seasonal predictability at all. I do not think that this difference is because Charlie can see his otters from the kitchen window, while I am relying on spraints.

Otter spraints

Spraining is another aspect of otter behaviour about which we make assumptions. It is perforce the main focus of our attentions, so much so that it has been said that we study the natural history of spraint, not of otters, yet there are many unanswered questions. We know that it is used as part of the mechanism for spacing otters out along a river. We do not know how much part urine plays in this essential defence of resources, but a wet patch is sometimes all that we find on a sand castle, so presumably, (unscientific word), its scent is also used in the same way as the scent of the spraint. (This urine mark can be used to identify the sex of the otter that made the sand castle, by judging the relationship of the wet patch to the hind feet; bitches leave the mark almost vertically between the footprints: dogs project it farther forward.)

We have no idea how much otters follow or identify each other by what otter hunters used to call their drag, that is the scent from the glands in their legs left on the ground as they go about their business, the trail of scent that a hound would follow. I do know that an ability for this type of scenting is well developed in the otter. You will not surprise an otter if the wind is from you to it, and they can certainly detect dead fish by scent, or taste perhaps, underwater. So it would be surprising if the plonking of scent markers on infrequent rocks was the only form of territorial marking they recognised, although it is obviously an activity of major importance in their lives. They go to a lot of trouble to make sand or grass castles, solely for this purpose.

An otter spraint (arrowed) on a low-lying rock – the perfect place for the next otter to find.

And the traditional sites are faithfully adhered to over many years. Neville Pitman, the jazz musician, holds the record for a long established site. He recovered 224 spraints from one heap in the bottom of Lovington Mill.

I do not know, however, what proportion of the digestive output of an otter is made use of for this form of communication. They have rapid digestions, to match their active metabolisms, and their diet of fish generates a lot of shrapnel to be excreted.

By following otters in the snow in Sweden, Sam Erlinge located some 30 or 40 spraints per session of activity, many of them so small as to be of inconsiderable worth as an excretion of waste products, but others much larger and probably a dumping rather than a message. I wonder how much this is a decision under the control of the animal? Or to what extent the output is a reflection of the input? Otters have frequently been observed to spraint after feeding

If there are no stones available an otter will leave its spraint on the next best thing – in this case a heap of dead grass and grass roots.

on the bank, before re-entering the water. This choice of spraint site is different from the ones used regularly to mark territory. For the latter, the otter deliberately travels to a predetermined rock to leave a spraint; that is its only purpose in going there; when feeding, the spraint place on the bank is governed by the chance of where the animal caught a sufficiently large item to need to go ashore to manage it.

Many books state categorically that otters spraint mark less in summer than in winter. I disagree. For a start, they still need to rid themselves of a similar amount of undigested material. In my experience, what happens is that they do not climb as often to the elevated places that serve them above the high levels of water in the winter. That would be unproductive, in that the scent would be carried across the river well above the head of a swimming animal. They spraint low down, close to the water's edge.

We measured the height above the water one year, as part of one of our Axe Surveys: the majority of signs were just a few inches above the water. This would make them useful as part of a defensive signalling system, but we do not know if that is what they were. Many of them may well have been just the almost automatic deposition that follows a meal. In that case, the books would be right, and we would have to assume that otters are for some reason less defensive or territorial in the summer.

I think I can demonstrate from my records that some otters are more given to making sand castlings, than others. We had one on the Tone that seemed to be obsessive about them. After every winter flood it would renew them vigorously; we once counted 19 in one meadow. I wonder if some individuals are more aggressively, or defensively, territorial than others. How many otters are hiding their spraints, as bitches are supposed to do when near their young cubs, by depositing them in water? Do dispersing juveniles dare to contribute to the traditional heap? Is it futile not to advertise their presence in this ostentatious way, since they will be found out by their foot scent, or drag, anyway?

Although there are still more questions than answers about much investigated spraint, we have even less hard knowledge about 'Anal Jelly.' We do now know that it is not anal jelly at all, but the name, a source of much vulgar humour to my young children, has stuck. It used to be 'known' that this marmalade-like substance was the neat excretion of the anal glands, the scent-laden material that the otter coats its waste products with. This has been shown to be wrong. It is now thought that it is a mucus from the lining of the gut, a necessary lubricant to protect that delicate tissue from all the scratchy fish bones and sharp scales passing through.

I do not know to what extent an otter can control this process. Does it in certain circumstances react by deliberately making an AJ statement, or is it just something that has to happen when the mucus needs replacing? It has been suggested that it is more frequent at certain stages in the sexual cycle, but I do not know whether from dogs or bitches, whether some otters, or classes of otter, are more prone to producing it than others, or whether some individuals do it more than others. It was more useful when we were looking at the DNA, in that it was purely from the otter, and, containing no degrading fish remains with bacteria, it lasted better and gave more chance of a full reading. And, unlike spraint, it cannot be mistaken for a

Years of sprainting on exactly the same spot make this feature — created entirely by otters — on the Spey in Scotland very obvious.

product of a mink. As far as I know, only otters indulge in AJ.

But although we do not fully understand the extent to which these things balance out in an otter's lifestyle, we do know that it is a mobile, social, playful, and yet territorial animal, prone to sudden aggression; this is what makes them dangerous pets. It is also what enables us to study them at all, as they attempt to eliminate conflict by means of scent markers. It has been pointed out that this safety system seems to be working rather badly at present, in that we find too many instances of severe fighting.

How this impinges on the process of the dispersal of grown young we do not know, partly because we have little knowledge about that part of an otter's life. We know also that they have to be mobile, to control so long a territory, and that a large part of each night's activity is spent in travel. This makes them difficult to observe.

Otters in the water

Although they swim under the surface much of the time – the physics makes it more energy-efficient to swim submerged than on the surface – we recognise that our best chance of observing them is in the water. We at least have a clear view of the surface. It is apparently logical to seek an aquatic animal in the water. Yet the otter, as a mustelid, is a land animal, and one that we know to be resourceful, able to adapt to differing circumstances, and types of prey. It is known to be very mobile, and we have observed it crossing the high ground between catchments.

As we seldom look for it away from water, we have little knowledge of how often otters are to be found elsewhere. There are of course records of occasional, incidental sightings of otters in unexpected places, but I sometimes wonder if the word 'unexpected' is entirely accurate.

But it must be easier, and more appropriate, to concentrate on the rivers for most of the time.

We can recognise that this animal, although basically terrestrial in structure, is beautifully modified for its adopted water environment in the fine tuning of its design. *Lutra lutra* is an able swimmer. It has short, powerful legs with large webbed paws. The hind feet are especially large and well webbed, but much of the power comes from its long flexible back and its muscular tail. The length of its back makes it a poor jumper, but it can climb well.

At the otter sanctuary in the New Forest, the trunks of the oak trees are sheathed in tin, to prevent the otters from getting a purchase in the roughness of the tree bark. It has a short coat, which produces little drag in the water. Despite being short, it is well designed to insulate so fat-free an animal from the cooling effect of the water, by being in two layers. The under layer is of dense wool, which holds air, and the outer layer is of hair that traps that air in the fur.

All our otters are basically brown all over. This matt colouring reflects little light and makes the predator hard to detect. Moroccan otters are paler than ours, a more sandy colour. English ones are a chocolate brown, which looks almost black when wet. Irish otters are darker, almost black. For some reason, 'Celtic' otters, those from Ireland and Scotland, have white throats, or even almost completely off-white chests and bellies, a feature seldom found in southern England, where a few creamy chin spots are all the variation one usually finds.

Occasionally freak colourings occur, such as white otters, but these did not occur as frequently as the number of stuffed specimens would suggest. Because they are so very rare, there was a prestige in having a stuffed one

When otters dive they can adjust the lenses of their eyes to a more convex shape to cope with the different light conditions underwater.

in a collection, so the Victorian taxidermists soon perfected the art of bleaching skins. But otters with white spots in the pelage are not uncommon; some people call these 'royal otters.' Less common is the occurrence of white toes, and some people consider that this can indicate an outcross of smooth-coated otter in the ancestry.

Not only are the swimming mechanisms well adapted, the head of an otter works well in water. Its ears, eyes and nose are all on the top of a flat skull, so that a submerged otter can protrude just a small area to investigate all it needs to be aware of. Its whiskers are sufficient sense organs to enable it to operate without sight, yet its eye muscles can adapt the focal length of the lens to suit the different refractions of air and water. Its teeth are sharp enough and narrow enough to hold a slimy eel, yet strong enough to crunch through a fish's backbone. It has not adapted its lungs for prolonged periods of underwater activity. Had it done so it would have disadvantaged its capacity for long distance travel.

Everything that we know of these animals makes them fascinating. The enigma of the parts of their lives that they hide from us makes them tantalising. The infrequent sightings that their secluded lifestyle permits us leave strong impressions of power, competence, and independence. They cast a powerful and compelling spell: those that try to enter their mysterious realm invariably become 'besottered'.

CHAPTER FOUR

THE LIFE OF AN OTTER

Otters are difficult animals. Their colouration makes them impossible to tell apart as individuals. Their nocturnal and mobile way of life gives one short glimpses rather than prolonged observations, too short to base firm conclusions on.

Much of what we think we know has been from the study of spraints; this may be fine for working out their distribution, but tells very little about the animal itself. Despite these frustrations, we have over the years pieced together much of the jigsaw puzzle of their way of life.

Like many animals, they are secretive about breeding. The birth of cubs takes place in a quiet

and secluded place, and the bitch is at this time even more shy. Initially, she is out and about very little, spending most of her time with her tiny cubs. They are born after a 9 weeks gestation in a holt or nest specially prepared for them.

The bitch chooses a small place, and avoids the large, rambling tree root systems which might well be attractive to another otter. She will draw out a rabbit hole; surprisingly little enlargement is necessary. Or she may use a stick pile or smaller tree root up a side stream. The breeding holt may be away from water, up in a wood for instance, but frequently it is close to the water. The aim is for seclusion, and snugness. I have been surprised by the lack of space in these nests. The polish on the earth walls shows that the bitch would fit tight to the sides when curled up, with the tiny cubs nestling between her legs, and little spare space to absorb and waste precious heat. The nest is well provided with bedding, grass and moss, although adult otters often do not bother with such comforts for themselves. They will lie on bare stone or earth, even when in holts that they occupy frequently. But even in those cases where the cubs are born above ground, which might be presumed to be warmer than a damp, sunless burrow, good depth of bedding is provided.

Reed holts

In reed beds and swampy areas, burrowing is impractical; any digging will flood. There otters make a big nest of reeds and grass. I have heard it said that they will have their cubs on a swan's

Two big otter cubs venture out cautiously across the ice on a frozen lake.

nest, but I have never seen this for certain. It may be that they use an old nest as the foundation, but I suspect that the nest itself is an otter construction. I am sure the best example I have seen was entirely of the otter's creation.

One warm summer an otter bred on a small island in the river Culm. The Culm is not wide, and the island would not have been sufficiently secluded, but the farmers had let all the surrounding fields up for hay, and as country people used to respect haygrass, that cut out all access to that stretch of river for a while. The otter had found a small, wooded island in a large peaceful area of tall grasses, a quiet area with lots of cover, just what a bitch otter likes. It all went wrong when the farmers cut the hay. That opened up the fields to people again, and the footpath became attractive to walkers. Two Jack Russells got the scent, and nipped across before their owner was aware, and killed the cubs. The small island was no longer secluded.

The nest had been disturbed by the dogs, of course, but not much. It was the nearest I have come to seeing a reedbed-type nest as the otter had made it. Usually they have been long gone before I find out about it, and the structure has been flattened. This looked a bit like a swan's nest in size, and shape, but the construction was different. Swans gather reeds and leaves by small beakfuls, so the nest has a uniform texture, but this one was made of rolled bundles of dry grass. I almost said hay, but the otter had made the nest before the grass was cut, so each bundle of what now looked like hay must have been gathered as grass. What a major undertaking, to bite off and bundle up

enough material for a swan's nest. Each bundle was the size of a rolled up tea towel, a sort of long sausage, and these had been piled loosely rather than interwoven. There seemed to be the remains of some sort of lid or covering, and I have read, but never seen, that a reedbed nest can resemble domed wren or dipper nests in shape.

New-born cubs

Cubs would certainly need some sort of protection against rain and cold. There are usually two or three in a litter. One bitch killed on the road recently had seven placental scars, but that must be very exceptional, and there was no evidence that the young had thrived long enough for her to have to suckle them much. As this early stage takes place out of our ken we do not know what the early wastage rate is, nor what sort of congenital problems very small cubs are subject to.

Occasional abnormalities, such as hydrocephalus, probably caused by pollutants, have come to light, but only the basically healthy

All otters sleep a lot, especially during the day. These two are drying their fur in some warm sunshine.

ones leave the nest. When born they are very small and helpless, and like puppies or kittens, their eyes are not open. Pregnant predators cannot carry their young to an advanced stage without being impeded from hunting by the bulge, so their young have to do some of their important development after birth. The eyes are an example.

Vic Simpson's series of ongoing post-mortems has revealed a problem with this. He has demonstrated that bitch otters carry a lesser burden of PCB pollutants than dog otters or immatures. As it is extremely improbable that bitches have in some way a different, pollution-free, diet, the explanation must be that they are off-loading much of their contamination via the fat-rich colostrums given to the cubs shortly after birth. The mothers are giving their tiny offspring a slug of contaminants, just at the most vulnerable stage, particularly as far as the still developing eyes are concerned. The molecular shape of the PCBs is similar to that of

Vitamin A. The messenger platelets that should carry the essential Vitamin A to those tissues that continue to develop after birth, the eyes and reproductive organs especially, are clogged with bits of PCB, and so there is a vitamin deprivation. Even though the food may have provided it, the cub cannot access it.

There is evidence of permanent retinal abnormalities in several otters. Just what the practical consequences of these are for the animal is speculation, but it is at least possible that some otters may be night blind. As otters operate in the dark anyway, using their whiskers instead of sight, this may not be as desperate as it sounds, but it may make avoiding cars more difficult, perhaps.

The growing cubs

The bitch keeps the cubs in the holt after their eyes open, long after. She may move them to a different holt, by carrying each one, but how frequently she would do this unprompted, as a hygiene measure perhaps, is hard to tell, in that we know only about those bitches whose cubs we have discovered, which may of itself be sufficient to prompt a move.

A radio-tracked bitch in Scotland was recorded as moving very frequently, and as being very secretive indeed about her nests. Perhaps she was just trying to get away from the intrusive antennae. The mother keeps them underground in the cramped confines of the holt for a surprising time. The cubs grow fast, and are lively and playful, but they are kept in the dark of a small space for far longer than puppies or kittens would be. They do not get out until about the eighth or ninth week, when they are quite large. This would be cruel for dogs, but is a necessary safety precaution for an animal close to water.

Flooding of holts

The rivers can be treacherous at any time of year, of course, but are more regularly in spate or flood in the winter months. Yet this seems to be when many of the bitches have small cubs to look after. There is no fixed breeding season for otters as there is for foxes or badgers. These land animals all have their young at the same time of year, and they breed every year. This they can do because they are free of the demands of the family after only 6 months or so, when their offspring are sufficiently well grown to be viable on their own.

Otters are different. As they have to keep the family together for as much as twelve months, they get out of phase with each other, and can breed at any time of year. Down here in the south of England there seems to be some sort of peak of births in November and December, which means that the cubs will be out and about when the weather improves in the spring. However it also means that some cubs may be lost in the nest to sudden floods.

When this happens, the bitch will have a period of rest, and when her physical condition has lifted sufficiently, then she will come into season again, seek a mate, and produce her next litter some 9 weeks later. As she must look after her cubs for a year or more, a bitch otter cannot breed regularly every year, nor at the same time of year as her last litter.

Scientists debate about whether our otters use the process called delayed implantation, when the foetus can be held in suspended animation in the womb for a long period. *Lutra canadensis*, the very similar North American species, certainly does, but they have tougher winters to contend with. Although the otters in the north of Scotland seem to have a more co-ordinated breeding season than our southern ones, I think this is a product of the weather and the feeding difficulties they encounter in

Calm and storm: the same view of a Somerset river in very different conditions. Spates (below) can be hostile and dangerous conditions for young cubs.

winter, rather than a physiological trait. I find cubs at different stages of growth at any time of year, and the evidence of placental scars and lactation from the post-mortems seems to back this up.

Weaning

Weaning brings problems for the bitch; she has to catch all the prey, and to be away for longer; in a natural situation it is hard work, so it is at this stage that she is more likely to focus on the concentrated, artificial food supply of stocked ponds and fish hatcheries. A family of otters

eats more than a single otter, so this can cause friction from the pond owner. Normally an adult otter takes the easiest fish, which means not the largest, and usually an otter eats the whole of each fish that it catches; many of them will be so small that the otter crunches them up where it catches them, out in the middle of the water. Only bulky fish are brought ashore, so that the otter can use its forepaws to assist in the slippery meal, but even here the whole item will usually be consumed.

This means there is very little mess or fall-out after a normal visit from an otter, and many pond owners do not realise that they are being visited from time to time by a territorial resident who uses the facility when it is in the area. As otters do not kill more fish than they need, the damage is not only unobtrusive, but also negligible in economic terms. In any stocked lake, some fish will die from time to time, and as the otter is careful to economise on the time spent in the cooling medium of the water, they may well take the sick or damaged fish as being the easiest. There is often no sign to the owner that this is happening, and even if he knows, it makes little difference.

Wasting food

However, if a family moves in, there is more evidence, as well as more damage. Cubs are messy and competitive feeders. They do not share a fish. Most captures are too small for that to be feasible, so the pattern is for there to be a scuffle as to which cub is to have the fish mother has just caught. When the next mouthful is brought in, the lucky winner may well join in the scrum again, even though he still has quite a bit of head or tail to finish. So bits get left about, and attract attention. Even when the fish is large enough, or long enough, for two to eat at it at once, they do not. I watched two cubs with a large sea lamprey on the Taw. Once one had established possession, it was able to eat in peace, although the other was waiting nearby. As soon as it paused in its feeding, the second one had a go, and it too was allowed ownership, until finally it gave up and number one had another turn. This seemed to me much more efficient than puppies would have been, with perpetual squabbling and snatching to prevent both of them from getting a decent feed. Finally they moved off with the bitch, leaving a useful chunk of the head end on the bank, a sure betrayal that cubs had been around.

Adults do sometimes leave good food. The classic example is the lovely, fresh salmon with a bite out of its shoulder, (although fish do not have shoulders). The hole is more than a single bite, of course; the otter has probably eaten its fill. The point of attack is always the same, just behind the gills, because the animal's aim is to get in to eat the more nutritious organs such as the heart and liver.

An otter's diet is restricted, and unbalanced. Fish muscle is all very well, but unrelieved steak is not the best way to feed a family. Happily, they eat the whole of many smaller fish, so get more nutrition than just the meat would provide. In captivity, zoo keepers often supplement the diet by feeding beef balls with added nutrients and oils in them. I have been told by two keepers that the otters prefer these to the fish they get. Fishery owners do not, however, see it as sensible and economical for an otter to eat the innards and a little of the muscle before leaving the rest of the body as incriminating evidence. To the owner this seems like waste, especially if the otter does not come back for more the next night. On a salmon river, it may well be too many miles away to make that feasible, or more economical than catching another fresh one.

Adults are also tactless at carp lakes, in cold weather in winter. Carp are at the northern limit of their range in Britain, and can only just tolerate our cold winters. They go torpid when the water temperature drops, and burrow into the muddy bottom of the pond to await more reviving temperatures. The otters, always on the lookout for easy protein, exploit this disadvantage, and haul out great lumps of carp far bigger than they can eat. They have to learn to catch the fish by the face, as the only part narrow enough for an otter's small bite. The bigger the carp, the more valuable the resource, so this can annoy the owner even more than the cold winter weather that has given him chilblains, as well as closing down his fishing trade. But big, somnolent carp apart, when I hear of fish fallout strewn around the banks of a stocked pond, I suspect a bitch with cubs.

Evidence of cubs

There is another symptom of cub presence. They rootle under the turf, like little pigs. So do badgers, but they are more like big pigs, with untidy and vigorous demolition of the lawn or riverside fields. Otter cubs are neater, and roll back the carpet of turf without delving deep. I watched them doing it in a zoo once, but could not quite decide what they were after. Some say they are getting worms and larvae, others that they are eating the taproots to obtain the trace elements pulled up by the roots, elements lacking from a fish meat diet. But they frequently do it, so finding turned-over turf near the river bank is a sign of the presence of cubs.

They can betray themselves by noise, too. They call to keep the family together, with a penetrating sharp cheep. People call it a whistle, but it is quite brief, something of a bleat almost, and very like a bird call. Its sharp note carries across water well, and is used to maintain contact,

A large otter cub already showing the extravagant whiskers which are the hallmark of the species.

"where are you?" or "wait for me." Otter cubs are anxious, and very dependent on their mother for reassurance, until they are almost as large as she is. We were waiting patiently in one of the bird hides on the Somerset Levels, hoping to see the otter family that was frequenting that area. There was also a small group of birders in the hide, pointing out the birds to each other in what I considered to be a too enthusiastic and rather noisy way.

That sound carries across water does not seem to bother birders. The angles of vision were such that their end of the hide could see farther through the gap between two reed beds

than we could, so one of them picked up the approaching otters first. Very excited, they showed each other where they were, in an audible way. The bitch otter, who was ahead, came through the gap into the clear water in front of us and stopped abruptly. She listened briefly, then crash dived away. The next we

saw was the whole family hurrying away along the side of the far reeds, hugging tight to the cover, with the two big cubs actually touching the bitch, so that they looked like one creature. The only problem had been human voices some distance away, a sound the otters out there must be familiar with. But whether from the excited nature of the birders' babble, or because it was unexpected in some way, anxiety had taken over and the instant reaction of the quite large cubs was to keep as close as possible to mother, literally to maintain contact. I was cross with the noisy idiots at the time, (their reaction was, "Well, we saw them first", which struck me as a tad immature and certainly unsoothing), but later I realised that it had been a good observation of otter attitudes, and more interesting than seeing them catch a few small fish.

Young hunters

If we had watched them hunting, even at that stage of dependency I think they would have been hunting each for itself. I have only once seen what could be called co-operative hunting, but even then I am not sure whether it qualified. I have never seen otters after really challenging prey, such as a salmon, so maybe they both work together in the same pool as a team for that sort of thing.

My only possible instance of co-operation was on the Taw, when I watched from a high bank a dog and a bitch fishing side by side in shallow water. They were working together, turning over the stones and getting the bullheads and minor fishes from under them. Each turned over its own stones, but the bitch kept station on the dog at what a cricketer would call 'first

There is little space inside the family holt, but this is where the mother will keep her cubs for the first eight or nine weeks of their lives.

slip'. She found fish of her own, but also picked up several which he disturbed into the current, and missed. It was not exactly co-operation, in that she contributed nothing to him, and he intended no benefit to her, but it seemed to work well. I watched them for over an hour, feeding hard. Most items went down quickly in situ, but a few catches were big enough to warrant one or other swimming ashore, while the other carried on exactly the same. I wondered why they needed so much to eat in mid morning.

Teaching the cubs

I have never seen a bitch educating her cubs by releasing prey for them in shallow water, but I have heard that it happens. Peregrines do the same sort of thing, and the adult then leaves the eyasses to get on with it. She does not take a helping part in the subsequent chase, and nor does the otter, I believe.

Otters fish singly, even when they are with their young. Learning the skills of hunting will be done by imitation, but the first part of their education is indeed a lesson, the introduction to water. An initial nervousness betrays the species' history, that they are the descendants of a land weasel that returned to the water after a successful period as a land animal.

Water is not as natural to an otter cub as it is to a duckling. They have to be taken, encouraged, and even deposited by the scruff for their first acquaintance with it. Nor are they very able, at first. Their fluffy baby coats and their "puppyfat" make them very buoyant, and they ride very high in the water. I suppose this is safer, but they bob about, and have difficulty diving. I am not sure how long this lasts, but they soon become more confident than their infant strength warrants.

The currents can defeat a quite large cub. This happened on the Tone, when a man walking his dog heard a series of piercing calls, and found a cat-sized cub trying to get back up a weir in a rain-swollen January flow. He went home for a net, but when he got back the cub was dead. He fished it out anyway, to take to show his children.

On the way home, the corpse wriggled, so he put it by the Rayburn, and it revived.

Abandoned cubs

Presumably, this was a fit cub that made an error of judgement. The bitch did not appear to look for it, so perhaps it had been washed a long way on the turbulent spate before going over the weir. Or perhaps she had abandoned it deliberately.

There is a distressing scene in a television documentary of this happening. The bitch takes the other cubs on with her, and ignores the cries of the cub she is leaving. She did not lose it, she abandoned it. Several abandoned cubs that have been taken into care have turned out to be suffering from a defect that would have made them not viable as independent adults.

One cub that appeared in films a lot never really grew to full size, and despite a caring and knowledgeable home, died suddenly at an early age. It had been found squeaking in the rain a few yards from a drain from which the bitch had moved her other cubs, but had left this one.

Charlie Hamilton-James took on a Scottish otter that had been found on its own. Honey did well for quite a long time, but then took ill and died under anaesthetic. It turned out that she had had a major defect in half of her heart all her life. As a wild otter she would have starved, so one presumes this was why she was abandoned originally.

Otters are very dutiful mothers, and take excellent care of their cubs for almost a full year, so there must be a strong reason when a bitch abandons one of them.

Orphaned cubs

Other cubs have been rescued because their mother has been killed. Rearing such orphans is a very tricky business, and the right milk preparations have to be used, and then the correct weaning procedures. If the cubs are very young when found, they need more hands-on attention from humans than is suitable for an animal which one hopes to return to the wild. If the cubs are older, they can be treated more as normal animals, and kept at a distance from personal contact. But for these ones, the stress of capture and transportation and veterinary checks can induce weaknesses which cause their premature death before they become adults. As I said earlier, young otters are anxious animals, and vulnerable to stress.

Zoo otters

I suspect they may be more anxious in the daylight. The species is hard wired to be nocturnal. In zoos Eurasian Otters make disappointing exhibits, because they tend to sleep all day. Some collections try to force them to appear by feeding only in the middle of the day, but although the food is put down, the otters will often wait until later. Other zoos lock them out of their sleeping boxes. The otters would not mind this if they had sufficient cover in which to rest.

Wild otters spend as much of their sleeping time lying rough as they do down dank drains and holts. They are not averse to having some sun on their backs. But most pens for captive otters have few bushes to hide in – that would defeat the purpose. So, too often, what one gets to see is an otter trying to curl down into some exposed hollow in the grass to keep out of the cold breeze, or an unhappy animal pacing back and forth and trying to break into its own bedroom. We were the last group to leave the Otter Trust's place in Suffolk one grey winter's day. The otters had been a bit energetic just before feeding time, but otherwise the mood had been one of inertia. However, at sunset, they switched on, and their outlook changed completely. They became vigorously mobile, and started to interact with the animal in the nextdoor pens. They were now worth watching, so we delayed, and lingered on past chucking out time for visitors.

As we slowly made our way towards the exit we peered over the wall into a pen we had looked at previously. Its occupants were startled; they had obviously thought all visitors had left, so at our appearance they reacted like truly wild animals, and dived into their pond, where they swam about suspiciously, venting only briefly and in hidden corners. They had been indifferent to the public all day; now it was hard to tell there were any otters in there, so self-effacing had they become. The setting of the sun had awakened their true ottery natures, and they gave a superb display of why it is so

Curled up and resting at the root of a tree. Adult otters often choose to sleep above ground.

hard to catch more than a fleeting glimpse of an otter on a river bank. If we had not known in advance that there were two otters in that small, bare compound, we would never have discovered it once they decided to hide from us.

Splish, Splosh and Splash were three cubs taken into care at a very early age. They were looked after and bottle-fed by Ellie West, who devoted a lot of time to them and gave them the social care and reassurance young cubs need, as well as food.

Once they were fully weaned, they were put into a well designed pen, away from all the activity at Secret World, and human contact was kept to a minimum. Ellie told me, sadly, that they became nocturnal almost at once, so she could no longer watch her babies even from a distance. This was their doing, not anything the sanctuary arranged. Even when small, they were by instinct nocturnal.

There is a photographer about so the two cubs, although nearly full-grown, are keeping close to mother.

Night fishing

It makes sense for a fish eater to be more active at night. Many species of fish lurk in crannies or under stones in daylight, to avoid sighted predators. Bigger fish stack up in shoals in deep pools, and idle the day away.

"Fish, fly replete in depth of June,
Dawdle away their watery noon."

With dusk, the riverbed comes to life. Eels emerge, gudgeon and bullheads have a living to make. Even the sulky salmon come alive. Cock salmon especially tend to move about in the dark, changing pools up and down river much more than we fishermen realise.

Between sunset and dark can be the most productive period of the day when fishing for salmon, when the fish have woken up, and are getting their danders up, but before they have set about their night's travel. However, seatrout fishermen have to wait patiently on the midge-infested bank. The accepted formula is that one should not start to fish the seatrout lies until

one has seen the second bat. We sit up on the high bank of the Taw, and watch the seatrout starting to drift back from the deep security of the Hurdle Pool into the shallow run-off under the big oak tree at its tail, where they take station, and start to feed. It is an exciting time of great anticipation, made the keener because as the minutes pass the chances of seeing an emerging otter also increase.

One night I had gone upstream to wait by the Rocks before starting to fish. This is a favourite place of mine, because you can see right up past the holt in the ash tree roots, and there is a good chance of a long view of the early otter. This evening the otter did not come from upstream but from below.

I watched a smallish otter swim up the Rocks Pool right up to the outcrop of rocks itself, quite close to me, too close in fact to see what it did once it was obscured by the raised edge of the stone outcrop. All ripples ceased. I scanned in both directions, but in the decreasing light I could not make anything out. I waited, but nothing

Swimming purposefully, with only its head above water, this otter is ready to dive quickly at the first sight of danger.

happened. So I knew, as an experienced otter watcher, that the animal had caught my scent and made itself scarce as only an otter can, without a clue as to which way it went. So I stood up, picked up my rod, and stomped out onto the rocks in my nailed waders, stripping line off my clicking fishing reel as I prepared to fish. Suddenly there was a splash. My otter had been sound asleep in a hollow on the edge of the rocks, and only woke up after I had approached quite close. This was before dark, say 10 o'clock.

Like most mustelids, otters have very high metabolic rate; when they are active, they are very active, and in compensation they rest for long periods. That juvenile otter settled down for a nap after travelling upstream against the current at just the time I was expecting otters to become active. I wonder if it was unwell, or perhaps as an immature on its own it was finding life very difficult, and not getting enough to eat to keep it in prime condition. In my view, that is why otters are seen more by day. One school of thought argues that since otters are no longer persecuted or hunted, they do not need to shelter in darkness, and can come out to hunt more easily in the daylight. I do not follow that. Fish are still nocturnal, otters do not rely on sight for hunting, and as I have explained, there is strong evidence that they are themselves naturally nocturnal.

I think the problem lies with the fish supply. All the angling organisations are agreed that fish stocks are much lower than they were, or should be, to maintain a healthy and sustainable future population.

Trout fishermen have a scheme for monitoring the fly life in their rivers: the results are worrying. The invertebrates are the basis of the food chain from which the fish, and then the otters, depend. They are in very reduced numbers everywhere, but in areas where enhanced synthetic pyrethroids have been used as sheep dip, invertebrates can be completely absent. One damp sheep can sterilise miles of a stream completely.

The otter's diet

Eels are the preferred prey of otters, and their staple diet, some 80% of what they eat. Eels have undergone a catastrophic reduction in the last twenty years, and electro-fishing shows that they are below 5% of their former stocks, in all European countries. The suggested causes are various, and all of them may contribute to the disaster: warmer oceans, changes in the Gulf Stream, over-exploitation, cumulative pollutions, to which fatty and long-lived eels are very vulnerable, and especially a recently introduced foreign parasite, a nematode worm that takes up space in the swim bladder. This matters very little during that stage of an eel's life that it passes squirming about on the bottom of a shallow pond, but it may well be a lethal impediment when the mature eel finally sets off to swim the Atlantic back to the spawning grounds in the Sargasso sea. The eels with the heaviest burden of parasites may just sink.

But whatever the reason, life for an otter is harder than it was in the days of plenty. It is great to see many more otters nowadays than I recall seeing as a lad (although I was seldom away from the water) but it is probably a sign of difficulties for the otters. They are having to fish when they should be sleeping. This means that the bitch with cubs is further stretched to feed the hulking great scroungers for a full year, as she must. It must be a relief when the family group breaks up and disperses, and she can rest and feed up before starting all over again.

An otter jumps clear of the water in a hurry to get down to its prey.

CHAPTER FIVE

LIFE AS A PREDATOR

Most of what we know about otters has come from research based on spraints. This limited approach has largely been forced on us by the nature of the otter. Its way of life prevents the adoption of the sorts of tactic which people looking into the lifestyle of other animals routinely follow.

Deer biologists rely on direct observation through binoculars, and they use cameras to identify individual bucks or stags. Even though the males discard their identifying features, the antlers, every year, they conveniently grow new ones which are sufficiently similar to enable that stag or buck to be followed for all its life. We would have learnt little of the biology of roe deer, for example, only by poring over their excretions.

The extent to which sightings are normally essential for intelligent appraisal of a species was made clear recently on the Quantock Hills, when an almost completely white hind was born. Apparently this is a very unusual occurrence in red deer. Although white specimens are commonplace in fallow, white red deer are unheard of except in heraldry and pub signs. At the time of the white hind's appearance, there

was rumoured to be only one other white deer, on Arran, and some people were sceptical about that.

For the first time there was a recognisable individual among all the scores of drab brown female deer, a unique animal whose movements could be studied. It had previously been accepted that the herds of females were pretty fluid, and prone to move at will across most of that small range of hills. But to everyone's surprise, during the 17 years of her life she remained in one restricted area, and was seen north of the bisecting road only once.

There is a strong culture of deer appreciation among the people of the Quantocks, and the fortunes of the deer are followed closely and in considerable detail by a lot of well informed people, who talk often of what they have seen. But they started to have to revise their opinions when there was one animal that could be followed by sightings.

This very rare albino otter was spotted eating a fish on the rocks in Aberdeenshire. The photo was taken by Karen Jack who was out walking her dog. She watched and photographed the otter for some 5 minutes before it disappeared, never to be seen again by her.

There have been white otters recorded in the past, but I have not heard of one in my time. I am almost glad. Should such a miraculous benefit be granted me, as a reward for persistent and unwavering devotion, perhaps, what a burden of responsibility it would pose. I know that it would not conveniently remain in one small area, but I would be obliged to follow it far and wide, upstream and down, miles at a time, nearly always at night, when its whiteness would not serve so well.

A cow-sized white deer on a russet hillside is visible from miles away: a white otter swimming with a low profile through broken water in the dusk would be much less easy to observe.

Spraint analysis

So naturally we have been spraint enthusiasts, and it seems to me that if we start our elementary researches by looking at what comes out of the otter, we should try to graduate to a study of what goes in. But we can do this only by looking at the end product. We know that otters are carnivorous predators, and we think we know that they are specialists, with a diet very much restricted to fish, or to fish and other water-sourced proteins, like frogs or crayfish. Any study of otter spraint will reinforce this belief.

Foxes are by design and metabolism also meat eaters, but they are not particular, and opportunistically turn to whatever is available. They eat a lot of blackberries, for instance.

Badgers, of the same family as otters, are notorious generalists, worm specialists that prefer peanut butter, whose population has boomed on the back of the massive increase in the growing of maize as a crop. Maize provides the young of the year with a rich and reliable food source at just that time of year when young badgers are in danger of starving because dry summer weather has driven their staple worms too deep.

Otters swimming in calm conditions. It is typical to see their heads followed by the humps of the lower back and the occasional swish of the rudder.

The pine marten, another mustelid, also eats a lot of fruit, especially rowan berries. However, I have never heard of an otter turning to fruit or veg, although raging rivers must sometimes make their normal, specialist fare very hard to find.

Mink are like their very similar relatives, the otters, in sticking to the food they are adapted for, a carnivorous diet, but they are not so narrowly focussed; over time, they eat about a third fish, a third fowl, and a third flesh. In other words, they will have a go at whatever is available. This is a sensible and successful strategy for a sub-arctic animal. Food in high latitudes is not so plentiful that a predator can afford to walk past any possible meal. But the otter, adapted to temperate areas where the water does not freeze for long, has become a fish specialist. This was a good strategy, to focus on a plentiful source of prey which was largely ignored by all other air-breathing predators. Lots to eat, and little competition.

Otter as fish-hunter

They have a body well designed to cope with the needs of an aquatic predator. The slim, tubular, basic shape of the average mustelid has become even more streamlined; their head, neck and shoulders taper in one line, so an otter can eject any form of radio collar over its head without difficulty; their tail is now a powerful rudder; their feet are large and spreading, with webs; the whiskers on their face have become a sense organ delicate enough to hunt by; they have developed special muscles which can adjust the focal length of their eyes to the different refractive demand of air or water, whichever

medium they are in. And most famously, they have a double layer of coat which traps air for insulation.

This is most necessary, as, being warm blooded, they have an especial problem maintaining warmth in water, which conducts heat away some 23 times faster than air. The strenuous nature of their patrolling life, which involves extra expenditure of energy in combating rapid currents, demands that the animal be fit, muscular and blubber-free, so the coat is their only insulation. To provide the extra energy for all this activity, they must spend more time hunting, and as fish eaters they hunt in water, which drains out heat and energy at an expensive rate. This is a classic catch-22 situation. In extreme circumstances it can prove dangerous to the otter's wellbeing.

Shetland research

Hans Kruuk calculated the heat that would be lost during the amount of time otters would have to spend in cold water to catch the calories they need to maintain their body weight, or to maintain their fitness to catch the fish that they need to eat to maintain their ability to catch those fish. His researches "show how vulnerable otters are when fish populations become very low". He found that in normal winter conditions otters need to fish for 6 hours a day to replace the energy sucked out by the cold water. "However, if prey availability were to reduce by half (which is not a very drastic reduction in fish populations), otter survival would become impossible in winter." A combination of low water temperatures and low fish availabilty would mean that an otter would have to fish more than 24 hours a day to replace the energy lost in feeding itself. "Otters are living rather close to the limits of their possible existence in fresh water".

That research was done in Shetland where things are more extreme than they are in southern England. Shetland was selected by Hans as a place with a strong otter population where continuous daylight enabled the sort of direct visual observation I referred to at the beginning of this chapter as impossible for me. He and his team consequently achieved much, and moved things forward a long way. But Shetland has continual daylight only in summer, and almost total darkness for much of the difficult winter. The otters there are all based on the sea, which in times of storm can be an even more difficult environment than a river. And weather extremes and seafish breeding cycles may force a seasonality on the otters which is not to be found elsewhere. His findings need to be re-evaluated in the light of our experience down here.

Below: Even on a bare rock an otter will often blend perfectly into its surroundings and its presence is given away only by its movement. This one has caught a small yellow fish, possibly a blenny or rock gobby.

A bitch otter reading the sprainting rock. The messages she receives from it will inform her of any other otters in the vicinity: possible mates, possible rivals and competitors, or simply that she herself was the last one there.

How to conduct spraint analysis

This brings us back, as always, to spraints. I said above that any study of spraint will reinforce the belief that otters are fish specialists. But I also said that spraints are a limited tool. There is a built-in bias in spraint analysis. What one does is cleanse off the goo from the spraint, using the sort of fierce preparation sold to de-soil babies' nappies.

One is then left with a sieveful of shrapnel, which can be teased apart and identified by means of a bought key and a magnifying glass. It is exciting to find the differently constructed vertebrae, and to learn the shapes and sizes of fish scales. Jaw bones and gill plates feature, too, and at certain times of year frogs' leg bones.

The initial process is to identify the different species, or in the case of the very similar smaller coarse fish, just the family, cyprinid. It is harder to decide how much or how many of any item the otter has had; if an otter made a major meal off a salmon kelt, and then snacked on minnows or sticklebacks, the spraints would contain lots of tiny vertebrae, but few salmon bones, salmon being a meaty fish which can be gnawed at

rather than consumed whole. The impression would be that sticklebacks were the major item of diet, but in fact by weight they would be an almost negligible portion. However, clever men have devised formulae for overcoming these discrepancies, and put them in their books, so judgement can be passed on which fish the otter mainly ate.

The head-scratching problems begin when feathers turn up in the spraints. Firstly, one has to be certain that what one is looking at is a spraint, and not a mink scat, in which one would expect to find feathers.

Then there are all the questions of frequency and quantity. If an otter makes a major meal of one moorhen, in how many spraints will feathers be found, and for how long? Is this an aberrant occasion, or is it to some extent habitual, in which case what is the ratio of fowl to fish available in that area? If habitual, is it the habit of all the otters in that area, or just the learned shortcut of one animal? Is the learned behaviour cultural, that is taught or encouraged from example, by the mother, or is it the reaction to adversity of an injured or sick animal, as is often the case with man-eating tigers?

In some cases I have known, the adversity which pushed the otter towards the ducks was the inexperience of youth.

A recently independent, immature otter found fish too hard to rely on, and started to raid nextdoor's ducks. It found a way into a fox-proof pen of ornamental waterfowl by squeezing on its side under the gate, through a slit so narrow that even the rabbits were not using it. The mud on the path outside the gate was scarred and ploughed by the effort of his back legs pushing and striving to insert this large animal under the bottom metal bar.

The river Tone in tranquil mood – a place where the local angling club stocks trout but the resident otters seem to prefer eels and bullheads.

When a badger had all my ducklings it prised the gate upwards by force: at this gate the otter had to flatten itself. Coming out again with a full belly must have been most uncomfortable, but he raided the pen two nights running before my neighbour, the farmer, reinforced the threshold.

The point is that the otter had sought out the pen, which was up by the farm, and two big fields away from the river, and had had to locate a very difficult way in. It must have been driven by considerable hunger, which means that it was not coping as a fish specialist in the normal way. A similar instance has recently occurred on one of the nature reserves on the Somerset Levels.

There a family of two cubs took out most of the production of young ducks and grebes one summer. In the warm weather the fish have increased energy and are hard for a young otter to catch in those wide, open lakes, so the cubs learned their trade on the equally inexperienced and underpowered hatchlings.

That the otters were at least partly to blame for the wipe-out of hatchlings was verifiable from their spraints, though of course the resident gulls and crows will have also been involved. Studies from Scotland have shown that otters frequently take birds in the summer. We were pleased when a mallard brought off a brood of ducklings in our garden, and we enjoyed their presence on the stream. Then an otter found them and had the lot; the spraints from that massacre were totally composed of juvenile feather fragments, no fish at all.

The bias in the interpretation of spraints occurs because only hard parts show up: bones, crayfish shells, fish scales and indigestible feathers. Softer items, such as freshwater mussels, leave no residues in the spraint, yet the empty shells on the riverbank disclose that considerable quantities have been eaten. For many years there was speculation whether otters condescended to catch such inconsider-able items as dragonfly larvae or similar invertebrates. Many people were reluctant to consider this; in some way it would seem to detract from the image of the otter as an intrepid hunter, a valiant creature on a par with the noble peregrine, and reduce it to the level of the ignoble and pedestrian buzzard, often seen scuttling about the fields after daddy longlegs. But recent research in Wales has proved that some otters regularly prey on dragonfly larvae, and also on snails and worms. This portion of their food is inaccessible to the amateur student who uses only a magnifying glass and a kitchen sieve, so it is not known how widespread this habit is, nor whether it is a regular method of feeding or an extreme response to difficulty and hunger stress.

Otters have very high metabolic rates, so it seems to me unlikely that they could base their regular uptake of energy on so slow a process as foraging for worms and snails; literally, life is too short for that approach. Yet I have twice found a small nemoralis shell in spraint, evidence of an otter having eaten a land snail. And last winter a small group of us watched an otter fishing in good light in front of Decoy Hide at Shapwick Heath. It was the second otter we had watched that afternoon. The first had been fishing normally, that is diving and foraging gradually forward, to seek what it might find. Many dives were unproductive, but some would produce a small fish which was gnawed on the surface, by being switched from side to side in the otter's mouth. We could see the protruding tail, flapping at first, but then moving only in rhythm with the methodical chomping; chomp, chomp, chomp: three or four crunches on the left, then a swift switch, and three or four bites on the right.

Then the otter would dive again, and continue slowly forwards across the lake. We could clearly see the chain of bubbles on the surface, and sometimes this would increase in intensity as the otter concentrated in one spot. On these occasions the trip back up to the surface for air would be as brief as possible, a quick rolling dive, almost like a leaping fish, and rapidly back down to the same area. This more vigorous procedure might result in a bigger fish, one which necessitated a trip to the bank, with the wretched roach protesting feebly on either side of the otter's narrow mouth, as it swam on the surface like a retriever.

After a short pause the otter would reappear, some distance out from the bank, (you seldom see an otter entering the water: the first few yards are underwater), and start fishing again. The concentration, agility and intensity involved always make this an absorbing spectacle for me.

Yet I was puzzled by our second otter. At first glance it seemed to be doing the same process. But not quite. It was not moving slowly forwards, but diving repeatedly in the same small area. The chain indicated that it was not exploring far during each dive, but seemed busy in one place. The dives were short, and almost every time it came up it seemed to eat something, but we could not make out what.

Whatever it was did not take much chewing, three or four quick gulps at most, and there were no projecting ends to give us any clue. From several dives the otter's face emerged with a moustache of water weed, which it scuffed off with its paws. This went on for a considerable time; dozens of items were consumed, and the show only ended when it caught a jumbo tench, more than enough for any otter. It carried it to the bank, and disappeared into the scrub.

I could only think it was deliberately and methodically foraging on dragonfly larvae.

Although all otters look alike and lack distinguishing features, they do vary in build and skull size, so from a close view in good light one can hazard an identification. I thought the first otter was the bitch of the family that was

The unmistakable silhouette of an otter showing its arched lower back and huge tail.

at that time in the process of breaking up, and that the second one was one of the nearly full-grown cubs, resorting to a labour-intensive but reliable method of compensating for its inexperience.

Unfortunately I cannot spend all my time watching otters. If I could have gone more regularly to Decoy Lake, I might have been able to find out whether that otter often used this resource, and whether its sibling also did. I wonder if they grow out of it, as I did from drinking pop. Watching an otter about its business in an undisturbed situation is such a treat. I am always totally absorbed, and far too involved to do anything sensible like timing the dives or counting the prey. Afterwards I ruminate on what I have seen, and learn a little more, perhaps, but I always come away with questions that I would like to know more about.

The quantity of dragonflies in those lakes on the Somerset Levels is a great wonder. There are several wildlife spectacles to amaze one out there, but the weight of invertebrate protein in those waters must be one of the greatest.

Many people know of the spectacular starling roost in the reed beds in winter, when several million birds fly round in a dense flock, in some years a flock of more than 4 million individual birds; with the noise of their wings, and even the pattering of their droppings as they circle over the water, it is indeed something to wonder at. Fewer people turn up in early May to see the congregation of hobbies. These graceful little falcons, having recently completed their arduous flight from Africa, gather here to feed up on the hatching dragonflies, before pairing up and dispersing to their nesting places. For a couple of weeks one can see up to 70 swift and agile falcons feeding in loose flocks on the emerging insects. This whirling and dipping ballet is another absorbing spectacle which pulls one's eyes and closes one's mind, so that it is only later that one realises just what one has been watching.

The birds are first to be seen sitting on the dead top branches of prominent trees, dotted about around the lakes. As the day warms up, the first ones start to fly, circling up to a moderate height well above the trees. More and more appear, and they start to catch insects. You can see them using their feet like hands, and if the light is good you can see the discarded, glittering wings spiralling down like sycamore seeds. The feast is continuous, and if you draw your focus away from the full swirling, darting flock and concentrate on one bird, you see that prey is plentiful and success frequent. I have never managed to stay on one bird for long enough to see how much it eats, or whether it drops out of the feast when full. But all day long there are busy birds eating hard.

The total amount they get must be prodigious, and they are of course not the only beneficiaries of this bounty; sand martins and screaming swifts are up high with the falcons, while gulls draw your eyes down towards the surface of the water. When, as an otter watcher, you sweep your binoculars across the surface of the water, you find that it is shimmering with dragonflies, spaced no more than a yard apart.

Scientists now recognise that small food items such as dragonfly larvae can be significant in the otter's diet.

There must be thousands in the air at once, and this level of productivity goes on for most of the summer. On more than one occasion I watched an opportunist greater spotted woodpecker feeding its young on the emergers. The system it had devised was to fly from its nest hole down to the water level on one of the line of drowned dead elms that project in front of Noah's hide. Here it could clobber the larvae as they crawled up out of the water to hatch into their final and most glorious stage in the sun. It was so easy, and so economical of effort.

On reflection, the real wonder must be the enormous weight of insects living under the surface of that lake before the start of the summer. It is peaty water, yet massively productive. I wonder if the sprinkling of starling droppings from the aerial ballets in winter helps to increase the fertility. With such a plentiful resource it is little wonder that the otters make some use of it.

On the whole they usually need their food in more efficient lumps, which is why they prefer eels to other fish. Eels are pound for pound more nutritious than other fish, and less well able to escape from an otter. Ordinary fish are very agile and swift in acceleration when the water is warm, so their speed to some extent governs the proportion of each species eaten by otters. Most research into whether otters prey preferentially, or take fish in proportion to the numbers available, misses this aspect of availability. These studies consider the amount of fish in the area by means of netted samples, a method which cancels out the varying abilities of each species to evade a predator. That this is a considerable factor was shown in a valuable piece of research done by Sian Bishop from Leeds University in 1991. She looked at the use by otters of the fish available in three distinct parts of the Tone.

"This part of the Tone undergoes extensive restocking schedules by the Taunton Fly Fishing Club, and nearby a trout lake has recently been restocked and reopened. It was surprising that so few trout vertebrae were found in the spraints examined. Other species were taken rather than trout, despite the large number of the latter." Eel was the commonest prey item at all three sites, and little bullheads the next most prominent item. Availability, ie. catchability, is a major consideration for these specialist predators. It reduces the length of time that has to be spent in the cooling water. In the spring they make good use of the concentrations of spawning frogs. They also go for the toads, but they have to be careful to skin these, and to avoid the toxins in the skin glands. Failure to take this precaution has resulted in the death of a few otters. The lake we lived beside had a good stock of large tench, but the otters only ate them in early summer, when they were spawning, and easier to catch.

It would be interesting to see whether the proportions found by Sian Bishop are still valid nowadays. Eels have undergone a massive decline. Had one of the more glamorous species of our national wildlife collapsed as comprehensively and rapidly, there would have been an outcry, and remedial action. Big efforts are being made to rescue the grey partridge, for example. But who cares about slimy pseudo-snakes writhing about unseen in the ooze? Recruitment of juvenile glass eels is below 5% of what it was some 20 years ago, a decline measured across all the European countries that have an elver migration.

As eels are long-lived, and remain in our rivers for up to twenty years, we will not see the full effect of this for some time, but already there has been a worrying reduction in the adults. Electro-fishing samples from Somerset recorded a drop of almost half between 1991, (Sian's year!) and 1993: density of eels fell to 63% of what it was, and biomass to 52%. It has remained stable at that reduced level to 2006. In his researches on the sea-dwelling otters of Shetland, Hans Kruuk did calculations to estimate the values of the prey to the requirements of the otters. Remember that he said, "If prey availability were to reduce by half, otter survival would become impossible in winter." If the depleted level of recruitment continues, the adult eel population is bound to reduce even more, as the remaining mature fish finally leave for the sea, and this must affect the diet of the otters in this area.

Typical evidence of an otter kill and a real problem for the carp pond owner. The flesh and innards have been eaten out behind the gills and there is evidence of a bitten nose-tip – the only place an otter can grip so large a fish.

scent. People mind more now, when their water features are raided; it used to be that goldfish were a give-away fish, a few scooped out of a neighbour's garden, or even won at the fair. Now people go in for designer fish, expensive koi carp, shubunkins and the like. The otters do not mind; it is all free food to them, whatever the price to the owners.

Most owners of small ponds give up after a couple of attempts at restocking. Otters are almost impossible to fence out by any method that can fit visually into a normal garden. The best method we have found is a low electrified fence of the white tape used for pony paddocks, which can look like some kind of decorative edging, but, as it can also sting up the children a bit, it is not suitable everywhere. There are compensations for having no fish, such as more tadpoles and dragonflies, so on the whole the gardeners grow accustomed to the change.

Domestic fish-pond raids

I think it may already have been an influence on the amount that otters are attacking domestic fish in garden ponds. Ornamental fish pond have long been a feature of our gardens. Winston Churchill's was famous, because he painted it. In my childhood we had a pond at our first house, before we moved to live beside a large lake. Grandfather had a much better one. Both drained into streams which fed the Lune, a good river for otters, but I do not remember raids. Nowadays such visitations are common, even in ponds with enclosed water-circulating systems situated far from streams, and with no drainage to the river for an otter to follow the

Put-and-take fisheries

Not so the lake owners however. In my youth, before the otters declined, such stocked, 'put and take' fisheries were unknown. At school, a friend boasted to me about catching rainbow trout; I had never heard of rainbow trout. They were a newly introduced novelty. Carp fishing used to be an abstruse pastime practised by only a few pioneers like the writer and artist, BB. I remember as a young teacher assuring a boy who came to me for careers advice about freshwater fish farming that he was wasting his time, that apart from a few salmon hatcheries to produce parr for restocking rivers, such places were not to be found. I like to think I was right at the time, but he now runs a most successful organic trout farm. Aquaculture took off while the otters were absent.

Consequently, large enterprises were established without any need for fencing. Mink could be trapped, herons would avoid overhead wires, and cormorants were mainly sea-birds, and much fewer in number before the easy availability of stocked rainbow trout ensured the survival of all the young that fledge, a success rate that nature never anticipated. So a fish farm had a lower set-up cost than nowadays, and the increase in our habit of eating-out gave a growing market for trout.

The industry had developed well when the otters started to return, by gradual infiltration from the west. The timing was bad; the otters started to revive in the late '80s, the eel population nose-dived in the early 90s and the fish farms and stocked lakes were there, unfenced, to provide an easy alternative. As commercial enterprises they could not afford to shrug and forget it, like a pond owner with some fairground goldfish.

Responses varied. One Somerset farmer, proprietor of some rather shallow carp ponds, put a television in a polythene bag up a tree, and played it all night. He showed it to me with pride, and assured me of its success. Luckily the set was quite high up, so his gaze was above the level of my wellies, which were sneakily erasing the fresh spraints containing obvious carp scales on the path where we were standing. Another carp man called me out to a lovely lake, much more suitable than the other one, to confirm that he had an otter problem. When I got there it resembled a scene from a Bond film; there were men in wet suits, men in rubber boats,

netsmen, and electro-fishers, all hard at work for the second day running. His idea was to remove all the rubbish fish, every last one, from his three acres, so that it would finally contain only adult carp. There would be two advantages to this. When fishing, his friends would not be troubled by pesky little perch, roach and tench pinching the bait all the time before the cautious carp could get to it. Secondly, the pond would be much less attractive to otters. I was not sure about that. Certainly, the easy prey would have gone, but if one did turn up, the menu would be very restricted. It was obvious that he had had an otter, and that his lake was situated

where otters were bound to pass, so he erected a good fence, as he did not want any conflict, or to harm them in any way.

Katie Etherton also showed a good attitude, but to be fair she did not have an investment to protect. In her parent's garden is a lovely pond, with a good flow of unpolluted spring water which never fails. For her birthday she asked for some trout. In term time she delegated the care of her fish to her grandfather, who, being a tad forgetful, would sometimes feed them several times a day, so they grew immensely and became a pride to all the family. Imagine Katie's consternation when they started to be killed and eaten, or rather, at that size, partly eaten. There were unsightly and distressing fragments on the rockery to draw her attention to yet another loss. When I told her that it was not mink, and that I could not set my cages, because the culprit was an otter, or more probably a family of otters, she beamed. How wonderful. In that case she knew what she wanted for her next birthday, some more fish, please. Good girl.

An otter chases a rainbow trout. Pressure forces air bubbles from the otter's coat and its ears are closed when swimming underwater.

Even though water is still dripping off this otter's whiskers, its coat has already opened up to replenish the insulating air.

A similarly generous-minded attitude was that of Ben Hanson, who ran a major trout hatchery not far from Minehead. He had lost 6000 fingerlings from one rearing tank in a week and the raiders had been seen in the river behind the pub, a bitch and two half-grown cubs. Obviously things could not go on at this rate until the otters reached maturity, so electric fencing had to be installed. But he was anxious that too strict a defence might cause the cubs to starve, so he concentrated the security round the core of the farm, and left at the top end a biggish lake with some strong adult fish, not very easy to catch in quantity. Then at the bottom end, as a concession to the inability and inexperience of the cubs, he re-commissioned a disused

pond into which he would put any damaged and unmarketable fish, a sacrificial pond to protect the rest. A generous attitude, considering the cost of such fencing. Cost depends on the shape of the ponds, and the neighbouring terrain. One long-established set of lakes with a long river frontage has had to buy wire by the kilometre.

The defences have to be thorough, too. Mary-Rose Lane was at a riverside fish farm in Devon, showing a group the design of an effective anti-otter fence. While they were discussing the set-up, a small otter came up out of the river, ducked through an unperceived hole and took a trout, which it carried back to the river. The hole (see photo on page 67) had been missed because they thought it was a rat hole, far too small for Britain's largest predator. It was about four inches in diameter.

It is hard to keep an otter out, but impossible to fence against mink. They can climb whatever they cannot penetrate. Unlike otters, they kill and hide more food than they need for one meal. They used to be a nuisance at fisheries, but happily they are now rare in most of this area. Only in the widespread reed beds of the Levels have they been able to avoid the aggression of the otters, and maintain a presence.

I used to have to be careful when called out to a raided pond, to decide which species was involved. But on one occasion it was neither. I

The almost imperceptible hole (no more than four inches wide) through which an otter passed. The film cartridge gives an idea of scale.

was called to a small trout hatchery at the top of a sidestream. There was another fishery lower down, which would have attracted the predators first, but I could find no signs of any animal activity. That confirmed the owner's suspicions; he had been robbed by people with nets.

Dietary Preferences

The idea that otters take whatever prey is easiest and most accessible to them holds good in most natural situations, where the otter's focus is on getting a full belly. But I have found instances

of otters in artificial situations of great plenty showing a preference. Both instances involve a large waterboard reservoir where rainbow trout are reared for day ticket fishing. The trout are farmed in dense quantities in unprotected ponds, but the resident otters bother them very little. The spraints reveal that they are concentrating on the now abundant signal crayfish in the lake.

We are all supposed to be sad that the (formerly legal) release of this American species has caused the demise of our much smaller, native crayfish, the white-clawed. But the introduction of this successful new food source must have been of great benefit to the returning otters, helping them to re-colonise their former haunts despite a big reduction in their staple, eels. So, although theoretically I ought to, I do not join in the chorus of disapproval about signal crayfish. Besides they are delicious, and big enough to be worth eating. Another point on which the otters and I concur.

It was at the same reservoir that another, more strange instance of preferential predation happened. The hatchery manager bred a blue strain of trout one year, and had a pond devoted to these unusual novelties. When the otters found them, they worked their way through the lot, by-passing similarly sized fish in nearer ponds to get to this particular colour. The manager had given a batch of the blues to his chum at another reservoir, so he rang him to ask for some back. But the same had happened. The otters there had also gone for the paler coloured fish and finished them off. I can understand that in the wild, in a big river or lake, a fish lacking in protective colouration might be a better target to aim for, but here all the fish were equally concentrated in the holding tanks, and dead easy to catch. They must have been exercising a choice for some reason or other.

Scottish studies have shown that otters take some sorts of salmon more than others. Cock fish are more likely to be eaten than hen fish; this may be because they cruise about much more at night, moving from pool to pool, and exposing themselves more on the intervening shallows.

At the time of year when otters utilise adult salmon most, the spawning season in late autumn and early winter, they take mainly kelts, and mainly cock kelts, probably because these tired and spent creatures are the easiest to catch. Opinion differs as to the extent that they make use of dead fish.

A small group of otters in the Mull of Kintyre learnt to visit the fishing boats in the harbour, and steal a meal, but I am told that when those individuals died the habit ceased. It was an aberrant trick, and confirmed the general supposition that otters are averse to eating carrion. However, my friend Derek Myhill took a series of photos which show definite and considerable eating of a dead kelt washed down the Teign in Devon, and that the otters continued to eat it when it was no longer freshly dead. Charlie Hamilton-James also filmed an otter retrieving and eating a far from fresh kelt on the Taw.

If this sort of thing happens more than the traditional view in the literature supposes, the otters are less of a nuisance on a river than they were formerly reputed to be. If a salmon is found with the familiar bite taken out, the assumption has always been that it was the otter that killed it. That is true, sometimes, but at others it may be that the salmon was dying anyway, or had finished its breeding cycle, and was of no further value in the scheme of the river.

Although they may not be the "vermin" that they were formerly labelled by the ghillies that reacted with anger to every dead fish, any large and mobile predator is going to be to some extent inconvenient. I know of one otter which met its end because it had decided to concentrate considerably on a diet of grouse eggs. For some reason otters leave the main rivers at a time of drought and low flows, and go up the side-streams, where one would suppose the lack of water to be more acute. In the fells of the north they go right out onto the moors, and live on the 'mosses' and peat bogs. This otter had found the living easy, and was there unscathed for some while before my friend Roger discovered what it was that was doing such systematic damage.

I know of a few instances of an otter killing lambs. In two of them it turned out to be an old and debilitated specimen that had turned to this unusual but easy prey. The point is that most of them don't, although they easily could. At the right time of year lambs are plentiful in the north, and the rivers carry a less dense amount of fish than our southern streams. Otters are at least as big as a fox, often half as big again, so they could equally cope with the killing.

There are fewer otters, so they would not be such a regular nuisance as hill foxes are. But if otters were opportunists and if they now take a wider range of prey than they used to, or than they were formerly known to, which is slightly different, one would expect them to make use of the spring abundance of lambs as they do of the autumn abundance of salmon. But, undoubtedly, they don't.

Are we back at the basic idea of a specialist, fish-only predator?

CHAPTER SIX

SNOW

How I long for a good fall of snow. I do not want feet of driven drifts blocking the roads and causing untold amounts of inconvenience and extra work. But I would like a good, even covering accompanying a spell of weather sufficiently cold to let the snow last for several days. When we lived in the north of England we used to have such weather nearly every winter, but I believe the snow in the Lake District is much more intermittent nowadays, and only on the high fells does it linger long.

Down here in the warmth of Somerset, such snow as we get often falls in the night, as the temperature drops, and the following morning immediately starts to thaw when the sun rises. This means it is no good for tracking. Such footprints as were made earlier in the night are filled in by the continuing fall, and the last few marks made before dawn are soon melted out. But very occasionally a sufficient layer is put down before midnight, and the snowfall then ceases for the rest of the night, so that, by breakfast, clearly displayed across the grass is the story of the comings and goings during the second half of the period of darkness. If these conditions would only remain for several days, I could get a good count of the local otters, and establish a baseline of knowledge from which to assess the rest of the year's activities.

But even the brief glimpses that I am occasionally given are always very revealing, and one must not be ungrateful. It's just that to be shown so much, and then to have the rest of the information wiped off before there has been time to get round it all, that is very frustrating. Especially when it is probable that such an opportunity will not occur again during the life of the otters involved.

Tracks in the snow

The last such opportunity occurred in February 2006. We awoke to a bright, clear dawn and as the forecasts had predicted, a fresh covering of snow. As I drew the bedroom curtains I noticed that there were two clear sets of fox prints across the lawn below me: that meant that the snow had stopped falling sufficiently early in the night to be useful.

There was enough of it to make hurrying tricky, but the marvel of four-wheel drive got me down to the Tone quite readily. The time spent driving there was taken up with planning what use to make of this chance. The most interesting thing to do is to find an otter's tracks, and to try to follow what it has been doing, where it went and how far it wandered. But, as the opportunity is so limited, I tried to plan a sort of count. I would sample the river at various places, and try to pick up the traces of as many otters as I could. At the back of my mind is always the idea that a census of breeding bitches is the only way I shall be able to establish the size and health of the population, and to monitor trends over time.

Mink Tracks

At the very first place I tried, the tall weir at Nynehead, I found mink tracks heading upstream. Without the snow, that mink would have been undetectable as it bypassed the obstacle. Typically, it had run the bank of the river quite close to the water's edge for some distance, but as there is a good cover of grass in those fields it would normally have left no tracks. That explains why people often overlook the presence of mink on their farms. Mink follow the river's edge closely, and they cut across the bends much less than otters, so they do not leave exit and entry tracks in the same way.

I found more mink tracks later in the morning, on my way home again, as the snow was being burnt off by the sun. About three kilometres downstream there was a similar set of upstream mink padding on the last bit of snow on a shaded bank. As mink are now much less common than otters, I assumed it was the same animal, although they do not regularly travel the river in the same restless fashion as otters. What I think these two brief snapshots showed me was a mink undertaking its spring dispersal to a new range for the summer.

I do not think in this instance it was a case of a hitherto undiscovered resident being revealed by a late fall of snow. The lower stretch of the river is so degraded by the presence all summer of an unfenced suckler herd of cattle that there is plenty of silty river's edge to betray even a mink. This was probably an instance of a mink that had been resident in winter quarters since the autumn, moving on in the spring to find a mate and a summer territory. They are reputed to move quite long distances at this time of year, and again in the early autumn when the litters break up.

Then there is a second general movement of mink, away from their depleted and prey-poor summer territories, into individual winter quarters. This accounts for the surprising spread of this species. They do not fill outwards into the nearest available vacant space, but leapfrog over large distances and suddenly appear in a new area which can be a considerable distance from any known stronghold of mink. This must have considerable survival value for the species, as it must make it very pointless for any predator to try to move in onto a mink population and exploit it as a resource. Now you see them, now you don't. And they move away from the area where they have been hunting intensively to feed their kits, to find a place with more plentiful food.

Following the Clues

The only snag to using the tracks in snow to decipher the night's activities is that there is no indication of timing. Coming downstream past the weir were the pad marks of a medium sized otter. It had cut out round the weir much more freely, so it had not crossed the mink tracks. Which had been there first? And was there any reaction by either of them to the presence of the other animal? It is now thought that otters take deliberate steps to seek out and kill mink that come into their territory. But their method of travelling along a river is the opposite of a mink's; the otter swims for much of the distance, only landing to get round obstacles, or to cut across a bend, so its tracks are very intermittent and spaced out, and do not reveal what it was doing for most of the time.

An exception to this took place on this same river, about ten years ago, when there was a good fall of snow at the spring half-term. I had gone further up to try to find signs of otters. I almost wasted the opportunity, by stopping my car to watch two dog foxes and a vixen, intent on courtship and rivalry in a roadside field. But a passing tractor broke up the party, so I carried on, and just as well, as I came across otter tracks that were equally as fascinating.

A big-footed otter had followed the Tone downstream, in a normal sort of way for a foraging otter, emerging briefly, and swimming much of the way, but always making downstream progress. When he came to the weir at Greenham, he went into the old mill culvert, and met another, smaller otter. The tracks became very confused. They had spent some time together, rubbing and rolling and playing in the snow in the field beside the culvert.

The smaller otter did not seem to have gone very far from the culvert, not on the snow, at least. But the bigger otter, probably a dog, had left in a hurry, crossed the road through the gateway rather than under the bridge, and had set off downstream at a good gallop. Four

Whitelip bounds fearlessly across the ice. Sometimes otters appear to enjoy ice and snow just like children.

splayed padmarks together in a bunch, then a long gap to the next set; he was bounding along, and following the river very loosely, galloping straight across each field and ignoring the windings of the meanders.

I got my car and drove on to where the lanes came back to the river. There were the tracks again, and he was still hurrying. Back into the car and on further. This time he had crossed the road through a field gate, and in the next field had turned under the hedge, and followed it directly to the far end of the field, and onto the path across the footbridge. I drove on again, and again, until finally, about 7 kilometres downstream from the culvert, he met another otter, again a smaller-footed one, and the tracks became all confused and friendly again.

There was a lot to be learnt from that one morning. It was a good demonstration of the scale on which otters habitually work a river.

I followed that dog otter for over 8 kilometres, without discovering either the holt he originated from, or the place where he finally rested for the day. It was good to be reminded of this. In the days of otter hunting such a drag would not have been uncommon, although the line would usually have been much less direct, and more closely allied to the course of the river. It was interesting to see just how far the otter had departed from where one would expect to find evidence of his passing. Had I been trying to work out what was going on under normal conditions, when I would have to rely on spraints or padding in the riverside mud, I would have stood no chance of realising that it was the same otter all the way. I would have decided that the intermediate bit of river was devoid of fresh evidence and that there were two dog otters involved.

There was also by implication an indication of the comparative size of the ranges of a dog and the two bitches. The dog's territory covered those of two bitches. It also seemed to show that only one big-footed otter is to be found working all that length of river, that they are indeed territorial. This was later to be confirmed by our research using the DNA from the spraints on the Tone. The study proved that many otters stick to their own stretches of river over several months, and that they seem to have the exclusive use, for their sex, of that length. It is natural for fishermen and others who go on reports of sightings to overestimate the number of otters on a river; they underestimate the size of each individual's range.

That was of course an exceptionally successful bit of tracking, especially for a river so far south as ours, where sustained snow is a rarity. However even a short-lasting covering can be useful, as the rest of my recent morning showed. After finding the mink and the otter at Nynehead I missed out the town of Wellington, and went on upstream to a farm where a bitch and cubs had been seen before Christmas, to try to find out if they were still in the area.

Initially I was disappointed. At the first place I looked I found the track of a small adult otter crossing a bend and heading downstream on its own. So, a little disheartened, I set off downstream too, across the same footbridge that the long-distance otter had galloped over many years before. I had not gone far before I found the tracks of a similar-sized animal, hurrying up the riverside footpath for quite a long stretch. At a bend below I was able to work out that the otter had gone downstream first, and then hurried back. This cheered me up, so I drove on upstream to the top of the farm, and there I found evidence of confused trampling by more than one otter right beside the water. I could not find enough of a straight stretch of padded snow to work out how many animals were involved, but some of the footmarks were encouragingly small, and I probably distinguished two sets of cub prints.

The temptation to exaggerate one's degree of certainty is very strong in such circum-

stances, but I could not really be sure. One of the restricting factors was the limited distance that this evidence seemed confined to. However, I got the impression that the bitch otter had exercised her cubs in the vicinity of a tree root holt where I knew some other cubs had been born two years before, and that they had kept strictly to the water's edge along a short stretch. Then she had left them, and gone by herself downstream, presumably to fish. But anxiety had set in, and she had hastened back to where she had left the cubs on their own.

The Tone is not very large up there, and I wonder how readily available fish are for a growing family. Further down there is a big mill dam, and a good supply of coarse fish. I think that is where the cubs were born, in the autumn. But there are more people and dog walkers down by the mill, so she moved them up to this secluded farm. It will be easier to get them to catch their own prey in the shallower water at the farm than in the depths of the long mill pool, but I doubt if an adult can easily keep herself and a good milk supply without a quick foray away. That is speculation, of course, but it is based on the evidence of the snow.

Given a more sustained period of winter weather, much could be worked out about the extent of the movements of these mobile creatures, and one would arrive at some idea of just how many, or how few, individuals are responsible for all the widespread activity and signs we normally base our studies on.

There would be an assumption behind such a snow scenario, of course, that the weather had not caused the otters to change their habits. I think it would have to be much more severe than we are normally accustomed to in England to affect them as much as a period of extensive rain and full spates does, for instance. When I was a schoolboy at Sedbergh there was every February a period when winter conditions set in and all the games pitches were unusable.

Good. Skating took over as the main outdoor activity, when the whole school went to our lake of about 50 acres high on the fells above the Lune valley.

The prefects would organise transport; our lot used to hire a cattle wagon, into which we would all pile for a fare of two shillings. No seat belts: no seats; no harm. Most of the hearties in mourning for the rugger pitches would get up a game of ice hockey. But not me. The game kept everybody nicely out of my way, and left me free to skate all round the perimeter of the ice, looking for tracks. A few rabbits, and their attendant stoats.

Solitary foxes would cross the lake; they were less plentiful on those moors than they are in the richer farmlands of the south, and much less welcome, in a sheep farming countryside just before lambing time. My father would try to use the snow to track them back to an earth and dig them out. This was more difficult than

it sounds. The tracks would cross and recross each other, and the distances involved were very long, I suppose because food on the moors was very scarce at that time of the year.

One would have thought that 50 acres of thick ice, thick enough to carry five or six hundred skaters, would make the lake a place of scarcity for the otters too. But the light covering of snow revealed that they would remain there regardless of the ice. They seldom crossed the open expanse of the centre of the lake. But day after day I would trace their intermittent progress round the shores. There were always one or two holes in the ice. The mute swans would keep one area open, and there were often apertures near the only inlet stream, and by the low weir at the outflow. The streams

Even this degree of human intrusion did not drive our otters from the lake.

themselves never froze, but I do not remember that the otters tended to frequent them much. They would have held little to attract them at that season. The spawning trout were back in the lake, the juvenile trout were minute, and the crayfish in the outlet would be deep and dormant in the crevices that gave them their name.

I think the otters were after the tench which were lying torpid in the peat at the bottom of the quite shallow lake. Certainly they had one of our Muscovy ducks. Its apparently uneaten carcass lay under the ice, not far from the hole by the boathouse where we used to feed the ducks and the swans. Gradually, as the skating season progressed, it rose up with its layer of ice, until it came to the surface, where it was shaved off level with the ice by all the passing skate blades at that busy area of the lake, a duck in cross section, and a different slice each day.

That it had been taken down by the otters there was no doubt: their bubble chain lay frozen under the ice too, and rose with their victim. I wonder why they did not eat it, for food cannot have been easy or plentiful for them, and I remember no bones or bits of tench at that time. I remember plenty from the early summer, after the spawning season, at which time I suppose the tench were easy victims, but in winter I found no awkward heaps of fins, bones and head to impede the skaters.

Finding an otter holt

My enjoyment was to skate after the otters, and to follow their every twist and turn. As the shoreline was partly wooded, and as some of it had a dense fringe of rhododendrons overhanging the edge, there were gaps in the snow cover, so I never really found their winter lying up places or holts. We knew that in summer they lay up on top of the bank under the bushes, just a couple of bounds from the water's edge. As far as we were aware there were no deep holts in the stony banks of the moorland tarn. The padding in the snow revealed that they remained in the area for many days, despite the yelling hordes of skaters and ice hockey players. I wonder where they were by day; probably curled up back from the bank in a snug and impenetrable bush.

As a small boy I found one such couch. When I was crawling in under the dome of a large, arching rhododendron in search of moorhens' nests, I spotted a smoothly polished patch in the angle between two major roots, rather like a deep armchair with high back and arms. A short path led into the water. Over the years it remained in frequent use, as a favourite place for an otter to pass the day. Yet it was at the nearest point to our house, and only a hundred yards or so from our kennel of dogs, who often rushed through that bush when we let them all out for exercise. There were many other similar bushes dotted all around the two mile circumference of the tarn, some of which the otters also used. Yet despite all the frequent disturbance, they continued to use the one by the house, and always to curl up in the same snug set of roots.

It is tantalising to be afforded these brief periods of increased insight into the nocturnal life of the rivers. In the presumption that, with a more prolonged period of tracking snow, all would be revealed and I would finally learn to understand all there is to know about this mysterious species, I long for more snow. But one deludes oneself that such yearnings are fulfillable. Such thinking is wistful, and in steadier moments of sober realism I admit to myself that there is bound to be a limit, a surprisingly low limit, to what we can learn about a major carnivore merely from tracks and signs. Indirect evidence cannot match observation, alas.

I was born just before the war, in 1939. In the forties and fifties there were other priori-

Creatures of habit – this well-used otter tunnel has been pushed through a heap of old rushes to reach the lake.

ties in rural Britain than investigating the private lives of wild animals which seemed to be plentiful and healthy. Most of the effort went into the preservation and restoration of some sort of normality in the lives of the people. I was too young to be aware of how difficult things sometimes were, but I can just remember my parents discussing how much longer they could last out without proper food before they had to put down all their pedigree dogs. And the doctor in Sedbergh told me in the fifties that malnutrition was an important factor in the health of the farm children from the fells.

Then, just as things became more comfortable again, the otter population crashed. The focus of such wildlife research as there was turned to investigating the presence or absence of these now rare, or totally vanished, animals, and to trying to identify the cause of their demise. In those days we were all busy measuring their return from the brink of the abyss of extinction. That took us through the 1980s and 1990s, and is important work still in the first decade of the new century in most parts of England. We in Somerset are luckier than most, in that we have now had an established otter presence for about ten years, so monitoring and recording are less of a focus for us.

Yet we still know remarkably little about them as a species. As could be seen from my experiences in the snow. Even one night's worth of information is a valuable addition to my knowledge, or at least confirmation of some theory I have assumed from a book. I reckoned that the dog otter covered more than 9 kilometres in one night, and checked on two bitches in his territory. Lots of theoretical assumptions there: to start with, that the ones with big feet are dogs. I suppose we do know that, as they say, for a fact, because we have had plenty of dead otters to measure, and on the whole the dogs are larger when full grown than the bitches.

But I have recently made notes on the diary of the master of the Courtenay Tracey Otterhounds. He killed 10 bitches over 16lbs in weight, and two of them weighed 22 and 23 pounds, so to say that my big otter was necessarily a dog is a supposition. As it is to say that he was territorial.

The study of Tone otters that we did by using their DNA seems to confirm that there was a resident population of both dogs and bitches, each of which was located in only one stretch of river. But their DNA was not discovered very regularly, and they could at least in theory have been absent from their territories for much of the time. I incline to think that the pattern for

enough of the otters identified is sufficiently consistent to support there being a system of territories on the Tone, and that the apparent absences are best explained as problems in the science labs in getting an adequate reading from enough spraint samples. But this still leaves unresolved the status of all the otters we found only once, a new individual every month on what seemed to be a full system.

Charlie Hamilton-James, the wildlife cameraman, told me that the two bitch otters that he filmed for the BBC's *Springwatch*, "Ebb" and "Flo"; kept to their own patches very rigorously. They lived with their cubs on a very short stretch of coast, within sight of each other most of the time, yet they kept strictly to their own side of the boundary marker, a wall that came down to the sea's edge at right angles. Bitches with cubs are of course restrained as to their mobility, which is why they are so disproportionately the subject of films and research projects. They are the only type of otter you can be reasonably sure of seeing again.

Radio collaring of otters is not often attempted because it has generally been found to be too hard on the researcher who has to try to keep in contact at night. Was the notorious Dee otter that covered 80 kilometres of that rugged Scottish river in any meaningful sense territorial? Or was it just a wanderer which kept

One or two? It is often hard to be sure.

to a catchment? Another Scottish otter that had been injected with a radio-active isotope, to enable its spraints to be detected, vanished out of the area altogether, so even the sort of scale of 80kms was inadequate for that one.

Things are even more complicated away from linear rivers, in a system of lakes or swamps. Here otters seem sometimes to tolerate very chummy densities, but I suspect that, like "Ebb" and "Flo", they have their own living areas. My best morning's otter watching was when I saw eight before breakfast from a mile of the main track on Shapwick Heath.

The situation was similar to that of the two bitches on Shetland: there was a bitch with three big cubs to the north of the track, using the extensive area of reed bed and lagoons known as Meare Heath. To the south, based mainly on Noah's Lake, was another bitch with two smaller cubs. And I also saw what I assumed to be the proud father, the dog common to both lots. These otters are often seen from the several bird hides, and there was no record of either litter crossing the main rain and the track alongside.

They appeared to be 'territorial', yet there was no sign of any interaction with the neighbours, no need to defend the territory, so perhaps it was just that the resources of the area each bitch had chosen to have her cubs in were more than adequate, so she had no need to move, and the smallness of the cubs would have prevented much mobility anyway. Lack of movement is far from the same as being territorial.

Mobility is the attribute mainly associated with the otter, however. During his adventurous, fictional life, 'Tarka' covers the whole of the system of the Taw and the Torridge, Williamson's *Two Rivers*. Williamson knew what he was writing about. When Charlie Hamilton-James and Phillipa Forrester made a film about the wild otters on the Torridge in 2006, 80

A well-worn otter path can be seen crossing the grass enabling the animals to skirt the reservoir dam.

years after Williamson finished his marvellous and evocative book, they found that the otters were to be found in exactly the same places, and holts even, that Williamson had written about. They could not of course verify that any one otter would travel so far or so often. As is inevitable in order to produce a coherent film, their programme was based around the fortunes of a bitch and her litter of cubs, so, of necessity, restricted to disclosing what was happening on one stretch of the Torridge only. Williamson obviously had experience of what the otters did on a wider area of those rivers, both from following the Cheriton hounds, and from his searching for the lost tame otter which took him to the river so often at about the time he started his book.

However, I do not know what evidence he could have had for the extensive wandering of a single otter; that must be supposition, or a carry-over from the earlier book by J C Tregarthen, *The Life Story of an Otter* (1907), which gave him the idea for *Tarka the Otter*.

Road-killed otters

The records of the dead otters we have found and sent for post-mortem do provide some evidence of such mobility. Enough of these have been found on roads along the tops of ridges and hills to provide significant proof that it is not unusual for otters to cross from valley to valley. Those of you who have driven down the M5 will have noticed the proud finger of the Wellington Monument, prominent on the very summit of the hills at the border between Devon and Somerset. There was a dead otter on the road past the monument recently. It must have been crossing between the Tone and the Culm. There is a precedent; the Culmstock Otterhounds started a drag on the Tone above Wellington which led away from the river, through the fields, and over Culmstock Beacon, down to the river Culm at Whitehall, where they put off their otter. That was a cross-country trek of about 5 miles by crow, and a major journey for an otter.

We have had other otters killed on the lanes along the summit between two branches of the same river; it seems that the otters of Clatworthy reservoir forage up one of the feeder streams, and then use the road to canter over the ridge about half a mile to the top of the next similar stream, before making their way back down that one to the lake again. I have had several reports from drivers who have seen them in their headlights, and three have been run over. These otters do not count as otters away from water. They know where they are going, and are just taking a short cut between two parts of their territory.

However this is not the case with the otters crossing from the Tone to the Culm, or the many otters we have found dead on the North Devon Link Road. They were leaving any useful system of streams and travelling across country. This is not a recent development, part of the spread of the depleted species as it re-establishes itself, but something otters have always done. I remember as a boy shooting on the moors near Sedbergh when my father pointed out to me a spraint on a tuft of rushes, right out on the tops, well away from any stream or watercourse.

'Tarka' crossed from the Taw to the Torridge on the top of Dartmoor, but that does not count as leaving water in the same way, since the Two Rivers rise back to back from the same small bog at Cranmere Pool. When I went there, I looked hard for spraints, to try to establish that an otter had recently done the same, but it was some time ago, when otters were very scarce, so there were no signs.

I was more successful one day on Exmoor, when I followed a series of fresh spraints up the Hoar Oak Water, which is the top of the West Lyn, and then found equally fresh spraints at the other side of the bog, where the infant Exe has its origins. I think, but cannot prove, that an otter crossed the spine of the country, from a river flowing north into the Bristol Channel to one flowing South into the English Channel. I

The sad form of a road-killed otter. An all-too-frequent sight as otters travel cross-country, seeking to colonise new territories.

searched hard, but could not find any evidence in the boggy ground on Exe Plain to link the two. However, on another occasion, I did find fresh spraint on Swap Hill on Exmoor, on dry ground well above the streams and bogs, which could have indicated that an otter had crossed from the Lyn to the Exe, and in this instance had abandoned all water and wetness to do so.

Roaming otters

So there does seem to be evidence to support the assumed theory of wandering and perpetual motion otters. Tarka's roaming is not inherently improbable. But there is so much we do not know. Do otters that cross from catchment to catchment do it only once, or infrequently? Or is it a regular part of their lives?

My interpretation of the evidence from the DNA study had one bitch otter crossing over from the Batherm, an Exe tributary, to the Tone, a north coast river, and then back again. If this was so then she knew what she was doing. For otters to cross the bogs from which two rivers emerge back to back is not unlikely, and may well be something that they find themselves doing often and incidentally, when searching for frogs to eat perhaps. But what drives an otter to cross over Swap Hill, or Culmstock Beacon, or the high fells of the Howgills? Will such an explorer ever return?

An otter surfacing from a dive. Few creatures are so well-adapted to the elements of water and air.

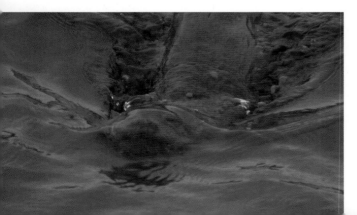

Above all, if conspicuous sprainting is part of their territorial behaviour, a possession marker by established residents, why would a transient deposit spraint high on a watershed? Did it have any idea what it was about? Did it expect that remote spraint to be read by another otter, or was it some sort of refugee, a dispersing youngster perhaps, forced out of its homeland by the pressure of its parents, or by other territory holding otters?

All we can say is that some otters seem to be resident, and not just the bitches with cubs that have no other option than to settle down for an extended maternity leave, while other otters wander about, sometimes well away from the sort of watery places we would normally look for them in.

Otters and intruders

Aggression plays a large part in the lifestyle of this species. All animals growl and snarl and nip, or whatever their equivalent form of ill-natured warning to back-off is. Yet otters, more than most other species, go farther than threats. They are of the weasel tribe, and that clan is known to be hard, and quick to use its teeth.

A ferret makes a delightful and affectionate pet, yet if the handler is abrupt and startles it, the instant response will be a sharp bite, without any warning; no raised hackles, no low growling, nor exposed teeth: the mustelids go in at once with an attack. This is consistent with their way of life. Whereas stags, being herd animals, can avoid much of the aggravation by ostentatious roaring and thrashing of vegetation, the solitary weasels do not have time for such a parade of strength when they come across a rival.

At one moment they are alone, going about their business, and the next moment they are in a confrontation. Another of its own kind has emerged silently from the shrubs, or has swum round the bend of a river in the dark, completely

Alert – and about to vanish!

unannounced. To dither would be to invite defeat, or even death, so they attack at once and without warning. This is why zoos have Asian otters rather than Europeans. Our species, being solitary by nature, is too unpredictable, and can cause severe damage.

Vic Simpson, the vet who did the post-mortems of all our otters, has found that over half of them have been in recent fights, and that the resulting injuries are often so severe as to be life threatening. Land animals meet head on, and attack from the front. They are protected to some extent by their thick skulls, and their strong neck muscles, especially the males; many species carry antlers or horns at the front, or business end, for defence as much as for attack.

But otters tend to meet in the three-dimensional medium of deep water. A head-on offensive would be to go for the strongest part of the opponent, and to offer little defence to any other direction of assault. So otters try to get under each other, and to attack the soft underbelly and the sexual areas at the base of the tail. This is serious stuff, much more dangerous than the nip on the nose that two members of a more civilised species might give to drive a rival away.

Vic has some appalling slides of the sort of the damage he has found, otters of both sexes castrated, penis bones snapped in two, soft belly flesh ripped open. These wounds are prone to infection and sepsis, which in several cases has proved fatal. Remember that an otter has to catch its prey in a difficult, strenuous and at times even dangerous medium. Any severe damage is going to reduce its ability to feed itself, and an inadequate amount of food will prevent resistance to infection and slow down healing. Otters do not often fight to the death, but death can often result from a fight.

Injured otters

This is the conclusion from the examination of the dead ones we find. We do not know what happens to the victors. Despite what one might expect from their clean habitat, otters carry a lot of bacteria in their bite; the old otter hunters knew that, and always stressed the need to disinfect any bite from an otter very carefully.

The defensive hold for an otter in a fight with another otter is to bite and hold the cheek of the opponent. That keeps his (or her) nasty teeth up at your front end, and away from the vulnerable parts near your tail. So otters that have been in a slight fight often have puncture wounds to their face, as well as their hind feet.

Otters have sharp teeth, but a very narrow bite. Their incisors (canine teeth or fangs) are only 20 mm apart; their mouth is designed to hold slippery, tubular eels, and can inflict very little damage on a flat firm surface like a dog otter's neck muscle. It is probable that the victors have some inconvenient bite wounds too.

We do not really know what happens to them. Most of the dead otters we find come from the roads. Cars have killed them, but a significant number were probably going to die anyway, and it was their injuries that made them less able to get out of the way of the car. Had the car not chanced along at that particular moment of the night, where would it finally have died? We have found two otters curled up dead in garden shrubs, having crawled in to die, but there must be many more, some of them underground in the holts. So even what we know from the post-mortems is incomplete knowledge.

It is probable that much of their behaviour is driven by their food. This is normal for predators; they have to adapt to the nature of their habitual prey species, in a way and to an extent that grazers do not. Wildebeests may have to walk a long way to keep in touch with fresh

The games played by young cubs can be boisterous and energetic.

grass, but they do not have to think about it much while munching away in such a wholesale manner. There is more to being a successful otter than just diving in and swimming around a bit with its mouth open. At least, that is true for the natural, wild situation that otters have evolved to cope with; nowadays, in some of the artificial densities of prey they find in fish farms, goldfish ponds and match angling lakes, getting a meal must be more like shopping in a supermarket, so easy that even I can do it occasionally.

Energy expended in hunting

However, otters do not have the direct sort of competition for their meal that African big cats and hyenas have; if an otter catches a fish, there is no queue of similar carnivores seeking to deprive it of its catch. No other similar species followed the early, innovative weasels back into the water that the land animals had so sensibly struggled out of so long before. Despite this, the considerable store of fish protein which attracted them to get their feet wet does receive a lot of unwelcome attention from a variety of

Captive otters, like this one, show little of the muscle-tone and leanness of its wild brethren.

hostile and hungry creatures, such as other fish and many kinds of bird, so fish have become very wary as a defensive consequence. Fish are, therefore, hard to catch, even for an otter. And an otter has to catch quite a lot.

Lions, or a cheetah, expend a large amount of energy all at once, and may well kill a lump of meat sufficient for several animals for several days. Catching a fish does not use up as much energy as a cheetah chasing a gazelle, but an otter's food comes in much smaller parcels, and catching a medium-sized fish may well be similarly expensive of effort as a leopard stalking and pouncing, say.

But the otter needs to pounce on several fish to get a full meal, each of which is fully elusive and requires an input of skill, time and calories. As stale fish is unhealthy, fresh fish must be caught every day, and even the element in which the hunt takes place makes a measurable demand on the hunter's metabolism. The jungle may be neutral, but the river is not. One loses heat some 23 times faster in water than in air, so an otter that chases lots of little fish needs more in the end than one that gets very lucky with a sizeable pike. It not only has to replace the extra energy from the extra chasing, but also it must compensate for all the extra time spent in the cold water.

Compensating for the cold water

They do not go in for insulating blubber. The agile nature of most of their prey, and the demand for athleticism which a river swollen in spate imposes, mean that a podgy and unfit otter would soon be a hungry otter. Their size and build is an excellent compromise, adjusted very finely to the demands of their lifestyle.

A larger otter might be stronger, and better able to massacre more fish, but it would need a much larger food supply, which would mean a longer stretch of river to patrol and guard, which in turn would need more of its time, which would leave less time for catching all the extra little fish required to satisfy its bulky appetite. Any smaller, and it would be at a disadvantage in defending its fishing rights, and in catching agile and elusive prey.

Smaller bodies lose heat more, too, ask any shrew. Those minute carnivores have to eat every hour or so to keep any fuel in their tiny tanks. Smaller otter species, such as the Asian short-claw, are found only in much warmer parts of the world, where heat loss is less of a problem, and where they can more or less graze on abundant small and undemanding prey such as land crabs, without a major cost in calories.

Otters and badgers

Badgers, which are a similar size to our otter, also take mainly undemanding prey. They snuffle up vast numbers of small items such as earthworms, where the only demand is for time; no skill or strength or energy is required to mug an earthworm, so they vacuum them

Otters of all ages enjoy frolicking in the snow, sometimes creating slippery shutes between holt and water.

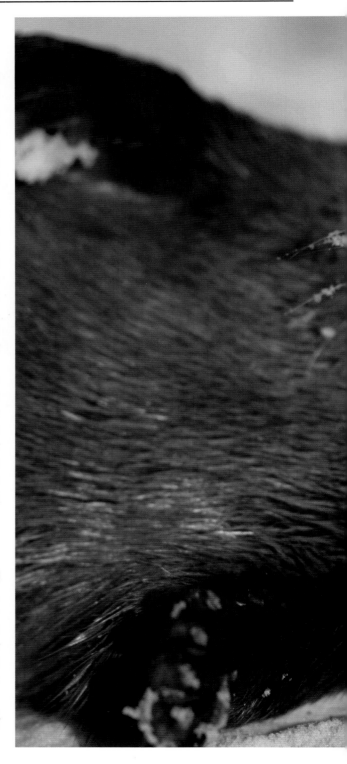

patiently up, topping up in season by maize cobs, apples and unripe barley. They lay down masses of fat, which sees them through any cold spells in the winter. It does not matter that they are pudgy and corpulent, as they do not need fitness to eat again, and they have taken to gang warfare for defensive purposes. What they lack in individual muscularity they make up for by calling in the other members of the sett.

How different from my admired otters. They must retain fitness, to catch the next fish, to cope with the strong currents and varying levels of the river, and to patrol enough of it to protect their fish futures.

Badgers also patrol their worm farms, but the circular shape of their patch means they are never far from the perimeter, and with so many of them in each sett, patrolling does not take up too much time. To patrol and secure a solitary otter's lengthy stretch of river does take time, and it is a finely tuned balance between the distance required to provide enough food for an animal of that size, the ability of an animal of that size to cover enough ground, and the amount of time this detracts from the primary need for catching today's meal.

It is a balance that works well most of the time, but it can be tilted quite easily into a condition which imposes hardship on the otters, and like all athletic predators, an otter which struggles to maintain its condition soon loses the ability to do so, and starts on a rapid downward spiral of deterioration.

Causes of stress

The hazards for a predator can sometimes be natural. It has been estimated that a prolonged Atlantic storm, with gales that prevent falcons from hunting for more than three days, can result in them becoming too weak to be effective. The abundant medium-sized fish that sustain the otters in Shetland sensibly migrate every winter away from the turbulent, storm-lashed shores into the comparative peace of deeper waters, where the otters cannot follow them. This imposes a period of stress on the otters at a time when the water is at its coldest and most difficult. Hans Kruuk calculated that an otter might need to hunt for 25 hours every day if it was to maintain its body weight. In other words, without some luck, some otters may not survive the lean period.

That dearth is caused by the weather, and occurs only for a short time every year. The similar lack of sufficient prey in many of the rivers in England is permanent, not seasonal: it is caused by our abuse of our waterways. We build more houses and overload the designed capacity of our sewage works.

Pollution incidents, many of them from deliberate dumping, are frequent; rainfall and the Environment Agency may soon clean up the stream, but they cannot as quickly restore the small life-forms that were obliterated by the short-lived poison.

Nor is all poisoning short-lived; diffuse and ongoing pollution is as great a destroyer of river life as dramatic, large scale dumping. Open-cast pig farming releases a lethal mixture of soil and manure into many small streams. The silt clogs up the gravel beds, and the accompanying manure particles use up all the oxygen as the bacteria break it down; this sterilises the basis of the food chain.

Free-range cattle are as bad. Near here there is a farm where 40 years ago they milked twenty cows, and put the milk out in churns for daily collection from the roadside. Now they milk 300. On a hot day the cows stand in the river for coolness, as they always have. If the farmer were to dump the manure from his huge herd into the river from a trailer, he would be prosecuted. That the same amount goes in full toss, straight from the cow's tail, is not preventable, but it is just as potent. Worse, while they are abominating the stream, the cattle cut up the banks with their hooves, and manufacture industrial quantities of silt, which chokes even the very plants. The river looks fine, and the cows look picturesque under the willows, but the catch returns of the fishing club show that fish are much less plentiful than they are a short distance upstream.

This is a general effect, common across many lowland rivers. Fishing clubs in every area are expressing anxiety about fish stocks, juvenile recruitment, lack of fly life, and the physical state of the river's structure. But for the large injections of money from the angling fraternity for restocking, gravel scouring, bank repair, and tree pruning, the supply of fish available to our returning otters would be even poorer than it is. I think that the difficulties they find in making an ordinary living may be affecting their behaviour sufficiently to amount to skewing it into the edges of abnormality. This makes my

self-imposed task of trying to discover how they live, and what sort of population structure they adopt, even more tricky.

The "dog" otter in the snow at the start of this chapter patrolled his territory, exhibiting considerable mobility, and cavorted with his females, or at least I thought that was what I observed at second hand from the tracks. The bitch otter seemed to leave her cubs and go downstream to deeper and more fish-rich water to hunt. All of these facets of activity will be affected if, as I suspect, the fine balance of the otter with its environment is out of true.

Can the territory still sustain a dog, two bitches and x cubs, or does such a group of otters, which, according to received wisdom, is a normal otter group, require more food than

Larger prey will usually be taken to the shore where the otter can use its hands.

can be regularly provided now by the length of river they can defend? If food is scarce, there will be pressure from equally deprived neighbouring otters on the ends of the territory.

Perhaps this is what accounts for some of the fighting, although closer examination of the detail of the post-mortem results shows that there are other factors as well, such as sexual activity. Mobility, too, may well be increased by hunger.

Bitch otters, cubs and food

Every bitch otter must leave her cubs to find food. The nature of their environment dictates that this must continue until the cubs are well grown enough to cope with the hazards of a river.

There is a scene in the TV programme, *On the Trail of Tarka*, where quite well-grown cubs are having to claw their way along the waterline of a riverside wall in order to make progress against the current; this struggle was not at a time of great spate. But how far from the nest would she normally go? In 2006 three lucky, very small cubs were found crying for their mum by a farmer at Gold Corner, on the Somerset Levels. They were taken to Secret World wildlife rescue centre, and made quite a name for themselves as 'Splish', 'Splosh'', and 'Splash'.

On the night they lost their mother, a bitch otter was killed on the M5 motorway, but she was 4 kilometres from Gold Corner in a straight line, and farther by following the waterways. The body was too mangled to see if she was lactating. Either two bitches came to grief that night, or the mother had gone a very long way away from her young, presumably in search of food.

I find that improbable, as otters need to protect their young. One November a lactating bitch otter was killed at Bishop's Lydeard, crossing the road when the river was starting to flood. We searched hard, and found two neat nests. One, above the road and out of the flood zone, showed little use; the other, in a drawn out rabbit hole lower down beside the stream, looked as if it had held cubs. We found no trace of the young otters themselves. I think the bitch had been killed during the process of shifting her family to safety. That the cubs were predated before we found their nests shows that bitches need to be very vigilant for their young.

Fighting otters

Defending the family against dog otters could account for some of the vicious bite wounds found on bitch otters. A severely bitten three month old cub from the Somerset Levels produced bacteria from its wounds consistent with it having been attacked by another otter. At that age it would have been closely dependent on its mother and no sort of rival or threat to whatever otter attacked it.

A more dramatic case was that of two dog otters, killed together by the same car while they were fighting on a road in North Cornwall. A lactating adult bitch had been killed 4kms away a few days earlier. Post-mortem revealed that one of the dog otters had recently eaten a female cub of about four weeks old. DNA analysis showed that the guilty dog otter could not have been the father of the cub, but that the other, older, one could have been.

Sadly, the body of the bitch, from her DNA probably the mother of the cub, was too badly flattened to show whether she too had been in a fight. But this episode shows that she might well have had to fight defensively against a larger, fit young male.

Why otters fight

Our discovery of such episodes is rare. We do not know whether this is aberrant aggression, a reaction to an imbalance with their riverside living space caused by the degradation of the habitat and depression of their food resources, or whether it is a natural part of their breeding strategy, as it is in lions. The first duty of an

Youngsters play-fighting — but look at those teeth! Otters are capable of inflicting serious damage on one another when the adults fight.

incoming male lion is to kill all the young cubs sired by his predecessor in the pride. Do incoming dog otters cleanse their territories ethnically?

Certainly bitch otters often seek out-of-the-way places for their natal holts, but

Rough and tumble in the reeds — two young otters are practising their combative skills.

swallows leave on migration before their young, or that hedge sparrows are amazingly promiscuous. Perhaps the smaller birds do indeed all conform to what their instincts permit them to do, but considerable individuality is readily observable in higher, more developed birds such as the peregrine.

Perhaps it is down to nurture rather than nature. Fledgling robins just hop overboard out of the nest and more-or-less get on with it; but young peregrines are educated by their parents in the same way as the cheetahs on the television. Prey is caught, and released alive in a battered and slowed-down state for her young to practise on.

Otters keep their young with them for a whole year, or sometimes more. Besides the problem for a half-grown, understrength otter of having to catch enough food at times of spate, there is so much to learn: the full cycle of the varying food sources needs to be shown to each individual cub. Instinct could not lead it to the spawning frogs in the spring or the lampreys in early summer, nor prepare it for the running of the salmon or the silver eels in autumn. It must learn these vital things from its mother.

If only otters were more observable, if they could be readily distinguished one from another, as stags are, what a fascinating revelation that would provide.

this is thought to be to remove their helpless young from the dangers of flooding. Yet I also know of breeding holts directly on the bank of large rivers. Perhaps some bitch otters are constrained by population pressure to do the best with the resources they find in the space they are permitted. Or they arrive at different decisions.

Otters are highly developed animals with advanced brains, and individual traits and attributes.

There is an inclination for people like me to try to establish a common norm of behaviour, to be able to say that otters do this, or otters breed in such and such a way. This is I think a carry-over from bird studies, where people have published that robins are aggressive, or that adult

Chapter seven

THE LOSS OF THE OTTERS

It is amazing that we still have a large, specialist predator roaming the rivers of our over-populated country. Politicians tell us that over 90% of the people now live in the towns and cities, which is some comfort to a rustic like me. Other authorities tell us that the last decade of the 20th century was a period of massive movement back to the rural areas, and that there are now more people in the English countryside than at any time since the Industrial Revolution began. The barns where I used to find barn owls are all converted into attractive dwellings, and there is a social crisis from the lack of affordable rural houses for indigenous young couples. I imagine that the otters of Somerset feel a similar lack of suitable and peaceful dwelling places, but, amazingly, they manage to survive.

How close they came to extinction in the 1970s is known, precisely. It was only by a whisker that they escaped becoming, like the wild cat and the pine marten, an almost-legendary species hanging on in low numbers

in the wilder and less populated regions of the Scottish mountains. The chemicals that did for our otters were widely used; arable farmers used them to dress seed corn, and to spray on bulbs; sheep farmers used them as a dip at a time when dipping of every sheep was compulsory; they controlled insect pests in orchards, and were used for moth-proofing in the clothing and fabric industries. Therefore their malign accumulation reached into every corner of England, and the otters, like the sparrowhawks and peregrines, succumbed.

It took a while for the full extent of the damage to be noticed, and another while for the scientific establishment to accept that what the otter hunters and fishermen were saying was more than what they scornfully dismissed as 'anecdotal evidence', (that is, no evidence at all). One particularly arrogant young woman actually announced that she would not even consider the records she was being sent by the hunts, as it was "ethically contaminated data". That she, and others, disapproved of the hounds did not lessen the accuracy of their scenting

powers, and while one might perhaps maintain that the interpretation of what the hounds did during a day's hunting projects too much human subjectivity onto the results, the use of scent to gather information about otters is of course very appropriate, as it is how the otters themselves communicate. It is much less haphazard than relying on the coincidence of sight to monitor a nocturnal, nomadic animal.

My early records

At that time there was no regular monitoring of British animals. Birds were counted, by a variety of schemes, which all relied on the enthusiasm, and assumed accuracy, of amateur bird watchers. The natural history club of my school in the 1950s regularly counted the wintering wildfowl on the tarns around Sedbergh, for a national census organised by Sir Peter Scott's Wildfowl Trust. We also sent nest record cards to the British Trust for Ornithology, and took part in the mapping of buzzards nests and dipper territories. We used to ring the dippers, too, but got very few returns, largely because dead dippers are swept away by the spates and never found, I suppose. But we would recapture some of the adults, and the rings revealed how faithful they were to their territories.

That schoolboys were doing such detailed studies of birds was not considered unusual at that time. Ornithology was well developed, organised and funded. Yet the records I kept of the otter signs I found while roaming the river valleys of the Lune and its tributaries were of no interest to anybody else. I used to keep a notebook of anything related to otters, and spend time making maps and lists – there was no telly in those days that far north! Then, when I went to university, I caught a bad case, almost terminal for a while, of intellectualism. One day, when my symptoms were at their most pronounced, I binned all those juvenile scribblings as no longer relevant to the high goals I was setting my mind; they were unscientific and childish, of no importance. How like the arrogant young biologist who considered the hounds lacking in proper systematic method.

How I wish I had kept them. They would be one of the very few sets of regular records for the otter from before the decline of the 1960s and 1970s. Now, in the year 2008, I am careful to check the "Otter Loo" on my stream every day when I walk the dogs, and like to think that the 21-year series of data is of some significance. Similarly, sixty years ago I recorded faithfully everything that I found on the shores of our lake. This was prelapsarian data, from a never-to-be-recovered world, from an era when there were far fewer people, when DDT was a novelty not in general use, when the otters were probably at their maximum density on rivers where salmon and trout were still plentiful, prior to the ravages of UDN (ulcerative dermal necrosis). Apart from the attentions of Christen, the rogue ex-keeper, they had had little depredation from

humans during the six years of war. The records I painstakingly misspelt as a child were of an optimum population, and would have been of great comparative value for evaluating the success of the otter's recent recovery from the chemical horrors which destroyed the idyllic world through which I roamed as a child of the moors near Sedbergh.

I do not think I am remembering my jottings through the rose-coloured filter of memory, any more than I am mystifying the departed ways and creatures of the countryside of my boyhood. We shot grouse and occasional partridges where now there are only conifers and sheep. Spring on the moors was noisy with calling curlews, bleating lapwings and drumming snipe. The blackcock still lekked at their traditional site beside the Old Scotch Road. Our ground had always been noted for them: The Kaiser's heir had been a guest especially to shoot them. There were no longer such numbers, so in our day we left them to breed. I can well remember putting up a small party of these powerful birds, and watching them fly right across the wide Lune valley to the Middleton Fells in the distance. We had high brown fritillaries, and roding woodcock in early summer. And there were otters on the lake irregularly but frequently, carefully recorded by me. But all that water went under those bridges long ago, and with them my notes. So we have only the hunt records to tell us of the otters of those halcyon times, unscientific and lacking in method though they may be.

First national otter survey

We do, however, have an accurate assessment of the reduced state of the post-pesticide, remnant population, an acceptable census which shows us exactly how near we came to losing our otters completely. After the authorities had become convinced that the otter population was indeed

very depleted, they finally instigated a survey, in 1977. When the results were published in 1980, the anxiety about the disappearance of the otters was confirmed. The score was even lower than anybody had predicted. 94.2% of the sites searched held no evidence at all of an otter; the 170 places where there was still some sort of a sign were closely grouped, and represented an even smaller number of individual animals.

The near-extinction of the otter

In the hope that any repetition of such an appalling situation can be averted, it is worth looking in more detail at what happened, or, too often, did not happen last time. This has been a large part of my motivation in following the otters all my life, besides a fascination and admiration of the creatures for their own agile and independent sakes. At first I wanted to help nurture the few survivors back to a reasonably secure status again, and later I felt I should keep monitoring them, so that we would have earlier and clearer warning should another serious problem occur. In theory, increased vigilance should enable a more prompt, positive and successful response. And this book should act as a warning and encouragement to others involved nowadays, who were not active in this area of conservation at the time of the last disaster.

How did it all start?

So I will try to retell the story of the decline. It did not have a definite start. A groundswell of opinions gradually grew among those who talked about otters, that the numbers were down. One of the ways in which "things" were different was that little was written about otters in those days. Otters were talked about in fishing and hunting circles, so the early information was indeed anecdotal. That, as you know, is a term of contempt in scientific circles nowadays, but of course it doesn't have to be synonymous with "inaccurate".

Anecdotal evidence dismissed

The anecdotes were that otters were undergoing some form of slight and slow decline. I first heard of it in 1964 or '65, when the Kendal hounds came to Somerset for a joint week of hunting. We were aware of nothing serious in the North, but the problem was mentioned by some of the people in the Culmstock country, in Devon. The older members could remember that there had been similar variations in the past. Several packs had recorded a barren patch in the latter part of the 19th century, and again

just before the First World War. Things had at one stage been so bad that the Dumfriesshire Hunt had imported Norwegian otters to top up their stock. We were also of the opinion that the development of the distemper virus into the disease 'Hardpad' in the 1950s had been as damaging to otters as it had been to dogs and ferrets. The matter was touched on, but not worried about. After all, there were in those days no firm statistics other than the hunts' own records of sport, and those had always been subject to the variations of the weather, the spates, and just plain luck.

That we in the North were not yet anxious fits in with what we now can see from the studies of peregrine falcons, for which there are precise statistics. These show that the decline was more pronounced in the South, and that the figures tail away as one moves north. This fits with what we know of the uses of the pesticides that we now blame for the whole debacle, but in the early days this cause and effect was far from obvious.

First report published in 1957

In 1951 the Scott-Henderson report looked into fieldsports at the behest of the Labour Government. It found that so little was known of the natural history of the otter that it recommended that it should be investigated. As a result, Marie Stephens was commissioned to do a study from 1951 to '54, and her report came out in 1957. No hurry, obviously. She reported by River Board Areas. She found 2 areas where otters were 'scarce', 10 with 'fairly small populations', and 22 where they were 'numerous' or 'very numerous'. So there seemed no cause for anxiety there, especially as she attributed most of the differences between strong and poor areas to physical causes such as polluted water and habitat destruction. The 1950s was an era when drainage engineers ran amok with recently-developed machines, draining and straightening rivers wherever possible, as part of the drive to make our expanding population self-sufficient in food. Everybody still remembered the submarine blockades of the war, when we were down to a week's worth of essential foods at one stage. Farming had to have precedence, we all agreed on that.

However, Stephens' leisurely approach and delay in producing her slim volume can now be seen to have been not just misleading, but positively harmful. That was not her fault, and the criticism of her slowness is perhaps unfair. She was after all the very first to attempt research in this difficult field, and she was working without any of the things we now take for granted. Even cars and telephones were different in those days. Do you remember having to book trunk phone calls? We used to calculate our longer car journeys on the basis of thirty miles an hour. She was charged to cover the whole country.

However, the year her reassuring report came out, 1957, was, ironically, the year the first pack of otterhounds, the Wye Valley, closed down because of a lack of otters in its country. The previous year, 1956, was "the year when the first unmistakable symptoms of the impending crash appeared" in the peregrines. (Ratcliffe 1980). There was a report of reduced breeding success from a series of eyries. In 1958, there were no successful eyries along the coast of North Devon and Cornwall.

But then as now, few people cross-referenced to other specialisations. Why should they, when physical factors along the over-dredged and mutilated rivers could be seen to be to blame for the discrepancies? But if they had, they might have picked up on the strangely accelerating rate of the decline. Yet the reassurance of The Otter Report of 1957 had caused a relaxation of attitude to the anecdotal chatter of the

hunters. It has also to be remembered that the Scott Henderson Report which had started this particular topic was a response to anti-hunting agitation, not a first stirring of conservation. So it, and the Otter Report, were put back into their box, and all was thought to be well.

Missed clues from the peregrine decline

And indeed, when I moved down to Somerset in 1967, and tried to start my researches in 1968, there were still a considerable number of otters. The accelerated decline that kicked in between 1971 and 1974 caught us all by surprise. Yet perhaps it might not have done, if a unique opportunity to understand the problem had not been missed in 1961.

My great friend and guru, Dick Treleaven, who had been involved in the Cornish studies of the peregrine that had drawn attention to the downturn in breeding success, submitted a dead bird that might have unlocked the whole mystery of the breeding difficulties and the accelerating rate of the disaster. He had been trying for some years to get the authorities to take seriously the possibility that the damage was being caused by pesticide residues.

Nobody seemed to want to listen to him. In November 1959 he published a paper in British Birds, documenting the lack of breeding success. Poisons were dismissed as unlikely by the few who responded to this warning. After all, either one is poisoned or one isn't. No near misses in Agatha Christie's world. Much more probable seemed the idea of an imbalance in the adult population, whereby a spare adult female would entice the tiercel away from the brooding falcon on the eyrie, so that she would have to let the eggs chill in order to feed herself. Instances of this had been reported. Too many birds, perhaps, not too few.

Even when Dick told of a falconer friend whose birds had been extremely ill after eating wild pigeons, he made no impression on those whose duty it should have been to listen. Three sick hawks in a mews somewhere, and one bloke down in remote Cornwall banging on about his own local patch; it's hardly a national crisis, and anyway, poisons seem very unlikely, there's no evidence as such, no dead peregrines.

But on 25th May 1961, Dick saw a falcon at one of his eyries on the Cornish cliffs attempting to soar out to sea, only to be blown helplessly back inland by a wind which should have been a dance floor to such a bird. Then, as he watched, she crumpled in the air and spun down from several hundred feet like a Sycamore seed, and crashed into a field of standing corn. After a long search he found her, and tried to revive her. But she died, and he sent the body to the RSPB, who were at that time looking into unexplained deaths in game birds and pigeons. This was not either of those, so they binned the body, and it was never examined. If it had been, the residues of the accumulated pesticides would have been found seven years earlier than the publication in 1968 of the research into eggshell thinning, and the chemicals might have been banned sooner and more decisively than they were. It would have focussed everybody's attention in a more chemical direction, and might have made the authorities investigate the effects of them on the otters as well, perhaps.

The chemicals principally involved were the replacements for DDT known as Dieldrin, Aldrin and Heptachlor. They are organochlorines, and very effective as killers and deterrents of insect pests and fungal infestations. They became very widely and freely used, in industry, especially in cloth or wool-based processes, and in farming, as a seed dressing and as sheep dip. All sheep had to be dipped annually, by law, to eradicate a nasty infection called scab. I remember the hares on the moor at home had it one year. You could see the poor thin creatures huddled in their forms, with nasty blisters and crusty scabs on their faces. A drop of sheep dip

would have been a mercy to them. The development in 1955 of such miracle potions must have been a blessing for the sheep farmers, too. The problem is that nobody realised its persistence, and its accumulative effects. A tiny drop zapped a sheep tick at once, but total immersion did not seem to harm the sheep at all. A farmyard hen could peck a couple of grains spilt from the drilling machine without any effect, but the wood pigeons and greedy pheasants that homed in on the field where the bulk of the dressed grain had been shallowly drilled soon found that they were accumulating more poison than was good for them. Little of it was excreted, but each grain's worth of very persistent poison was stored in their tissues. Comparatively rapidly these greedy feeders started to be found dead and dying across the countryside, but as the poison was not instantaneous, it took a while to connect the dead birds to the area that had caused the problem. The RSPB was set on to look into it.

The birds belonging to Dick Treleaven's falconer friend were fed on three pigeons only; that was enough to make them ill, but not enough to kill them outright. Perhaps, if they had died, more notice might have been taken, as pigeon is after all a popular human food, too. But the research focussed on the species that were succumbing, and ignored the falcons, and the otters, as no dead bodies had been produced as evidence. It was all still anecdotal. The scientists were looking in the main for avian diseases, which would be worrying for both the poultry and the pigeon industries.

Slow poison, hard to spot

There are several reasons related to the nature of these chemicals to explain why the otters reacted less dramatically than the birds of prey. In larger organisms the chemicals are slow and accumulative. Some small part of each tainted meal is transferred to the predator's fat, where it gradually builds up, and remains, stored in a fairly harmless way. Pigeons take quite a considerable load, and only feel the full effect when cold weather or long distance migration causes them to deplete their fat store.

So apparently healthy, but loaded, quarry is available to raptors, which eat much of the meat and fatty tissue of each bird. So they too accumulate all the stored doses from all their meals. Many falcons and sparrowhawks specialise in pigeons, so they are very susceptible. But the raptors, being athletes, do not carry much fat. The alternative store is the reproductive organs. If a fat person were to slim, such residues of these chemicals as he was carrying would not leave his body, but move to the reproductive organs. This explains why the onset of the problem in Cornish birds of prey was manifested through poor breeding performance.

Otters take the poison in more slowly. There are only three stages of accretion in a raptor, from corn to dove to hawk. In the river it may go from microbe to small invertebrate to a larger predatory insect to a small fish to a larger fish and then to an otter. This is a longer and more indirect process; a small water bug will carry much less chemical than a similar sized grain of wheat which has been deliberately washed in the stuff.

Whereas pigeons can and do fly about, carrying their doses of slow death with them, and spreading it to birds of prey all across the land, otters keep to their rivers, as do the fish they eat, so not all otters will get it at the same rate, and the overall effect will be, as it was, less noticeable. Eels are a snag though. They are the otters' staple diet, and are very full of fat. They can slowly accumulate a big dosage, which is why the effect increased in its speed in the later stages. Otters are low in fat, being predatory athletes like the hawks. So most of their dosage went to their reproductive systems, and the main effect was not sudden and alarming death, but prevention of breeding. Breeding in otters is always a secretive process, and so this insidious depletion went virtually unnoticed, and as late as 1969, people were still speculating widely as to what might, or might not, be going on, and following the false leads of water quality, destruction of bankside habitat, and disturbance, which had first been presented to them by the Stephens report.

These chemical goings-on were hidden from those of us out on the riverbanks with an interest in otters. Even with hindsight it is hard to be sure exactly what the mechanisms were. Did the chemicals poison or sterilise the otters directly? Or did they make them susceptible to diseases? To what extent was the effect of these pollutants on the populations of fish a factor in making life impossible for the otters? All the fishing literature of the time was full of gloom about the

A sign of pollution in a Somerset river. No healthy river should have foam like this and it heralds poison for fish and otters.

reduced carrying capacity of the waters. Salmon disease had been spectacularly obvious. But as far as I remember nobody at the time was making a connection to the possibility that the sheep dips

had weakened the immune systems of the fish. Nor did anybody connect the outbreak of fungus on the returning salmon with the lack of trout in the rivers. We were speculating; we had no real information to go on.

Our suspicions as to the cause of the lack of fish pointed mainly to physical factors. Grip drains on the high fells were causing fierce and devastating spates of very short duration, but savage in their scouring-effect on the gravels of the riverbed. The idea behind this large-scale progamme was to improve the moorlands for grazing. At about this time, vast quantities of lime were blown onto the moors and mosses. I do not know what improvements this made to the grasses, but most of it must have been rapidly washed down the grips into the becks. This is another example of the drive towards agricultural production of those times, a drive which ignored things like wildlife. We found that the deep, straight-sided furrows were a trap for young ground-nesting birds, and discovered many dead curlew, redshank and grouse chicks that had jumped in and been unable to scale out.

There were other factors to be considered. In 1957 the first feral mink bred on the river Teign in Devon. Mink may be easy to farm, but they are difficult to contain, so before long pockets of feral mink established themselves in many parts of the country.

One theory was that these mink carried infections from their high-density farms into the otter population, which had built up no immunity to them. It is similar to what colonial Europeans did to the inhabitants of various remote islands when we did them the honour of discovering them. Since we now know, or believe, that the main cause of the decline was the organo-chlorine chemicals, we tend to dismiss other factors as completely discredited. But I am still of the opinion that disease was to some extent part of the jigsaw puzzle. An article I wrote in 1969 discusses some physical evidence for a disease that has not been otherwise explained away. Otters killed by our hunt were again found to have distemper-marked teeth, a blemish we had not noticed for many years. Unfortunately, I did not keep a record of these instances. There cannot have been very many, as by this time the hunts were killing fewer otters, but it became sufficiently common to be remarked on "anecdotally".

My article also betrays the misled sort of thinking that was going on at that time; the chemicals still had not been identified as the prime cause. That acceptance came much later,

after the publication of a paper by Paul Chanin and Don Jefferies as late as 1978, which was based on retrospective analysis of the records of the hunts.

Red herrings

Mink started to increase very vigorously at this time. Although I saw my first mink in 1959, a dead one shot in the gardens of Levens Hall, it was not until 1968 that they are commented on in our hunt records as a frequent novelty

and nuisance. That they might infect the otters seemed probable. There is a well-documented catalogue of diseases which affect the fur farms. To what extent the very severe winter of 1962/63 had contributed to the problems of the otters was speculated about, too.

And this fog of misunderstanding was made thicker by those who sought to use it for their own agendas. There were those in the anti-field sport movement who were openly prepared to use the problem as an opportunity to banish a hound sport, and to stress whatever would most assist their objective. If the cause were chemical, a removal of the substances concerned could reverse the decline. That would not help their political aim, however, so they played down that aspect, and made much of the contribution from disturbance. Otters were fragile, and shy to the point of neurosis, they alleged. Some of this attitude remains. I am frequently told that otters will totally avoid a river where dogs are exercised, although there are dozens of obvious local exceptions. It was never fully explained why the otters should have so suddenly succumbed to

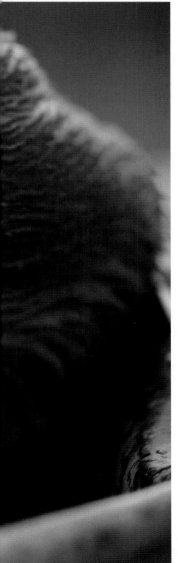

Otters in many parts of Britain have taken advantage of the growth of stocked fisheries and fish farms. A rainbow trout like this affords a decent meal for an otter.

their nerves when they had stuck out centuries of persecution as vermin, but disturbance and bankside clearance were for a while the front runners as causes for their disappearance. In *The Declining Otter* (Potter and King, Friends of the Earth, 1976) they claim, "Some creatures, such as the fox, are remarkably adaptable and co-exist successfully with man. Others, including the otter, are less so and are greatly affected by disturbance to their habitat. The great upsurge in the use of our rivers for fishing, boating and other amenities, together with pollution, abstraction and river management, has led to a sharp decline in the numbers of otters."

So the focus of most people's attentions was away from a chemical answer. The chemicals involved were receiving some attention, but not for reasons to do with wildlife. The motivator for progress was the effect that they were found to be having on the sheep, and the speed at which replacement substances became available. Dieldrin and Aldrin were found to dissolve in wool fats, and to be too persistent in the sheep. They also had been shown to impair reproduction, and to suppress the immune response to a variety of infections. These are the sort of considerations that I had speculated about. So they were banned in New Zealand in 1961, although they continued in use as a sheep dip here in Britain until 1968.

At that time the organophosphates started to be commercially available, and were able to replace the organochlorines, so a ban could be brought in without causing agricultural hassles. However, OC's were still legal as a seed dressing until 1975, a further 9 years of widespread use of a substance known to be accumulative and persistent. And Aldrin could still be applied to the bulb fields of Cornwall until 1992, 36 years after the first report of unmistakable signs of a crash in breeding in Cornish peregrines. The men in the ministries always proceed with deliberate lack of unseemly haste.

With the benefit of hindsight, it seems incredible that it was compulsory for sheep farmers to use organophosphates regularly from 1976 to 1992. The malign effect of these sinister substances was evident before 1992, and had been brought to prominent notice by the outrage caused by their damaging effect on our forces in the Gulf War of 1990, but it was not until the Synthetic Pyrethroids became widely available that the OP's could be withdrawn. They in their turn were hailed, as their dangerous predecessors had been, as the wonder answer to all the farmer's needs. SP's are lethal to invertebrate life in very small concentrations, so very good to cleanse sheep of their parasites, but also lethal to all forms of invertebrate life in any stream that is accidentally dosed. A single soaked sheep crossing a stream can drip enough poison to wipe out the basis of the food chain for an amazing distance.

The Salmon and Trout Association protested about this comprehensive and widespread destruction of the life of the rivers as early as 1996. Research by Moore, at CEFAS, a government organisation, showed that not only did the SP's wipe out the whole of the foundation of the food chain, they also had a physiological effect on the salmonids in the river, even at very low dosages. Their chemical effect was to block the production by the female of the pheromones which induce the mating urge in the male fish, and which are essential to ensure synchronous production of the eggs and the sperm by the two fish lying alongside each other.

Further, the government's Salmon and Freshwater Fisheries Review of 2000 recommended a complete ban on synthetic pyrethroids, which had by then been demonstrated to have even worse effects when synergistically combined with other chemicals. Without undignified rushing, and avoiding any suspicion of a crisp decision, DEFRA announced a temporary withdrawal of the licence for these

materials in 2006. Possibly, therefore, just possibly, the series of contaminants that people have been deliberately, and with encouragement or even compulsion introducing into the habitat of the otters since 1955 may finally have come to an end after 51 years. But I do not think that our system of dealing with this sort of problem can claim any credit at all.

1968 Mammal Society study of otters

In her ground-breaking report, Marie Stephens (1957) recommended that the otter be studied, and in 1968 the Mammal Society was commissioned to undertake this. Sensibly they turned first to the hunts, as the only source of comprehensive data then available. This occasioned two kinds of turmoil. There were those who wanted to have no dealings of any kind with so degenerate, immoral and untrustworthy a bunch as the hunters and their "ethically contaminated data", as one biologist haughtily said. This position was loftily principled, but would close the only practical way forward at the time.

On the other hand the hunters were, perhaps understandably, suspicious of the true motives of those who had so frequently bad-mouthed them. I remember much debate about whether we should co-operate or not. It was certainly felt that we should be circumspect, as whatever we said would be twisted and used against us.

In the event. it was the Kendal hunt that was accused of spin. The numbers for our hunt country showed a slight increase, and suspicions were raised about their trustworthiness. Our attempt to explain met with an indignant rejection, that hunters would always try to massage facts in their favour, and that it was for objective science to interpret numbers, not wriggling self-interest. All we were trying

least, even during a time of plenty. By 1971 the expectation had declined to from 42 to 55 finds per hundred days, and from 1971 onwards it had gone as low as 31 to 45. Sheep dip had been banned in 1966, so the continued acceleration of the problem rather threw people off the chemical scent.

But perhaps the ban had started to have some effect, as a second report in 1973, using the same method, showed a general stabilisation, except in the East Midlands. There was much doubt cast on this report at the time. Firstly, it, like the previous one, was based on the diaries of the 'repulsive' hunters. Secondly, hunting is in many ways an inexact sampling method.

It was pointed out that hunts would avoid areas where otters had totally disappeared. There is no point in searching for an otter where failure is certain. This would tend to hide the true extent of the decline. The hunts in return pointed out, not unreasonably, that the 1950s had been exceptionally strong years, so any decline could to some extent be explained as a return to normal levels. There is little doubt that the controversial second report might not have been published had not its author, the elderly Professor Hewer, died shortly before. It was felt that it would be demeaning to his memory to bin it, or to be too openly critical of what it told about the situation.

So the Mammal Society thought again. Their report, the first of the two, had emphasised that "without highly organised investigations little further information of value can be obtained."

to point out was that our success rate had gone up because we had changed our huntsman, and had been lucky enough to engage a new man who was experienced and skilful, in the place of a foxhunter who had found the mysteries of the different quarry beyond him.

Results from other packs

Briefly, the first report, which came out the same year, expressed the hunt records as finds per hundred days hunted. Those used to foxhunting would expect the answer to be in excess of 100, much more than one fox found each day, but the nature of otter hunting was always such that the score would be less than 100. The numbers revealed that sport had been stable to 1967, at a level very similar to that of the years between the world wars (64 to 79 finds per hundred days). Note that these figures give an expectation of one poor day in five at best, or in three at

They called on Paul Chanin, who had recently completed a doctoral thesis on the newly-established feral mink population in Devon, and who had also been investigating the otters of Slapton Ley, a coastal lake in South Devon. It was decided to build on the method employed by the Biological Record Centre of the Institute of Terrestrial Ecology. Their distribution maps were based on a grid of 10km squares, and each square was recorded as positive when one record was received.

1974 spraint-based otter survey

This scheme had been first mooted at the Mammal Society Conference in Exeter, in April 1974. A group of us went to the river Dart, and tested out a series of variations, to see which would be the most practical method of ensuring that one picked up some evidence from a thin population. A 500-yard search along one bank seemed to do the trick, so this method became the basis for all subsequent spraint-based surveys.

Paul Chanin contacted all the members of the Mammal Society known to be taking an interest in otters, and asked them to survey their area on this basis. My first such map covers 1973. In 1974 I was making a major effort to get around as much of Somerset and East Devon as I could, bearing in mind that I had a job and a young family.

Even then, as I did the survey, I had reservations about the worth of the method. Each 10km square is in fact 100 square kilometres in area. One spraint renders the whole block positive. A second spraint from the same otter can shade in another square if it just happens to lie on the other side of an invisible cartographic line. It was a crude tool, but times were very hard, and

robust information was badly needed. On 23rd June 1974, Sam Erlinge, the renowned Swedish otter ecologist, paid a visit, and I was privileged to show him my patch on the Tone, a river with a strong reputation for otters. We visited 8 places, but found only 2 tired old spraints on one weir. That was the best I could do for a man who could have shown me so much in the way of how to interpret evidence, a man who had a store of 14,000 spraints to keep him amused in the dark evenings of the long Swedish winter. Hard times indeed.

I made a major effort to fill in the 10km squares for the ongoing survey. As otters were scarce, this involved a commitment of time and petrol. To get the tick for my home square took more time each year. When I first moved to the Tone, it was easy; almost any walk out with the dogs would have provided some kind of otter evidence near our cottage. Later, it usually involved a trip in the car to confirm a report given to me by a friend. After confirming that, I would need to go further afield. Each tick needed to be 10km apart. Whereas in the times of plenty I could have just pulled up at a suitable bridge and expected to find some spraint, now that otters were scarce it became a game of hide and seek.

If the first stretch of 500 yards produced no work, it was back into the car and off to try somewhere else, and then somewhere else, until finally success was registered. Success was relative, of course. It was a fun game to play, and involved using one's knowledge of the country and one's experience of the habits of the otters, a sort of cross between a motor rally and a safari. Getting it right was satisfying, even when the sought-for prize turned out to be a dried up, and scentless pile of white bones, the ancient remains of a once aromatic and indicative spraint. Beggars have to be grateful for very small rewards.

The problem with this system was that the

harder one tried, the more likely one was to ink in the 100 sq kms as positive, which is exactly the opposite of what the survey was intended to show. Keen types like me were not only incurring a fair amount of domestic dissatisfaction for long absences with the car, but were producing an illusion of plenty in a land of dearth. The harder we tried, the less reliable the result. Except that in other areas of England, no matter how hard one tried, no result would be forthcoming.

By the time the exercise closed in 1978, 596 squares had been checked, covering 2057 sites, of which 30% were positive. This was disturbing enough, but the result from the first English National Survey, which overlapped with the end of Paul's Mammal Society one, gave an even more dismal picture. That found fewer than 6% of 2,940 sites had evidence.

The discrepancy can be accounted for by the eagerness of Paul Chanin's volunteers. It is a problem with all natural history maps; they tend to record the distribution of naturalists, not animals. The National Survey had got round this bias, to some extent, by getting one salaried surveyor to do the lot, and selecting the sites from a map in advance, to give a methodical network of coverage, without recourse to local knowledge. Whereas the network of volunteers

tended to look where they had most chance of success, or to persist until they did achieve a dodgy positive, Libby Lenton had to soldier on to all 2,770 negative sites, and search with unflagging enthusiasm some 1,264 kilometres of barren riverbank.

6% was a very conclusive score; no doubts about there being a considerable decline with that sort of number. It was much lower than we had expected, and caused great alarm, especially as several of the 170 positive stretches would have been indicative of the same animal, some frustrated and solitary specimen vainly wandering the waterways in an endless and futile quest to meet another of its own kind. Even Libby's methodical and comprehensive approach was in no way a count of otters. It was, like the Mammal Society map, an estimation of occupied range, valuable in that it seemed to disclose complete absence accurately, and because its strict method could be repeated exactly for the purposes of comparison and discovery of trends.

As it has been, although the spin on the statistics has been unhelpful in many instances. For instance, the 3rd National Survey of 1993 cheerily announced an improvement of an increase over the first, base line, result of 142%. This was hailed by the unthinking media as a triumph, and a sure sign of the otter's return to our waters, and of the rivers' restoration to health. But this massive percentage of increase was based on a score of only 22% of the sites checked having been positive, that is, 706 places

With a skilful mother to provide most of their food these big cubs have time and energy for messing about.

with otter evidence, out of 3,188 looked at. Or to put it another way, 4 out of 5 sites were devoid of any trace of an animal which habitually advertises its presence through deliberately sprainting on prominent rocks, that is 2,482 blanks. Even the 4th survey in 2002, also acclaimed as evidential of success, scored only 34%, that is two thirds negative, almost exactly the same score that we produced for the Mammal Society's first effort by our over-energetic volunteering 24 years earlier.

Meanwhile, people were attempting to put numbers on what had happened. It was easy for me on the Tone. On 6th April 1975 I noted that I had found no signs at 11 places, and concluded, 'I must assume no otters between Taunton and Wellington, including the side streams.' Others had a more tricky task. West published in 1975 the results of his surveys in Suffolk between 1969 and 1972, in which he claimed a population of 36 otters in space enough for 44. At the same time Macdonald and Mason, in neighbouring Norfolk, reported 'a significant further decline'. However UFAW examined some of the rivers in the Welsh Marches that Stephens had looked at, and concluded that the situation was relatively stable, as signs were frequent, and otters still relatively abundant.

Public reaction to the otter's decline

This was all very muddling and contradictory. It is hardly surprising that little progress was made towards the goal of many people to grant the otter some form of protection. To do this, hard scientific evidence was needed, and that evidence would have to demonstrate that things were desperate indeed for the otter, and that it was well on the way to imminent extinction. The relevant act could only accept an animal "so rare that its status as a British wild creature is being endangered." Badgers had had their own Act, designed to prevent badger diggers. There was of course a vociferous body of opinion which wanted to achieve the same sort of thing for the otter; their principle objective was the abolition of the hunts. This explains the over-emphasis in the documents of that time on disturbance as a major problem for the otter.

In the two reports of the Joint Otter Group, great prominence is given to prevention of disturbance of all kinds. Not only hunting, but also angling, management activities, boating and other recreational uses are all to be reduced or, in "otter havens", eliminated entirely. The idea had recently developed in the general mental furniture of those involved that otters were particularly sensitive to disturbance of any kind, and that they required absolute seclusion from people and, more especially, from their dogs.

This was a new concept at that time. There is no trace of it in the older literature. And common sense alone should have been enough to prevent so widespread an acceptance as it received. Once it had appeared in print, and been quoted and referenced a few times, it became part of the unquestioned background knowledge. That otters were to be found in towns, that they bred in the busy K Shoes factory in Kendal, such instances of unfazed otters were well-known, yet the myth persisted.

In *The Declining Otter*, King and Potter stated, " well-intentioned people taking part in otter surveys, or naturalists simply wanting to catch a glimpse of an otter can cause considerable disturbance to otters and could drive them away from an area." There is no doubt that this over-emphasis originated in the desires of the anti-hunt people to attack the hunts.

Times letter against the protection of otters

As late as 1977, a series of letters in *The Times*, after a committee of the House of Commons had discussed the protection of the otter, makes interesting reading. Sir Christopher Lever wrote, *"It is also, I think, not fully appreciated how shy and timid the otter is; if it is to breed successfully it requires both an absence from competing species,"* (by which he can only have meant mink), *"and above all freedom from disturbance by man, whether as angler, yachtsman, camper, hiker or huntsman."*

Ironically, in March 2007, the British Canoe Union lobbied for unrestricted access to all waters, and for unfettered enjoyment of their pastime as of right. The canoeists would not have appreciated Dr. Ian Linn's letter in the same series, written from the Department of Biological Sciences of the University of Exeter.

"I have grave doubts about the wisdom of placing the otter under legal protection at this juncture. There is no evidence that, over the country as a whole, the

It is understandable that people who felt so strongly should have sought to use every method available to them. Yet the consequences were not entirely to the benefit of the otter. People who intended no harm felt restricted or attacked, so became defensive rather than co-operative. The Otter Havens were intended to be total exclusion zones from all human activity. Fishermen found bits of their river closed and neglected. I remember when the hounds were drawing the Dorset Frome from Rampisham. During the course of a long day they located three places with mink, each of them a small "otter haven", so the mink were left in peace, at least until the hunt had gone. The local people were very angry indeed, and had no intention of preserving those mink. Traps would be set, and much less discriminating methods employed, to rid the area of unwanted mustelids. As it happens, I do not think there was an otter in the vicinity at that time, but its cause had not been advanced by the events of the day.

The over-heavy emphasis on the harmful effects of the removal of bankside vegetation was a mistake, too, in my view. I am told there were areas in the flatter parts of Eastern England where machinery operatives were encouraged to canalise the watercourses, and remove the bankside vegetation. This must have inconvenienced any surviving otters, but flat areas have field drains, and bushes and woods up side streams where otters could lie up during the day, as they always have.

It was a good idea to try to curb the mechanical enthusiasms of the drainage engineers. Their main harm was not to render the otters homeless, but to wreck the necessary habitat for the fish they depend on. But the blanket mantra that bankside despoilation was a major factor in the decline, a hare which had been started in the Stephens report, took everybody's attention away from the real causes of the problem. As had the exploding mink.

killing of otters occurs on a sufficient scale to make the slightest difference to their numbers. The otter is not yet endangered. What it needs, if it is to return to anything like its previous numbers, is good clean water, plenty of secluded riverine and lakeside habitat, and the peace and quiet to enjoy them.

"To provide that would involve society in paying a high price. The activities of many people and organizations (farmers, anglers, boaters, water authorities, huntsmen, industrial and domestic polluters, to name but a few) would have to be firmly curtailed. Is society prepared to pay that price?"

Mink distraction

We were still very suspicious of the role of the booming mink population in this sad situation. A note for the 13th July 1974 records a day on the River Exe by the minkhounds. With what they killed, and what the farmers had recently shot or trapped, the note concludes, "there must have been 18 mink at least between Cove and Tiverton last week." That is a distance of about 6 kilometres. The same page records that the hounds killed 7 on the Yarty from their previous meet. Mink are supposed to have first bred in the wild in Britain in 1956, on the river Teign. That they had established such a prevalent presence across the whole of the South-west in only 18 years is remarkable. Little wonder then that we were focussing on their introduction as a likely cause or factor in the concomitant decline of the other, and senior, mustelid

of the rivers, the otter. That the chemicals are now seen as the principle reason does not, in my opinion, entirely exonerate the mink from all blame. In 1997 the first report of the Joint Otter Group, in summarising the situation, discusses the effect of mink only in terms of inter-specific competition. The contribution of disease is airily dismissed as 'a possibility, though without any evidence'. There was evidence, in the distemper-marked teeth. Subsequently there have been other instances, with the virus that causes Aleutian Disease as a prime suspect.

Benefits of hindsight

From the distance of thirty years one can see how it was that we otter enthusiasts were groping in the fog of uncertainty. We did not realise that the persistence of the insecticides, especially in long-lived eels, was preventing an upsurge in otter

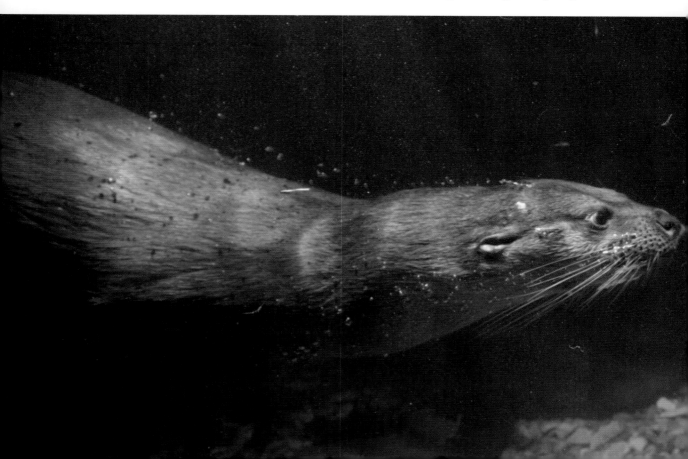

numbers after the poisons had been withdrawn. So it is understandable that we naturally tended to the view that it was physical and reversible factors that were impinging on the otters. Mink could be eliminated, as the Ministry of Agriculture tried hard to do. Bushes could be replanted. Intrusive people could be fenced out. At my level of involvement, the important thing was to try to discover some hard numbers about how many otters were left.

It was in the early 1970s that the Mammal Society said, in response to the first call by Marie Stephens for research, that "without highly organised investigations little further information of value can be obtained." These surveys, and other smaller and more local ones, were set up as a response to the need for better knowledge about the otter. All these efforts were our resulting attempts to measure what is largely unmeasurable, the kaleidoscopic, shifting, nomadic and fluctuating population of the otter. And there have been two good results. We established that there was a decline, as the anecdotal otter hunters gossiped into their beers all those years ago, a massive decline which has to some extent been reversed. And we have also established that we still do not know how to evaluate the current population of these elusive creatures. Forty years after Libby Lenton first set forth in her Dormobile to start the National Survey, we are still inking in 100 square kilometres on the strength of one small spraint. As I write this, the talk is of repeating the exercise for a fifth time, at a cost of some £258,000. I do not think that is the use of the money that would most benefit the otters, although it will cause us to comply with required monitoring targets. I do not think the result will be worth it.

Ears and nostrils clamped, eyes wide open; an otter in hunting mode.

The method is ponderous and is not sufficiently sensitive. Better by far, and much cheaper, to employ the method that I find just as good as anything we have so far managed to develop from all these years of intensive research. To assess your otter population, count the vicars along the river, and divide by three.

Try it, it works.

THE OTTER'S DIET

At a time when there is much misleading speculation and damaging allegation about what otters eat, here are the factual results of some studies.

Sian Bishop looked at two rivers in Somerset in July 1991. The Tone had recently been stocked with 500 medium-sized trout by the fishing club. From the Tone, 82% of the spraints contained eel, 68% cyprinids, 37% bullheads, 34% perch and only 26% had trout in them. Out on the Somerset Levels her study revealed 83% with eel, 58% cyprinid and 33% bullhead.

Dr Rafael Miranda and others did a more detailed study on the Somerset Levels in 2004, identifying the prey species from 358 spraints collected over a period of a full year. Despite the crash in eel numbers since Bishop's survey, eels were again the prime target of the otters: 38%. Sticklebacks were 19%, roach 11%, perch 6%, gudgeon and bullheads 4% each and pike 2%. Carp, the angler's favourite, formed only 1.5% of the diet. 6% of the diet consisted of birds.

A further study in the same area by Daniel de la Hey in 2006 found that birds were recorded in 41% of the spraints. Coots were the main species, followed by mallard and cormorants. Eight other bird species were recorded. This looks to me like opportunist hunting rather than deliberate targeting. The incidence of birds is much higher than in the two earlier studies which recorded 4.7% (1975) and 4.6% (1981). This big increase could be due to the decline in eels or the presence of some new cubs learning to hunt for themselves. It has not been echoed in other areas of Somerset.

My overall conclusion is that otters take whatever is easiest to catch. The percentage of birds was highest in summer when there are fledglings and moulting adults on the lakes. The Tone otters took surprisingly few of the recently stocked trout. You might have expected naive stock fish to be sitting targets for an otter, but in warm summer water a trout is probably too fast for an otter to catch easily.

These studies make no mention of incidental items such as frogs, newts or water voles although at certain times otters eat considerable numbers of them.

CHAPTER EIGHT

OTTER HUNTING

This is a chapter about the sport of otter hunting. Before you slam the book shut in high moral disgust, reflect a while. Like the British Empire, for better or worse it existed, and it is perhaps as well to consider what it was and what it did. After all, the otter hunt was for over 800 years the main source of information about our largest and most secretive predatory animal.

Be reassured: I am not about to attempt to justify something that many of you abhor, but neither am I going to apologise for my participation in it. I cannot see much point at this belated stage of trying to apologise, like some do for slavery, the crusades, or the Norman Conquest, for what I did in my younger days; besides, I no longer know the girls' phone numbers.

To start with, I must make clear what I mean by 'otter hunting'. Nowadays the words 'hunt' and 'hunter' are used very loosely for any kind of attempt to take or kill a wild animal. That is a modern and slack usage. Fish farmers, gamekeepers and people who wanted to sell skins used from time to time to go forth to kill an otter, but that is not what I am referring to in this section. I am talking only about those organised packs of hounds that met to provide

Our rough-coated otterhounds at work.

nature of the quarry, and the terrain in which it was conducted, it had to be significantly different in many ways from the better-known sport of fox hunting. In 2006 I wrote a portrayal of what went on, for the magazine of the enthusiasts who still breed, but of course cannot work, the pure-bred otterhound.

a leisure activity for their subscribers. Because there were no horses in this form of hunting, the interest came solely from the hounds; that this was engrossing, fascinating, and infinitely compelling should come as no surprise to a generation familiar with wildlife films on the television. Millions of people who would never dream of killing an antelope themselves regularly sit enthralled by the hunting attempts of a pride of lions or a cheetah. That this is natural and necessary behaviour for the predator, but not for the hunt follower, is an irrelevance to appreciating the absorbing nature of the contest.

Recently there was a film taken from a plane of a pack of hunting dogs in pursuit of impala. A gyroscopic device enabled for the first time the showing of the whole pack from above, so that their strategies and skills could be appreciated, as well as the speed and agility which filming from the ground can more usually display. If you get a chance to see it again, do so, and notice the excitement and involvement of the commentator. No hunter he, but he is caught up in the tension of the action.

But whatever your views on this, it was a popular sport, with a pack of hounds in most rural areas of England and Wales, a sport with hundreds of regular followers. Because of the

A typical day with the otterhounds

As it is now 30 years since the otterhound packs in England went into voluntary abeyance, I suppose that most of the present breeders have had no chance to see what sort of activity their hounds were originally bred for.

So I thought I would try to conduct you in imagination through a typical day. Although of course it has to be said that one of the great sources of interest in this hound sport was the way in which the days varied so much. Was there ever a typical day?

Our hounds met at 10.30am, usually at a bridge. Sometimes we would go to a pub, and occasionally a big house for a lawn meet, but the serious hunters did not want to be hanging about at a prolonged social event while the drag was evaporating. 10.30 was quite late enough to make a sensible start, they held. I suppose in these over-regulated days I had better explain that "the drag" had nothing to do with an artificial scent laid by a man towing a sack. It is the vestiges of scent left from the otter's ramblings of the previous night.

And to those familiar only with fox hunting it is necessary to point out that, as the otter is a territorial animal, we couldn't just trot about trying hither and yon until we bumped up one of the many suitable quarry animals in the parish, and to emphasise that if we should lose our otter, there was little point in drawing for the next one. A pack of foxhounds may find half a dozen foxes in a day; otterhounds used to find one every other day, perhaps. Hence the need to get going before the drag went off.

People turned up at the bridge, the members in their blue uniform, but most wearing practical country clothes, and all with stout shoes or boots; wellies were a great waterlogged nuisance, and nobody ever wore them twice. The hounds were let out of the van and held up in the corner of the field below the bridge for all to look at over the parapet, and for the children to pat and fuss. Another distinguishing difference of this sport was that everybody in the Field, (the followers, not the enclosure), knew each hound personally, and the speed of proceedings was such that their individual progress could be monitored by all throughout the day. The really alertly interested could recognise each hound by voice, and comment on what was happening in a wood by ear. I still hear Regent's tree-trembling roar in my dreams, and often see Deacon throwing his great skull at the sky to give full vent to his enthusiasm for a swimming hunt.

After ten minutes or so, the Huntsman would touch his horn (blow a short note) and the day's endeavours would begin. Today the

With my hounds on the Rawthey with Tommy Harrison, huntsman (right), and Wilf Atkinson, whip (left).

master has indicated that we start downstream. First go the two whips (Whippers-in), one on either bank. They are the brakes on the proceedings. If young hounds get impetuous and enthusiastic they will dash ahead too fast, and hounds may well draw past their otter.

So the pack is held back, at a pace at which the huntsman can control and direct their endeavours to locate their quarry. Most of the hounds are ranging the riverbanks ahead of the huntsman, who directs them by incomprehensible cries. Behind him wander a few old and wise hounds who are saving their energies for when some action starts, and one or two puppies who haven't really entered yet. Young otterhounds were much slower to get going than foxhounds, and patience was required.

At a respectful distance behind this procession of workers comes most of the Field (spectators). It was important not to crowd the huntsman and his hounds, so a gap was to be observed. The old and bold of the Field have taken to their cars and are on their way to the next bridge, the one just above the junction of the rivers. Like the old hounds, they are conserving their energies.

Nothing happens. It fails to happen in a spectacular and interesting way, a part of the proceedings which was always incomprehensible to fox hunters used to the excitement and dangers of their nappy and over-corned horses right from the word go.

The whole hunt walks along the river bank, and the hounds cross and re-cross the river, in silence, sticking their noses into tangled tree roots, and checking for drag on exposed islets of rock. The huntsman yodels away in medieval welsh, or whatever, and nothing continues to happen. Dippers and kingfishers of course, yellow flag-iris, or a patch of

ripe wild raspberries, or scenery, stuff like that all the time, but no hunting.

Except of course there is, to those who are watching with their brains switched on. Which hound is trying best, look how that puppy is starting to have a go, did you see how Remus remembered to swim across to the root where he found an otter two seasons ago, strange that there was no drag at all around that favoured place. And now there is some interest. The deepest scenting hounds dwelt on those rocks, and two old hounds tried to feather across that bend in the river. They could not speak to the scent, but there was enough stale drag left for them to flag their sterns (wag their tails). There was certainly an otter hereabouts the night before last (the thicker breed of fox hunting thrusters never could see any virtue in acknowledging a scent over 48 hours cold, but never mind, it takes all sorts).

So on we all go, with the interest increasing, until we come to the junction pool. Here the drag becomes much stronger, and the hounds start to own it (speak to it). The huntsman tries them across the inside of the junction, to test whether the otter has cut the corner into the tributary, but they find no trace. This makes him think that the otter has gone on downstream

'Drawing' the river on a sunny autumnal morning. No scent yet.

bits out. The huntsman encourages them ceaselessly. The Field has stopped its idle chatter and all eyes are on the pack and the famous favourite hounds. Surely they will find the otter any minute now.

Suddenly the huntsman blows two long notes and calls them back. He has decided that the drag was fading, and from the way it skirted all the fast water and the rapids he estimates that they are heading the wrong way, and that his otter went up, not down, last night. So he gathers up his hounds and retraces his steps to the junction.

Several of the followers think that he has got it wrong; the fading of the drag was to be expected, from the lateness of the hour, and surely he ought to have made good as far as the well-known ash tree "where we always find".

Although criticism is easy, in many cases it is also informed. In this form of hunting, the Field can watch the hounds at work, and make their own attempt to make sense of the separated clues the wandering otter has left as to its whereabouts. What the huntsman has thought is also based on observation of his hounds, but unlike his critics he has also to calculate what would happen if he did continue to the big root. OK if they find there, but if, as he expects, the otter left there at dusk the night before to go up the tributary he has just passed, it will be too late to return.

He has to trust the evidence his hounds give him, and try up the side stream. If they find up

(you should realise that an otter will normally travel some seven or more miles in a night).

He blows his horn, and the whips turn the hounds, by voice not by whip, of course, and we all progress down the now much larger river. For some it means wading across to the other bank, but not to worry, most have got wet knees by now anyway, from avoiding the hazards of the first three miles.

The drag is good and strong here, so the hounds are very busy, swimming back and forth, wading along under the overhanging banks, scrambling up and down over rocky ledges, forcing their way through the rapids at the head of every pool. The people watching are mostly on level meadows, but for the hounds every mile is a full obstacle course.

For the next two miles the hounds are at high expectation. All have joined in and there seems to be drag everywhere. Their great voices resound across the valley as they drag back and forth across the bends, or find a sprainting place (otter poo) out on a fallen tree trunk. The whips have to be very agile to restrain the foremost hounds from surging ahead and missing vital

Evidence of an otter: the hounds follow a touch of drag along the river bank.

there, he will be hailed a genius. If they don't, the know-alls will have the satisfaction of being right, and they will have no less a blank day, if that is what you can call a day when the hounds have been working a drag for two hours.

Up the tributary, there is plenty of drag, but rather less strong. Proof that the otter is below, or just the effect of the hot summer sun on a scent now ten hours old? Watch every move the hounds make, for they will be first with the answer. Then they stop speaking. They try just as thoroughly, but cannot even feather up those stones. Nor across the grass. The drag has run out. I told you so, the otter is below. Obvious from the way Dragon and Cherish were pushing forward; even the puppies wanted to get on. Too late to put things right now. Still, we had a good drag, but rather a shame to miss him.

None of this gets to the Huntsman, of course, nor is said too loudly near the master.

The huntsman has turned the pack, and instructed the whips to keep them tight to the river bank, as he patiently draws back the way he came. He stops them rerunning the strong drag across the big bend, and gets them to draw all the way round.

All at once the entire pack surges into the water and swims across the deep curved pool to the steep bank opposite, in full cry. There they struggle and strive to haul themselves up a small cliff into a bramble bush above them, but the water is too deep for them to get a purchase. They are so frantic to get up to where they have winded their quarry that they do not see the brown flash of a big dog otter slipping off the end of the ledge into the deep, but the huntsman did. He doubles his horn, (rapid notes), and calls them away. Young and inexperienced hounds continue to try to back their own judgement up the cliff, but the older ones turn at once, and swim downstream at his instruction. A couple of yards below, they catch the scent on the water, and boom out their finding to the rest. Now they all swim after the departing otter, full cry down the middle of the stream. Right to the tail of the pool they power, and down at a splashy gallop over the shallows.

But Regent has stopped, and Royal, and now Forester and Gameboy. The huntsman blows a recall, and the whips hasten to turn the impetuous younger hounds which have continued down with the current-borne scent (the wash), while the otter has turned back at the tail of the pool, and is now heading back into the safety of the deep water.

The young hounds have to come back up against the fierce current of the rapids to rejoin those that have now refound the scent and are swimming steadily up the far bank. Tall Manton can wade safely up the rapids, but lesser Spitfire is swept back twice, and gets badly left behind.

Meanwhile the whips have dropped downstream: their job is to turn the inexperienced hounds that are following the current-borne wash well beyond the point where the otter turned, and to keep watch in case the otter should slip away down the fast water undetected. The Field has spread out, each person choosing a vantage point to savour the ebb and flow of the swimming chase round the big pool. With no charging about, with no horse to control, these keen houndmen and women lean on their poles (wading staffs), and can concentrate with critical awareness on

the whole of the action. Sometimes they have an idea of the direction the otter has taken, but always they can appreciate what the hounds are doing, whether in full cry on a strong scent, or at fault, having temporarily lost their elusive quarry, and trying for him again by questing to and fro.

Up and down the big pool they swim; for the otter it is a series of dashes from tree root to tree root, then a long pause while the much slower pack swim up to him. As soon as they locate him, off he dives, and they, without a breather, must turn and swim after him. But thanks to the skill of those hounds which do not go down on the wash, but turn where he turns, even though he is well beneath them under flowing water, they press him hard enough for him to leave the big pool and head down the river.

Nobody sees him over the rapids at the bottom of the pool, but by the time the hounds are surging down them the otter can be seen porpoising rapidly towards the far end of the next long straight, with a good lead over the swimming pack. Then they lose him. They stop of their own volition, and start to cast

Taking the pack across the river. The huntsman shows good control of his hounds keeping them well-bunched and orderly.

back, knowing that they have swum down on the wash. Melody stops at a tree root and gazes silently into its recesses. The other hounds mark, but in a muted way. The scent is weak, so the otter is obviously a long way in. The hounds are taken away, right back from the river to the far hedge of the meadow, while Smuts the terrier is put in. A wait of ten minutes, then the Master raises his hat as a signal that he has seen a chain of bubbles leaving the root. As soon as Smuts is safely back on his lead, the Huntsman doubles his horn, the hounds gallop across the field and splash into the river; the chase is on again. Downstream again, no pausing this time, almost back to the junction, where hounds halt and start to cast about. There is a short pause until the bell-like voice of Ramble is heard from a small thicket. She is marking in a heap of rubble and stones, the ruins of an old mill. The otter has gained a safe refuge, and the hounds have worked hard and well all day, so the Master nods to the Huntsman, who blows a last, long note on his horn: "home" is sounded.

It is a good three miles to walk back to the van, and some of the hounds look very tired. All the way the talk is of the hunt, which hound did what, and where they excelled. Everybody's favourite did best, and together they were outstanding, including Smuts. All idea of the sure-find in the big root that they turned back from is forgotten, as is the skill and judgement of the Huntsman who bravely followed his interpretation of events. He is forgotten about; the stars of this memorable day were the otterhounds.

That is what happened on a very good day, with an interesting drag, a good find, a spectacular swimming hunt, a clever refind, and a dramatic chase to the conclusion. On another day the otter might be found much earlier in the day, if it had been coming down the river in the night, and the hunt was drawing upstream. Then there would be no drag, just a sudden find. Or the hunt might not be so interesting; on many occasions there would be a short period of hunting, then the otter would just vanish. There were places where this regularly happened. At Underley Bridge on the Lune, for instance, we would often find in the roots of a leaning tree just upstream from the park bridge. As frequently, the otter would be seen to swim down under the bridge, and then that would be that. There must have been a hidden chamber or pipe of some sort at the bridge, which all the otters knew about. So a hunt from that tree root lasted about 150 yards.

Further on up the Lune, we would often have good drag around the junction of the Rawthey, but we never found there. My father spent a lot of time trying to work out the mystery of where he was leaving the otters, but never cracked it. So on those days there was no find, even, only a drag. Other days again would be entirely blank. The hunt and an otter had not coincided, so after a long walk everybody would go home. No otter, but they had seen the way the hounds had tackled the problem of looking for one. Blank days were never infrequent. Between the wars the Kendal and District Hunt used to have about one day in three blank.

Sometimes of course the hounds would kill the otter. In my father's time, he would kill about 12 a year, from 50 or 60 meets. The aim of the day was not to kill every possible otter; to the hunters they were not vermin. The aim was to watch the hounds at work, so the only reason to kill the otter was either because it had been causing damage to a fishery or to poultry, or to reward the hounds.

The hunts were scrupulous that the otter should have a fair chance of escape. This is exemplified by the story of the big dog otter on the Tone. He lived for a long time on the stretch of river directly above Taunton and from his padding he must have been a giant, although we never saw him. Several packs hunted his

drag, but they always failed to find him.

The Eastern Counties came on a visit, and had a wonderful drag, but were beaten, as were the local pack, the Culmstock, despite their advantage of local knowledge and familiarity with the river. It fell to my pack, the Kendal, to solve the riddle. Like the others, we were having an excellent drag, and had noticed the enormous padding in the sandy places.

As we neared Hele Bridge, some of the hounds came out of the riverbed and Peeler and Posy took a drag across the grassy field towards the railway line. They continued right to the corner of the field, where the scent led into a very small stream running beside the lane. Most people would have thought it just a ditch, but in fact it had sufficient flow to be a brook. Tommy, the huntsman, drew his hounds back down the stream to its confluence with the main river, but they showed no interest, nor was there any

An otter lies low in the water, surrounded by duckweed and looking to the casual observer like a floating log. Only his movement will betray his presence.

more drag below the bridge. The otter had not come back down the brook to the main river, but had gone on up the tiny tributary to spend his day in the brambles above the railway. It seemed probable that his usual route to this sequestered shelter was to follow the brook all the way up from its confluence.

Previous packs had never discovered this, because the mouth of the stream was so tight to the abutments of the bridge that it was in a little length of some ten yards of riverbank which had always been missed out in their searches. The hunt would leave the bridge through the gate onto the footpath, and start to draw the water after the path had come back down to the bank again, leaving the stream mouth in the tiny triangle of land they did not notice they omitted. I remember the interest and satisfaction that solving this ongoing mystery occasioned, but also the unanimous certainty that there was nothing that could be done; to disturb an otter in such a small stream would be an act of murder, so we all went home, and that otter was never hunted in quite a long life as occupant of that stretch.

This story may give the impression that the hunts harassed a stretch frequently, but that was far from the case. Each hunt had an agreed territory, registered with the Masters of Otterhounds Association, and worked its way round its waters according to a set and traditional rotation. The Kendal used to meet

at Devil's Bridge on the Bank Holidays in May and August. I believe this is now the tradition for a vast assembly of motorbike enthusiasts. This meant that each bit of river would be visited once or possibly twice a year.

Most packs hunted twice a week during a season which ran from April to September as long as the state of the water was suitable. Meets were cancelled for spates, and for extremely low flows. There were about twenty different hunt "countries" in the whole of England and Wales, and so each pack covered a vast area.

My father hunting the Kendal & District pack on the River Wyre.

The Dartmoor had all of Cornwall and all of Devon west of the Exe. Their neighbours, the Culmstock, were allocated all the rivers running into the Bristol Channel between Clevedon and Lynmouth, and those flowing into the English Channel between Exmouth and Portland Bill. With such a large area, the annual arrival of the hounds was quite an event locally, and the culling pressure on any one river was minimal. The number of animals removed by the hunt made no difference to the strength of the population as a whole, and was only just enough to prevent other, more lethal, measures being used against the otters.

Attitudes were different in those days, and the gin trap was still widely used. It was far more effective than any hunt, and also a very private and secret method of doing the deed. There is no doubt that in many areas, although not on the smartest of the top-rated chalkstream trout fisheries, the impending arrival of the hunt caused there to be less trapping and engendered a degree of toleration towards the otters which was not as automatic and widespread then as it is today. A hunt is open and above board. If unfair methods had been used, or if an undue number of otters had been killed, everybody would be aware of this. The system was to an extent self-regulating, in that there was a mechanism for protecting a duck farm or a fish hatchery when necessary, in a way that all could know about and recognise, but the method was not so lethal as to eradicate a local population, something that was well within the capability of an assiduous trapper.

Hunting had its critics, of course, in those days. There have always been people who dislike the idea of any kind of hunt, and there were also those who objected to certain aspects of otter hunting. Principal among these specific objections was the one that the hunts would disturb bitches with cubs. Over my hunting career I did see occasional instances of this,

HUNTING TERMS

Blank Day a day without a find and therefore no hunt

Bolt a terrier evicts the otter

Double the horn rapid notes of encouragement

Drag the traces of scent left by an otter in the night

Draw the hounds search for their quarry

Chain bubbles from a submerged swimming otter

Enter when a young hound has learnt to hunt

Feather vigorous tail wagging while silently following a scent

Field the followers

Find to start to hunt an otter

Hunt an organisation with a pack of hounds

Hunt the chase of one animal

Huntsman the man in charge of the hounds. Therefore only one.

Mark a hound indicates that an otter is in a holt

Meet the gathering before starting

Pole a wading staff

Scent the smell of a hunted otter; not the same as drag

Thruster an impetuous galloping rider

Wash waterborne scent, carried below the quarry by the current

Whipper-in the huntsman's assistant

but usually the huntsman became aware of the situation very soon, and the hunt would stop at once. Most often, the hounds would fail to locate a bitch with cubs.

Many of the breeding holts were up small side streams, where the hunt would not go, but my experience from those which the hounds did approach was that such a bitch had very little scent, and that the hounds were often unaware of her presence. Other objections were to the use of terriers to bolt an otter. Very many of the hunts would not have occurred without a bolt to start them off, so terriers were essential.

As terriers were normally used singly, the otters were not mauled by them; it was their presence that the otters bolted from, rather than a danger, and in many cases the otter would just remove to a more secure part of the holt from which the dog could not shift it. Our country was full of places which were known to be secure for the otter, the Casterton Rocks, Hell Ghyll, Nettlepot Drain, Jumbles, the Gasworks Caves, a long list of places where even the best of terriers could achieve nothing.

The known presence of such strongholds used in the former days, when otters were considered more as vermin, to give rise to the use of stickles (a line of followers in the water) in an attempt to turn the otter back from the impenetrable refuge. This had ceased long before my time, although it is described by Willamson in *Tarka*. Tarka is not deterred, and breaks through the legs of the people. In early Victorian days spears were used to stab the otter as it passed underwater, but the aim in those times was for vermin elimination, not for hound sport.

Amazingly, although I missed the use of spears by a century, there were still opponents of hunting who were objecting to it right up to

The cast for the recreation of an otter hunt for the TV programme 'On the Trail of Tarka' with the Stevenstone foxhounds and David Ford, the huntsman.

the sport's end in 1976. Some people do not like to let a few facts spoil a good prejudice. They convinced themselves that the long wading poles that every follower carried were really devices for bashing every possible otter.

The same sort of people used to object to the hunt uniforms. For a sport that involves wading about in rivers it is sensible to have special clothes, and it makes some sort of sense if the special clothing of all those officially involved in the running of the pack is recognisable and the same.

So the hunt officials wore a uniform which nobody saw any reason to alter over the passage of time, usually a set of plus-fours in blue welsh flannel, a lightweight material which is warm and which drains rapidly after wading.

That, then, was the nature of otter hunting. A group of people, some of them smartly turned out in outmoded uniforms, would repair once a year to a bridge on a river and endeavour to find and then to hunt an otter, using a pack of specialised hounds. Many people took part as spectators occasionally, and a significant number were enthusiasts who followed regularly. Like cricket or ballet, it was of itself an unnecessary activity, and it ceased in 1976. Why then bother about it now?

The contribution of otter hunting

It may not be relevant to the conservation of the otter in England in the 21st century, but I am certain my participation in it has given me an advantage which future otter enthusiasts will find hard to match. The sport was at the time the only valid source of information about the species, and that information was of a higher quality than what is available nowadays, in that it was provided by the sensitive noses of the otterhounds, interpreting scent, which is the otters' own medium of communication. I try to spend time guiding younger people along the riverbanks and to pass on what I myself was shown by the experienced hounds who guided me round the haunts of the otters.

No method available today can match them. Radio collaring is very impractical, and anyway it only tells you about the otters you manage to catch in the first place, a process that this species finds very distressing and disturbing. DNA examination of fresh sprants could tell you about every otter, but there have been technical difficulties with the interpretation processes, and at present this expensive method is still being developed experimentally. It would tell you nothing about the otters' interaction with their habitat, which bit they use most, where they roam, what nooks and crannies they explore, and most importantly, where they dwell. This information, considered vital for the conservation of any species, is in the case of the otters only really available by scent. As I was fortunate to have followed the hounds over many of the rivers I now study, I am sure I have a fuller knowledge of the habitat than I would ever have achieved by my own unaided efforts. On my study shelf I have a set of large scale maps on which I have endeavoured to record all my knowledge of habitat features. For a while I had doubts about the usefulness of this, and suspected that it might have been merely of historical interest.

However, I was reassured recently, when Charlie Hamilton-James set about making a film of the wild otters on the Torridge, and wanted to link his findings to the life of the otters described by Williamson in *Tarka The Otter*. Williamson had his information from the hounds of the Cheriton Hunt, of which he was a member. Although the story is a fictional tale, Williamson was at great pains to be accurate to the detailed life of the river, and depicts his fictional events in correctly described, real

places. Charlie found to his delight that the otters living in the same area some ninety years later were following the same haunts and places, using even the same tree roots, where they still exist. So my record of the habitats may have a more enduring value than I at first suspected.

Recording distribution and population density

The evidence of the otter hunters can help with another problem. Shortly after I first started to keep conservation records, the main aim of such a task was to record where, if at all, any otters were left. Later, as the otters recovered, we began to wonder to what extent they had succeeded in restoring their numbers, and more recently, to try to estimate the size of the population and to assess whether their recovery in this area is complete and whether we have a full house, or full habitat.

One problem is whether the rivers can support the same density of predators. After all, the invertebrates and fish have had a hard

An exciting moment as the hounds 'Find' on the far bank.

time in a damaged habitat as well. The other problem is that we have no idea what the level of the population was in the former times, when the human population was much lower, and the rivers were more natural and wholesome. We can make the assumption that, in the years directly after each of the World Wars, when the river keepers had been absent, and when the remainder rural population had had other things to occupy their time, the otters would have had the chance to increase undisturbed to their maximum possible density.

That the otter hunters were such dedicated diarists can tell us something about that population. What they seemed to find was that the otters were as spaced out along the main rivers as they are now. There must have been more food for them, and more cover for them to live in, but there do not seem to have been more otters per mile. The drags I have read about on rivers that I know well tell that the otters travelled just as far in a night as they still do, and that they were to be found at a very similar spacing along the banks.

It was by an analysis of the hunt records that Chanin and Jefferies were able to write their paper of 1979 which pointed the finger of suspicion for the root cause of the decline away from the physical environment and towards the chemicals which are now believed to have been responsible. As a former master I had privileged access to the Kendal records, and made my own analysis, the results of which will feature in the next chapter. But I hope it has been worthwhile to throw light on what the process was which produced these informative disclosures.

Waiting to move off. Followers watch the Kendal & District hounds from a road bridge.

CHAPTER NINE

GRADUAL RECOVERY

In 1976 the otter hunts closed down voluntarily at a meeting of the masters in London. They were perhaps the first to recognise the extent of the peril for the otter, and to their credit they took a decisive and difficult action. This removed a major source of information about the state of the species, and when two years later, the Mammal Society's first survey scheme collapsed, we were left with nothing at all. That survey had been rendered unreliable by the over-enthusiasm of the local volunteers. All it registered was their energy, really. As I was one of the enthusiasts, there seemed nothing to do but to carry on trying to monitor the local residual populations. But then, as now, there was no central co-ordinating focus to report to, no body with the power to initiate any action.

The only activity on any sort of widespread scale came from the Vincent Wildlife Trust, a private body set up by Vincent Weir, a wealthy man who funded various forms of research into rare species; initially he focussed on the otter. The trust's otter work went mainly into the Otter Havens Project, which set up a series of small sanctuary areas along the rivers to provide resting cover for otters. Many people considered that riverbank habitat destruction was the main cause of the decline, and this was a practical

Otters are attracted to eels and lobsters in traps and – just like the eels and lobsters themselves – find it impossible to get out. They panic and drown.

project to reverse the damage. The extent of their activities was considerable: in Wessex they set up 25 havens covering 39km of riverbank, and in the South-West, 42 covering 79kms. They also tackled the problem of the eel nets.

Otters trapped in fishermen's nets

Their report of 1984 disclosed a very significant accidental mortality in traps set quite legally by commercial fishermen. These deaths must have been a very considerable drain on the depleted numbers of those days. Two Scottish netters had five each in one season; another group of three netsmen had 23 otters in 18 months on south Uist. Even in Scotland, which was less affected by the decline, such slaughter must have been denuding large areas.

The traps are very simple in design, just a bag of netting with a series of funnels that enable the eel to move towards the bait, but not to find its way out again. Lobster pots also work on the same principle. The eels, or the lobster, become in turn bait for otters; the otters drown of course, and there are several instances of an abandoned net containing a whole family of a bitch and her cubs. As result of the Trust's researches, otter guards were devised for the mouth of the nets, and by-laws were introduced in many areas to

make it illegal to set an unprotected net. At the same time the Vincent Trust made the simple guards free to any fisher who applied. Practical conservation indeed!

Traps for signal crayfish

Sadly, the laws apply to eel nets, but not to crayfish traps, which were not a feature of our waterways at that time. They are now (2007) being set in many parts of the country for the recently introduced, and legally released, American import, the signal crayfish. The story of the introduction of these imposing looking and delicious creatures is yet another sad example of our inability to learn from previous mistakes, (ruddy ducks and grey squirrels), and of the ineffectiveness of the bureaucracies which are set up to protect and regulate such affairs.

Enterprising pond owners hit on the idea of releasing these large, saleable crayfish into their ponds, where they would live and grow for free, and whence they could subsequently be harvested for market by cage traps. It was a good scheme to raise a profit from an unused resource, their ponds, without any great expense of labour or fodder.

There were various snags, however. The crayfish could escape from any pond, either by the minute larval forms drifting downstream from the outflow, or by adults migrating overland through the wet grass. And the American imports carried a fungal infection which obliterated the smaller native crayfish, the white-clawed crayfish. In most places that was of only aesthetic importance, as the white-claws are of no commercial value. That we had endangered another native species by careless importation caused no great sense of urgency in the Environment Agency, (or its predecessors). The EA knew of the plague, but got around, not to action, but to a proposal for the consideration of some eventual action, about three years too late. Still, look on the bright side, it can always be considered an economy no longer to need to purchase a bolt for the stable door.

Signal crayfish are now well-established in many areas. They massacre many types of water life by their strategy of a rolling feeding herd, comparable to grazing, in that they live together in considerable density and eat invertebrates, fish eggs, anything containing protein, and as they deplete one stretch they roll on down the river, vacuuming it clean as they go. Enterprising people harvest them in traps which can be bought very cheaply on the internet. The traps are made in China, and have no guards against otters.

This week I saw a photo of two otters recently drowned in one such trap in Cornwall, and read in the paper of three others killed in Cambridgeshire. Earlier this summer an observant member of the Somerset Otter Group found that a Chinese chef was setting unprotected traps for crayfish in a lake in the grounds of the hotel where he works. We were able to inform the EA, who 'would look into it'. Twenty-five years after a private, non-statutory body, the Vincent Trust, implemented practical action, the danger to our otters remains.

Local surveys in Somerset

Meanwhile, localised activity continued here in Somerset. We still had some otters, so I assisted with various attempts to find out about them. The Somerset Trust for Nature Conservation, under Rob Jarman, wanted to initiate practical action on the Somerset Levels. The first stage would be to locate them. This idiosyncratic and

The native British white-clawed crayfish (left) compared to the larger American signal crayfish (right) which has escaped into rivers and lakes throughout much of Britain. The signal crayfish carries with it a deadly fungal infection against which the indigenous British crayfish appears to have little resistance. Both crayfish are eaten by otters. Unfortunately, some of the crayfish traps being used are also lethal to otters.

ethnic area of low-lying grassland, much of it below sea level, had long been reputed a stronghold of otters. Every field is bounded by four water-filled ditches, called in the vernacular, 'rhynes'. These were full of eels and other fish. 169,000 acres in extent, this area was esteemed a paradise for otters. Yet nobody knew how many there had been, how much their population was in decline, whether the otters had held on there better than in less suitable and more damaged areas. Evidence in the form of spraints and paths could be found scattered all through the area, but nobody had any direct knowledge of the strength of the population, nor of their main habitations and preferred dwelling places.

There were two reasons to try to find out these basics: firstly it might be that we had a residual population largely untouched by the habitat reduction so widespread elsewhere, which would be a valuable conservation asset at a time of such scarcity; secondly, the levels were under threat of severe agricultural improvement, which in their case meant drainage, to turn them into rich, arable fenland, such as is found in the east of England. The Somerset Trust for Nature Conservation, led by Rob Jarman, decided to make this research a priority. The first thing was to identify which parts were most used by otters, and to attempt to find out how many different otters were roaming across these wetlands.

I suggested that we could call in the hounds. My idea was to get several knowledgeable hound men and lend them a couple of experienced hounds each. We would spread them out in different parts of the Levels, all on the same day. The hounds would own any overnight drag, and indicate areas where otters had or had not been recently active. If several places of interest were found, we would get some idea that different otters were involved. Also the drag might lead the hounds to a mark in a tree root or other form of holt. This would be the first

indication we had of the whereabouts of these important places, and would enable the Trust to focus their protective attention onto the main features to conserve. With only two hounds in any area, there was no danger to the otters. At the worst, one or two might get wet. This plan was both economical and practical, and would have provided a vital baseline of information in only a couple of weekends. But it had to be stopped, as offensive to the sensibilities of the ethically high-minded. They offered nothing in its place.

The pressure on the Levels from drainage proposals was increasing, and it might be that we were about to witness the destruction of the last major nucleus of otters in England. The Nature Conservancy Council produced a consultation document in 1977 on the future of The Somerset Levels.
The preamble states:
"A fundamental conflict of need between wildlife conservation, agricultural improvement and exploitation of a mineral resource (peat) has developed. In conservation and agriculture, two socially desirable objectives are in conflict with each other. Government views both favourably and has appointed organisations in the MAFF, Wessex Water Authority, Somerset County Council and NCC to fulfil them. These organisations are competing for the same area of land and it is difficult to see how the differences can be easily reconciled. Peat working is gradually eating away the remaining areas of high scientific interest, and the planning authorities are having great difficulty in preventing it."

RSPB intervention

This conflict was being robustly but politely debated until the RSPB pitched in with a consummate lack of tact. They acted too quickly in the face of an emergency and an opportunity, and set the job back many years. The land on West Sedgemoor where a few pairs of rare godwits still nested became available, so they bought it, to save it from being drained, and promptly told all their new neighbours how all the land in that valley should be managed. Off-comers have not been very warmly welcome on Sedgemoor since Cromwell made his last and decisive cavalry charge down Crimson Hill, to cut up the west-country royalist infantry caught against the swamps at the bottom. Judge Jeffreys in 1685 did not increase their love of Londoners either, so resentment fermented to an ugly level. A meeting was held in Stoke St Gregory village hall, to calm things down. Some of the farmers came to it in a second world war tank, and the young farmers had erected a gallows with three dummies in dark suits dangling from it.

All this kerfuffle made a stir in the media, of course, so I took a group of my sixth form pupils down to see what all the fuss was about. We walked along a grassy drove until we came to a wooden field gate with an abusive poem pinned to it. We stopped to read it. The field was one of the flower-rich ancient grassland fields which were being cited as a main reason why this area should be preserved from the spectre of carrot farming. I was pointing out some of the species of flower in the impressively colourful carpet when a tractor which had been ploughing the far side of the field stopped its work and drove at some speed across the meadow towards us. It stopped at the gate, and the farmer descended. He immediately started to abuse us, in such intemperate terms as betrayed him as the poet. The pupils were amazed, and even frightened.

However, we were on a right of way, so I kept them there and eventually managed to explain that we were not taking sides, but had just come to see for ourselves something that we had read so much about. He calmed down a bit, and I was able to get him to talk to us about his farm. Eventually one of the pupils, a country girl who realised that it was rather unusual to

be ploughing grass at a time when the orchids were in flower, a time of year when most people let it up for hay, asked him what he intended to grow as a result. He exploded again. He was not ploughing in order to grow anything at all. His plan was not agricultural. He just wanted to get rid of all the bloody flowers and weeds so that he would never again have anybody coming along to tell him what to do with his own land.

Godwits no longer nest in that valley.

A year-long survey

This was the atmosphere in the area where Rob Jarman was trying to sustain a (possibly mythological) otter population. It is greatly to his credit that he managed to set up a scheme that proceeded smoothly for over a year without causing an outbreak of poetry anywhere, as far as I know. Four young biology graduates were employed to investigate the whole area as thoroughly as possible. I spent a little time with them to help get them started on the detection of spraint. They put in an incredible amount of legwork. Their report reads, "731 bridges were located and recorded during visit 1. Of these, 203 were chosen for further study, and four further visits were made to each." That is 1543 visits to bridges, most of which were footbridges or cart bridges, and accessible only on foot. No wonder their report was so useful and so comprehensive. Yet among their conclusions one reads,

1) Otters do occur on the levels; they appear to be widely distributed, but the size of the population is unknown.
2) There are a number of areas which have been found to be more regularly frequented than others. It is not known whether this is a real picture of otter distribution.
3) There are further areas where no otter evidence was found at all. It was not possible

to identify any factors which determined this.
4) No definite evidence of otters breeding was found.

5) It is impossible to estimate the size of the overall population from this survey. The subjective opinion of all who have commented is that otters are fewer in numbers than they were 15–20 years ago: most reported sightings of otters nowadays are probably wrongly identified mink.

So much work for so little real knowledge. The footsore four made two recommendations for the future conservation of the otters: the maintenance of the water quality and habitat in feeding areas, and the conservation of breeding areas. But they had not identified a breeding area, nor had they seen an otter.

Study of regularly-frequented otter areas

Rob Jarman decided to follow up their recommendations and locate breeding areas, if possible. In April 1980 he invited Libby Lenton and me to follow up the core areas identified in conclusion 2 of the report. He wanted us to comb through them in detail and search for features vital to the otters' frequenting of those places, so that the Trust could become involved in the conservation of specific habitats. Libby agreed to look at the areas in the Brue valley north of the Poldens ridge, an area she had long been involved with. I would take the Parrett/Cary catchment to the south.

I consulted the report for details of where to start. I looked at the list of bridges they had visited, and plotted onto my map all those where the surveyors had found spraints on more than half their visits. The resulting pattern seemed to give a sensible spread across the area. I started my checks on these in January, and gave up

in October, after 18 trips. I checked a total of 74 sites, with an expectation of success, based on the results from two years before, of more than 37 positive results. I found two places with spraint on my fifth trip, four spraints in total, none of them fresh. That was all I could find. My population had crashed, and it was many years before that area was occupied again.

A few miles further north, Libby had a better result, and found ongoing evidence of a continuing population of some sort, but not enough to enable her to home in onto the key features. So she rang round for assistance and held a consecutive day survey in July 1981. Everybody searches on day 1, and then again on day 2, when any new work can be identified and mapped. By joining the positive dots from day 2 appropriately, one can detect the number of different stretches of water used on the same night, which gives a minimum number of otters present. Eight of us took part, and on day 1 we looked at 99 sites, all in Libby's half of the levels. Only 26 of them produced evidence, but as these sites were quite well spread we were not too despondent at this. In fact we were really quite cheerful, I recollect. To come up with so many positive sites at a time of national dearth was a treat, and we set out on day 2 full of optimism. We found 2 fresh spraints, 6.5km apart as the crow flies. A freak result, we thought. So we undertook a third day, which confirmed the worst. Two only. 5km apart this time. Three years later, we did it all again, but still found only two set of evidence

We should not have been so surprised, perhaps. After all, the only reason we were doing all this was that we knew the species was in dire trouble. Our hope that this area would prove to be some sort of exception was based on its high habitat potential; despite the rate of agricultural improvement, there was still much 'natural' vegetation left. We still had not grasped that the problem was basically chemical in nature.

Habitat not the reason

This must have been bitter disappointment for poor Libby. It was she who had alone and unaided done all the sites for the first National survey in 1997/79, the one that came in at under 6%. The Brue was her home patch, and, being in a white square on the chessboard diagram of England, it had not been looked at in her national survey. To have such conclusive confirmation that it was equally short of otters, despite still carrying such good habitat, must have been a blow indeed. As it was to us all.

If such gloom had continued I wonder how much longer we would have soldiered on with our disparate and self-set scheme of ottery tasks and objectives. I can remember the dismal evening in January 1985 when I sat down, as I did every winter, to summarise the annual notes and jottings in my folder for 1984. I had just twelve notes, the total of all that I had found in my wanderings and fishing forays, and of all that my network of friends had also found. That is not twelve otters located, but twelve instances of otter evidence for the whole year. It must at that time have been literally true that most of the scattered remnant otters in Somerset would never meet another of their own kind except for their mother.

The only outcome of that is extinction, of course. It seemed that there was no further point in continuing the searches I had first started when I moved down from Scotland in 1967, 17 years before, and that all my anxiety and effort had been of no avail.

The first national survey had shown that the otters had gone from all but the fringes of western England, and it was sad but not surprising that the process had continued to include my patch.

Beam Weir on the Torridge – as good a place as any to catch sight of a West Country otter.

Peregrine come-back heralds hope for otters?

But, luckily, I was involved in helping other projects, so I could not give up entirely. The temptation was strong to switch my allegiance to peregrines. They too had been almost extinguished by the poisons, but were making a slow comeback, and some of us were recording and watching the first eyries to return to the cliffs. It was more fun than trailing about after otter droppings, and more worthwhile.

Not only could you see the birds, and get to learn some of their individuality, such as which prey species they preferred, or the differing degrees of aggression they showed to intruders such as buzzards and foxes into their territory, but you felt you were in some small way helping with their revival, by recording their progress and providing some degree of security against those, racing pigeon men mostly, who wanted them to fail. And picnicking in the sun on the coastal cliffs of Somerset and Cornwall was much more pleasant than thrashing a path through a nettlebed to examine a smelly patch of stagnant mud in the gloom under a low bridge.

But, as there were grounds for a little hope for the otters, I kept going. The following year, 1985, things on my patch got a little better, and there was a steady succession of increases every year after that. 1984 had been the nadir, the very worst year. I think it is worth stressing and emphasising just how bad things were.

Nobody had intended to reduce any of the species that were so badly affected. All the chemicals had been seen as helpful and safe to use. It was all a gigantic accident, but one which we now know affected not only the cherished species of wildlife. The accumulating chemicals are now known to have affected to some extent ourselves, people as well as animals.

So let me stress again just how dire the situation became, measured by otters. You could also show it in terms of peregrines, or barn owls, but I have numbers about otters, numbers that delineate fact, not opinion or supposition. Otters advertise their presence deliberately, so the numbers are reliable.

Slow recovery after 1984

In 1984 I had only 12 records for the whole county. Records, not individual animals. Even allowing for ones we missed, there were fewer than a dozen otters in this water-rich, predominantly rural area. That this was no freak result, nor a purely local effect, was shown by the second national survey of England, done at the same time. Of 3,188 sites looked at, 284 had otter evidence.

This was a "great improvement" on the first survey of 1977-79, when only 174 positive sites were located. The report considers the positives score of 8.9% "encouraging." Although it is a 61% increase, was it really "encouraging" that 91.1% of England was devoid of any sign of an otter? To put that in perspective, in 2007, the Somerset Otter Group checked on one weekend 309 sites, of which 227 were positive, which is 73.5%, as opposed to the 5.8% and 8.9% of the first two national surveys. I have seen more otters this year than were alive in the whole county at the depth of the decline.

Out on the Levels, Hilary Scott was employed by the Vincent Trust to continue the work started by the Somerset Trust's four surveyors, of which she was one. So she knew the area well. Her reports indicted that the otters seemed restricted to a small, central area of the Brue valley, now known as Shapwick Heath National Nature Reserve. They still are.

I concentrated on the rivers to the west, and continued to fill in the 10km map squares. My map held 41 such squares, and in the 1970s I had positive results from 33 of them, in one year alone from 23. Of course I could not search so large an area regularly and methodically, so some squares were omitted in some years. But I recorded the overall picture of a widespread population changing to one of fragmented dearth. In 1984 I could tick only 7 of the squares. The grid charts a steady recovery thereafter, by a spreading towards the east. Otters are generally considered slow breeders, so the initial speed of this spread still surprises me. It must mean that otters were moving on long before all the available habitat in the vicinity of their birth was occupied.

I wonder why?

★ Was it that otters have a built-in tendency to disperse far from their area of birth, an instinct to wander which prevents inbreeding?

★ Or was it a result of the unimpeded adults claiming far more living space or territory than is normally permissible in a more dense population?

★ Or could it be that otters have preferences for quality habitat of some kind, and given sufficient space into which they can expand, they roam about looking for the very best set of riverside circumstances before settling?

I think there is no doubt that some of the otters in strong populations are forced to live in inferior habitats, pushed out of the best places by their parents. I do the same with armchairs.

After 5 years the expansion slowed down, in the vicinity of Bridgwater. Here there was an area of several hundred square kilometres which remained otter-free for many years. We recognised that there was some kind of problem, and discussed the 'Bridgwater gap", but we had no idea what caused it.

By 1989 things were back to a level similar to that at the start of my researches: in 1988/89 at least 29 squares were to some extent occupied.

That this is a genuine increase, and not just an effect caused by a very few otters wandering very widely can be ascertained from looking at the number of records involved. In 1979, at the start of the decline, I checked 22 squares; half of them were blank, and I scored 74 negative records to 19 positives. But after the recovery had kicked in, in 1989 I found only 4 blank squares out of 25, and found 181 positives to 62 negatives. The population was rebuilding itself, almost as rapidly as it had crashed.

Lack of co-operation between researchers

It was a pity that my report concentrated more on the successful spread from the west than on the problem encountered at Bridgwater. Our anxiety at that time was still, understandably, whether the otters would return and remain, so this was our main interest at the time.

Although more detailed than the previous surveys, my report was dismissed as just showing what was already known from the national surveys: that otters had spread from the west. This dismissal was partly from reasons of not jealousy exactly, but professional protectionism. There were by this time an increasing number of trained zoologists and ecologists, all chasing slender grants and scarce jobs to do with animals. There came about a strong element of competition between them, which increasingly grew into nastiness and sniping in a jealous way.

One of the worst examples of what lay under the surface of the professional politeness was the scene at the Lampeter Conference of the Mammal Society in 1978. An undergraduate from Cardiff gave a paper on the spread of the polecat across Wales. Instead of this rare mustelid being confined to a small area around the Tregarron Bog in the far west, as was widely supposed, he had discovered that the polecat had undergone a revival, and was now present throughout most of Wales. This had happened after the removal from its environment of the gin traps of the professional rabbiters, when myxomatosis depleted the rabbits and made commercial trapping uneconomic.

The senior professionals had missed a chance, a whole new British species to study, so when it came to question-time they went for him as aggressively as any mustelid. Their questions were not designed to elict information, but to expose the limitations of what he had been able to achieve in this preliminary study.

Several of us amateurs there were amazed, even disgusted, but we subsequently came to recognise the extent of the competitiveness among wildlife professionals with CVs to guard and foster. It still continues at some levels; there are people who will not co-operate or contribute to studies they are not principals in, editors of county newsletters who ignore surveys they have not initiated, in case it seems to show them up in some way. So the early discovery of the Bridgwater Gap was another opportunity missed. In fact, if the Royal Ordnance Factory had not ceased the manufacture of TNT, the problem might still remain, as we amateurs had no chemical expertise, and were wise as to the cause of the problem only after the event of its removal.

Yet I did ask about it once, on an occasion when my son and I were conducted round the ROF by the chemist who was also the environmental officer. It was a fascinating place, in that all the buildings are widely spaced apart from each other, in case an accident at one should cause an explosion in the next, and most of them have ramparts of earth around them, to direct any blast upwards. These ramparts have been created by digging out a series of pits and ponds, so the whole site is very otter suitable, (except for the Acid Drainage ditch). The wide spacing of the buildings created a wonderful site for other kinds of wildlife; the birds and flowering plants were remarkable.

There were orchids and nightingales, and a strong population of stoats dependent on the rabbits which grazed the wide spaces between the buildings. My son remembers the tour chiefly for the excitement as a schoolboy of having to hand in his watch to a uniformed security man before we entered the world of James Bond, in case it contained a detonator. The thing that made the most impression on me was the reply I got when I asked why they did not put the extreme acid from the TNT process into a pipe, instead of allowing it to flow for 6 kilometres to the sea in an open ditch. It was rather witheringly explained that, obviously, it would corrode the pipes. No wonder otters that groom their fur by licking could not cope with it.

CHAPTER TEN

INVESTIGATIONS

In addition to continuing these surveys, and trying thereby to supplement the only national initiative, the big seven-yearly surveys, I was fortunate to be able to be a little involved in other, different investigations. The field surveys were aimed at discovering what otters still existed, but there were also more scientific studies going on into what might have caused the problem. Chanin and Jefferies, working from historical hunting records, had posited that the probable cause of the decline had been the sudden widespread use of pesticides, principally the organo-chlorines.

Not everybody was entirely convinced by their paper. For one thing, there had been no dead otters; birds of prey had been found, and dead foxes galore, but no otters. Secondly, what was the mechanism for this? Their conclusion was based mainly on the coincidence of the timing, that the otters declined at the same time as the pesticides were introduced. Other creatures had bounced back comparatively rapidly when the chemicals were banned, but not the otters. So different groups of scientists were searching for an underlying cause.

The mysterious death of an otter

Interesting work was done by Jim Conroy at Aberdeen and by Hans Kruuk at the Institute of Terrestrial Ecology, who initiated a major study of the coastal otters on Shetland. Scottish researchers had two advantages over those further south, plentiful otters, and long hours of daylight to disclose them to observers. Therefore it is not surprising that much of their attention was devoted to the study of the animals themselves.

In England there was more focus on the background and the habitat of these still-scarce creatures. There was very much an atmosphere of fire-fighting, of responding to an emergency and trying to identify what the problems were.

Holding a dead otter is always a sad moment but it does offer an opportunity for scientific research.

This was a different and complementary emphasis from the Scottish approach. They looked at the animals they had; we tried to make sure we still retained some animals to look into. I was lucky to have been able to help with some of these projects. I was in an area where there had been a strong otter population which was continuing to decline.

Only one otter had ever been recorded as having definitely been killed by these widely-used substances; that was the record-holding bitch found on the banks of the river Tone in May 1972, and reluctantly and belatedly analysed, after considerable pressure from us, in September 1973.

That the Monks Wood Experimental Station of the Nature Conservancy was still so leisurely in its approach to a major national problem seemed to us to confirm the need for independent research.

That this bitch otter had died in the middle of a bare field from a massive dose of a chemical that had been banned for more years than that otter had been alive seemed to raise no actions from the nature authorities. Nobody came to follow it up. I do not think that this was solely because they had allowed such a lapse of time since the date of death.

The problem was one of attitude. The investigations were being done by lab. scientists; their intellectual interest was in solving the chemical mystery, and their product was not the increase, by protection, of more healthy otters out in the field, but the publication of learned papers in the scientific journals, to show that they were on top of the problem. But not on top of the solution: that, to be fair, was not in their remit.

This is the same mindset that did not look into the death of the Cornish peregrine because their remit did not include birds of prey, but only species of commercial significance, game birds and agricultural pests.

Help from the anglers

The agencies were doing little that was practical. However, luckily we were able to do something practical about our dead otter, once we had the result of the investigation. I was on the committee of the fishing club, and by good fortune, the chairman was Dr. Alan Parry-Jones, the Medical Officer of Health. I alerted him, and he was able to initiate a search for the source of the dieldrin, on the grounds that it might be in similarly harmful levels in the trout we were eating.

It did not take long to trace it to a cloth factory in Wellington, where they made khaki puttees for the colonial forces. The government had given a derogation from their own prohibition of this accumulative poison, in order to protect these essential items of clothing from moth and termite damage in the tropics. Our rare and precious bitch otter had died that the Nigerian police might look smart on parade, but this considerable sacrifice would have gone unnoticed and unrecorded but for the efforts of a group of amateur countrymen, interested in the river through a fishing club. The Medical Officer was able to put pressure on the factory to clean up its waste disposal.

Despite being involved in this incident of proven pollution, I was still convinced that the story of the decline of the otters was more complicated than the general assumption about organochlorines. After all, despite the withdrawal of these poisons from most of Britain, and despite a lack of corpses, the scarcity continued. So I set myself to see whether what I knew from my own experience fitted in with the decline as written up by Chanin and Jefferies. You may remember that I was of the "disease" camp in the speculations about the probable causes. So I undertook an examination of the records of my own hunt; the pattern of the onset of the decline in our hunt country had not seemed to fit the overall picture, so I attempted my own analysis, and published my findings in 1980.

My analysis of the hunt records

I employed a different method from Chanin and Jefferies. They calculated their scores on a basis of finds per hundred days hunted. This ignores the technical meaning of the word 'find' in hunting parlance. A 'find' occurs only when an otter enters the water in front of the hounds, and a chase starts. This is more understandable in conventional foxhunting, when the pack enters a wood, the hounds rummage about in the scrub, then up jumps a fox, and off we all go. A 'find' is straightforward in those circumstances, but even in that degree of obviousness what it does not indicate is how many other foxes were lurking nearby. "Finds per hundred days" works only if one is trying to establish areas of presence or complete absence.

As I was more concerned to quantify the extent of the decline, and because otters are more tricky than foxes to 'find', especially in our hunt country, I needed a more subtle indicator. To find a fox is comparatively easy: there are several available. What I needed was a measure of when there was an otter present, one only in most cases, on the river being drawn by the hounds. Frequently the hounds can have a busy day, but never 'find'. It is easy to draw over an otter, or to mark it in an impregnable holt, where it remains, so no 'find', no chase, occurs. This means that there were in many areas more otters located than figured in Chanin and Jefferies' calculations.

To get round this technicality I looked at blank days compared to active days. On a blank day the hounds draw along the riverbank, looking for the scent of an otter, 'the drag', but fail to find it. They indicate by their boredom and frustration that no otter has been present thereabouts in the last couple of days.

The Kendal hounds were especially appropriate for this. The pack was made up of the true, old-fashioned, pure-bred otterhound, a rare breed of hound which some other packs preferred not to use, because the proper woolly otterhounds would acknowledge too faint a drag. This was considered a waste of time by some, but in our tricky country, with so many drains, caves, borrans and big root systems where otters could remain secure out of mark, and unlocatable by even the best-scenting hounds, a hound which would speak to drag was essential. My lovely, deep-voiced hounds could give an accurate indication of the presence or absence of an otter, even if they could often not 'find' it, or even find it. We often went home discussing where we might have left our quarry, which, according to the hounds, had undoubtedly been somewhere on the stretch where we had looked for it.

I analysed the information in the diaries into 'positive draws' and 'negative draws', i.e. presence or absence, and grouped them into five periods, 1936-39, 1949-52, 1953-56, 1964-67 and 1968-71. I was surprised to learn from this that before the war one day in four had been blank. Whereas in the mid-Fifties it was only one day in thirteen.

The Sixties saw things back to the state of the pre-war years, but the average is pulled down a bit by the vicissitudes in the fortunes of the hunt; a new, inexperienced huntsman in 1964 and 1965 undoubtedly affected the result. In 1966 the hunt had one day in six blank, a good score again after the two inept years, but by 1968 it had halved, and in 1969 it collapsed to one blank in two, and never recovered. The abruptness of the onset of the decline, and its extent and completeness, came as a shock when I worked out the figures, even though it had also been noticed at the time, as the diaries tell.

Mink appear

1968 is the year that mink are first mentioned in entries in the diary relating to the Kendal and District's own country. The previous year there were two mentions of mink, both referring to meets when the pack was on visits to other parts of England. There is no previous mention of mink at all, but early in the season of 1968 this entry occurs:

"Found 4 lots of mink in the first 5 days, and drew Halton Deeps blank- more signs of mink there too- this is getting serious."

Ten years after this first, anxious, diary entry, mink were everywhere, but their arrival coincided with the sudden demise of a previously healthy and robust otter population. Of that there can be no doubt; what is debatable is whether it was just a coincidence, or an effect. I tried to see whether the diaries could give any suggestion of guidance on this. Although mink later spread throughout the whole hunt country, they occurred first and most seriously in the Lune Valley, and at the same time as the decline. In the 1950s the Lune had been full of otters; in 1954 and 1955, for two magical seasons, it was never once drawn blank in a total of 28 draws.

In 1966 the population had settled back to the more sustainable level of the inter-war years. But by 1969 the expectation had become that every other day would be blank. The rest of the country did not decline so rapidly, and although the figures show that in normal times the Lune system was marginally better stocked than the rest of the country, for the rest of the period after the sudden onset of the decline, it remained much worse. The arrival and the prevalence of the mink seem from these statistics to be more than coincidentally connected to the collapse of the otter population.

It seems from all this that what happened in the north-west of England cannot be explained solely by accumulative exposure to sheep dip. I still incline to the theory that the sheep dips caused the immune systems of the otters to collapse, and allowed a disease, probably introduced by the newly-arrived mink, to be unusually devastating. I found doing the study interesting, but it made little contribution to what went on afterwards.

Polluted otter-food

I was fortunate to be encouraged by helping with other people's scientific researches. Sheila Macdonald and Chris Mason, of the University of Essex, were looking at the levels of pollutants available to otters through their prey. "It is essential that the supply of pollutants in the food supply of otters be determined to assess whether a contaminated diet might be contributing to cause losses or to prevent a recovery in the distribution and numbers of the species." I was well placed to assist. The waters of the Levels are fish-rich, a renowned coarse fishing area.

Although I know little about coarse fishing, I had plenty of pupils who were experts. They needed very little bribing to get them to disregard the regulations of the angling clubs about returning what they caught unharmed to the water. I organised an inter-house poaching competition, and every Monday morning proud and happy youngsters would roll up with soggy packets of roach, rudd and eels to the door of the Staff Common Room, for a weigh-in. My main difficulty was devising packaging secure enough for the train journey by Red Star parcel from Taunton to Essex.

The results were revealing. 10% of the fish submitted were contaminated, some of them "above the critical level which could represent a potential hazard to carnivores feeding extensively on fish. The majority of these were in areas where otters no longer occur. High levels of dieldrin were also recorded from fish

on the River Culm, Devon, and the River Tone, Taunton, and were probably of industrial origin."

They go on to say, "Eels were significantly more contaminated than other fish species and these observations support previous suggestions that eels may be important bio-magnifiers of chlorinated hydrocarbons." Important, presumably, for otters, as more than 80% of their diet is eels. Subsequently, they considered the importance of PCBs, and again we sent fish from the Tone. Our sample demonstrated that fish from the source of the river carried a basic level, scored as level 1, from general background pollution. As one progressed downstream the levels increased, until they scored a worrying level 4 below the outflow of Taunton's sewage treatment works.

It was we humans that were inserting into the ecosystem our excess PCB's from the burden stored in our tissues. They began to look at PCB levels in tissue from dead otters and found levels well above what had been shown experimentally to impair reproduction in captive mink. Yet, "it was concluded that chlorinated

A silver eel, partly eaten by cubs. Eels are a major part of an otter's diet.

hydrocarbon pesticides and polychlorinated biphenyls are unlikely to be adversely affecting populations of top carnivores, and especially the otter, at the present time." That left everybody wondering what was, then.

They next looked at accumulations of metals in the fish. There are more difficulties in this, as metals, unlike OC's, occur naturally in the environment, so their report contains many caveats and cautions. However, they do state,

"Our results indicate that eels carry higher levels of mercury, cadmium, zinc and copper than other species.

'Levels of mercury, cadmium and lead in fish are sufficiently high to present potential hazards to piscivorous animals such as the otter.

'Metals may be at levels which could impair the optimum functioning of an animal, thus lowering its fitness. Smith and Stephens have described how low levels of lead affect visual discrimination and the development of locomotor and exploratory skills in young laboratory animals. To a free-living carnivore, such skills are crucial."

These studies were useful in that they at last advanced our knowledge about the animal we were so concerned about, and for the first time provided hard biological fact on which to base our conservation efforts. Helping with such work was not only interesting, and satisfying, it was also fun. There was considerable glee among the schoolboy anglers at being encouraged to neglect their homework to go fishing in a way which also involved defying the regulations.

A large fish is held down by the otter's fore-paws, and crunched – bones and all – in its powerful jaws.

A blind otter

I put together another report at about the same time. This one did raise some interest, but as it was retrospective it had little practical effect on the fortunes of the otters at that time. It has perhaps been of some value more recently in that it suggested a focus for subsequent researches, and these could be of value in other parts of the world. As a member of the otter hunting community I had begun to be aware of stories and "anecdotal evidence" of blind otters. In 1966 our pack had killed an otter in unusual circumstances on the river Bela, in Westmorland. The otter was seen to land on the riverbank and listen for the hounds. That in itself was not at all unusual, but in this case the otter did not move as a hound approached and grabbed it, although it had plenty of time and opportunity to dive back into deep water and escape. The surface of both its eyes were found to be opaque and creamy-coloured. My notes tell that it was one of two found together, that it was in good condition, and healthy, or at least fit, as it had evaded the hounds for some time before it landed. The only possible problem was that it had a strong infestation of sheep ticks, but that was not uncommon in otters in the sheep farming area of the Lake District.

I saw another blind otter with visibly white eyes in the winter of 1967/68. This otter lived on Leighton Moss, near Carnforth, which had recently been taken over by the RSPB as a bird reserve. I used to go there frequently, to look for birds and to see the otters. This otter was one of a group of three that used to fish together in the open water for eels. The areas of open water were just flooded flat fields, and the water was quite shallow. These three otters used to swim out from the shelter of the tall reedbeds, and hunt for eels in the open water opposite the willow-fringed causeway track. There was no need for an observer to hide, as the bushes provided enough cover, and one could stand and watch through binoculars as they plied their trade not far away. To be able to watch otters in those days was most unusual, and there was no wildlife on the telly to accustom us to close views into the world of nature. It is impossible to describe my vivid excitement at being able to watch an animal, which would normally just be glimpsed as a departing shadow, going about its behaviour in a totally unconcerned way.

The blind otter eel-hunting

The method was always the same, and very effective. The otter would dive, but the water was so shallow that only the front half of the animal would disappear from view; the back half would be exposed in an undignified way to the air, with its well-muscled bottom and rudder projecting above the thrashing propellers which were its hind feet. The backside pushed the front end along, and the otter ploughed the bottom of the lake for eels. I could not make out whether it was ploughing with its forepaws to feel for the eels in the mud, or with its face to locate the wriggling of the eel with its whiskers. From time to time each of the three would come up for air, and gaze about before ducking down again to resume the search. Although they remained close together, there was no attempt at co-operation or co-ordination that I could see. It definitely seemed to be each otter for itself.

Sooner rather than later an eel would be ploughed up from the sludge. Then the lucky otter would dart forwards, with a massive convulsive effort from its exposed bottom, and grab the eel. There were few misses, and no prolonged chases. Grovel, grovel, grovel, a

sudden lunge and there you were, successful nearly every time. It looked easy, and showed the usefulness of the vibrissae, (whiskers) to this species. The murky colour of the peaty water must have prevented any visibility, and the whole process must have been done by feel alone.

This is why a blind otter can succeed in carrying on a comparatively normal life, whereas a fox, say, or a hare, would not last any time at all if both its eyes were opaque, as this otter's were. The one with the white eyes seemed just as successful at this method as the others. Small eels would be eaten where they were caught, but larger ones were taken to the reeds and eaten on land before the otter came out to rejoin the other two.

Sadly, at that time I was just so thrilled to see them that I did not keep properly detailed notes, of how many they caught, or how long their hunting sessions lasted, or even what time they came out. But I remember it as being in the middle of the day: that was considered sufficiently unusual for us to speculate in conversation whether the damage to the eyes of the "blind" one had anything to do with when they did their fishing. I am also sure it was only eels they caught; no fish, and no birds. That was what we expected, of course, and I recollect that when my son told us many years later that he had seen an otter at Leighton Moss pull a coot under in much the same place as these three used to eat eels, our interest was in the unusual nature of that sighting.

Possibly a good supply of eels was necessary for a blind otter to survive. And possibly it was easier for "White Eyes" to catch them in the daytime, when they were dormant, than at night, when eels are more active. But whatever the reason, that otter lived there for several years, and was probably the one that was picked up ten years later in a very sick state as a very old otter. Although the Bela is not far from the Leighton

Despite its intent gaze, this hunting otter is probably getting as much information from its flared whiskers as from its eyes.

Beck, and they both drain into Morecambe Bay only three kilometres apart, at that time I dismissed both instances of blindness as just isolated freak incidents, of curiosity value only. But over the years I came to hear of other stories from other areas, and in 1979 I decided to gather all these stories and instances together. I appealed through various sporting magazines for details of any other cases of blindness in otters.

Initially there was a strong response, but gradually the instances became less frequent, and by the mid-1980s there seemed to be no more. When I came to collate my findings, and to write it up, the limited period over which this had occurred seemed the most interesting aspect of the study. I asked all the oldest otter hunters

among my wide acquaintance in that close-knit world. Many of them were considerable diarists and record keepers, but they had no knowledge at all of any such cases in former times. Nor was there any mention of it in the many books about the sport. The first case I could discover was a big dog otter on the Cole near Lechlade in 1957. I learned of 23 cases between then and 1980, and one in 1989, when I wrote my report.

I had disregarded those otters whose blindness was obviously caused by something

external, mainly from being shot. There was also one otter with a non-functioning eye that had never opened after birth. This left 22 cases with apparently similar symptoms. They all seemed to have the same sort of obviously white opaqueness; two were blind in one eye only, and one was described as "nearly blind". Ten of the 22 were described as in good condition, but three were in a very poor case: one was described as 'starving', and the other two were in fact dying of liver disorders. One of these two was a very old otter indeed, so his reaching such an old age can be counted a plus, rather than a minus, but the other sick animal was a young dog that should have been in his prime.

One important thing that I had no way of knowing was how big a proportion of the problem the 22 were. A sick otter may well crawl into a hole to die, say some; others think that before it reaches that final stage it will make desperate efforts to feed itself somehow, and will then be more exposed to our view, as it raids a hen house or a goldfish pond, so we may well notice most of those otters which are dying slowly. I do not think it likely, despite my advertisement for instances, that I was told of *all* the blind otters that people knew about, nor do I think that those that were found would be even half of the otters affected.

But at that time, even 22 was a huge loss. The first national survey in 1977 found only 170 sites with evidence of an otter. So my compilation of the list attracted attention to the phenomenon, and in 1996 Don Jefferies published a paper that gave details of four more cases and looked at the situation in some detail. Three of his new cases were within my time span, but one was as late as 1986. This very sick and old (9 years) bitch otter from Norfolk was caught alive and

OPPOSITE: Even Hebridean otters, living in the cleanest of seas, have been known to have sometimes suffered from blindness.

examined thoroughly after its death four days later, by no fewer than three known experts. The blindness was due to cataracts in both eyes. But the symptoms which had caused it to be in such a poor state of health "closely resemble the pathological changes found in Aleutian disease in American mink. This is a lethal contagious disease first reported in captive mink, and its probable discovery in a wild mustelid, particularly an otter, is of some concern to conservationists."

After discussing whether the white opacity is caused by cataracts rather than Keratitis, Don Jefferies goes on to look at the distribution of this problem:

"The distribution of the records in time and space is sporadic, occurring over a period of 23 years and widespread over most of Britain. This suggests that the blindness is unlikely to be due to a contagious disease, or a congenital problem. The findings of Williams that several of the reports involved other apparently normally sighted otters living with the blind one would support this. This sample includes a juvenile and a cub. Thus the blindness is not solely the result of an ageing population.

"The distribution of the 19 otters listed with county by Williams is 10 (52.6%) in southern counties of England, 6 (31.6%) in northern counties and 3 (15.8%) in Scotland. This does not correlate with the numbers of otters in those regions at that time, but is, in fact, the opposite. The incidence of blindness does not follow otter density, as might be expected with disease or parasites. Thus the pattern of correlations which emerges points quite clearly towards the organochlorines (insecticides and PCBs) as the likely basal cause of the blindness noted by Williams. However neither of these two groups of compounds is known to have produced cataracts in the many laboratory tests to determine their likely environmental hazard."

In retrospect, I find Jefferies' heavy emphasis on the organochlorine pesticides as the cause very revealing as to what was going on beneath the surface of the conservation activity of that time. An intense and at times ill-natured debate was going on between two points of view. Chanin and Jefferies had published a major paper estimating the introduction of dieldrin and aldrin as the cause of the decline in the otter population. These chemicals had rightly been withdrawn from use, yet the expected rapid revival had not materialised. Mason and Macdonald had pointed out the continuing prevalence of the PCBs in the water environment, and were keen that further work should be done on this hazard. These points of view became two camps, and this polarity became at times more of a defence of reputations than an objective search for a way forward. Thus Jefferies, after his examination of all the aspects of blindness, plumped in his conclusion for those aspects which reinforce his earlier paper on the pesticides.

"In conclusion, although some of the later cases of blindness are almost certainly due to cataracts associated with old age, most of the factors in the earlier cases point towards keratitis and hyperkeratosis of the cornea with the main causal factor being the organochlorine insecticides dieldrin and aldrin. The incidence of this blindness started around the time of the initial date of use of these compounds, and ceased around the time of the final ban in 1981. The finding of a likely sub-lethal effect occurring over the period and area of their greatest use is of particular note in that it provides valuable confirmatory evidence."

He dismisses entirely all the evidence from the only animal to have been given a thorough post-mortem examination, an animal whose death fell well outside the cut off date for the pesticides. The Norfolk bitch that died in 1986 showed signs of having a disease caught from

feral mink. My study of the decline in the Kendal hunt country pointed to a sudden onset of the decline at the same time as the mink became well-established. In September 1990 the Daily Telegraph reported a widespread outbreak of Aleutian disease in ferrets, and at about the same time a dead otter from North Wales was found showing many of the same symptoms.

Was it pesticides or disease?

I realise that in writing this, I am exhibiting the same sort of bias. Jefferies leant in my view too much towards his theory of pesticides. I have always been of the 'disease' persuasion, and still am. Whether it matters so long after the events is not just a point of academic pride. If pesticides were to blame for the (nearly total) disaster, they have since been withdrawn, and all shall be well. However, if disease was implicated, the problem may be continuing. Happily, the recent series of detailed post-mortems on over 800 otters by Vic Simpson of the Wildlife Veterinary Investigation Centre has found no sign of any infectious epidemic, so it begins to look as if I may have been wrong, and we shall have to look at other factors to explain the present slowing down of their rate of recovery.

Blindness persists today

The instances of blindness have not entirely ceased, however. I now, (December 07), have a note of 38 cases. Dr Hans Kruuk trapped and released an adult dog otter in 1989 in Kincardineshire. Although it seemed fit, he thought its obvious blindness might make it atypical for the research he wanted to tag it for, so he just let it go, collarless. One was photographed in Shetland in 1993, and another at Lochinver in 2004. Three cases in 2006 can be put down to old age and infirmity, two in the Hebrides, and one an 11 year old captive bitch at the Otter Trust zoo in Cornwall, that developed double cataracts. The most interesting recent case for me was an otter of a different species in southern Chile.

DDT-blinded Chilean otters

Vic Simpson, the veterinary pathologist who did all our otter post-mortems, had gone out to Chile to help with scientific research into the rapidly declining population of the Southern River Otter, *Lutra provocax*. He managed to get a head-on photograph of the only one he saw, as it surfaced under a bush. The photo clearly shows a white opacity in each eye, of the kind we used to notice here.

This gave a clue as to what might be the fundamental cause of their decline. Previously the Chilean researchers had been concentrating on removal of riverside habitat and vegetation as being undoubtedly linked to the fall in otter numbers. The cause of the removal of so much bankside habitat was the system in use out there, whereby an impoverished settler can be granted a strip of land alongside a river, to try to develop it as a small subsistence farm.

The family moves in by canoe, and clears land back from the bank to plant a vegetable garden. The idea is that each season he can extend his holding farther back, and increase his productivity. The snag is that in the early stages his vital crop is adjacent to the raw jungle, which is home to all manner of ravenous insects and bugs. To protect his plants, he has to spray with DDT, which is still readily available out there.

The damage to the otter's eyes indicated that it may be this, rather than lack of bankside cover, that is killing off this very rare and restricted species. As is often the case in conservation, is it easier to identify the problem than to know what to do about it.

But this is further evidence that pesticides are harmful to otters. If these substances can damage their eyes, they could also attack their reproductive systems, and cause a gradual decline through lack of recruitment, or they could wreck their immune systems and allow diseases to flourish.

THE HEALTH OF BRITISH OTTERS

A considerable number of otters are subjected to post-mortems each year, so it is possible to give a general overview of the health of the English population.

The first thing to note is that there is no evidence of any kind of epidemic, or infectious disease. Two or three otters have shown lesions associated with a disease common on mink farms, but they were isolated instances. Generally, otters do not seem to be affected by TB; the first confirmed case was found in Northern Ireland in 2008. That is perhaps to be expected, as the solitary lifestyle of these animals would make the spread of any disease very unlikely, especially TB which thrives in circumstances of overcrowding, such as is found in a badger sett or a cattle yard. Several otters have been found with lung spots which look like TB infection, but they are a rare form of fungus. Anything that compromises the lungs of an animal which has to dive for its food is going to eliminate that predator very quickly, so we probably do not see all the cases of this.

There is little evidence of starvation, but stomach ulcers are not uncommon, mainly in cubs that have been captured and handled a lot. The physiological stress is considerable in this species. A Spanish study monitoring otters being fitted with radios found that it was a very damaging process. Another stress-related condition may be frequent enlargement of the adrenal glands. To what extent this is caused by, or is the cause of, the alarming amount of fighting that we are finding, is not clear. A fifth of all the otters looked at have been injured in a fight, but in the south and south-west regions, up to a half are wounded. Some have minor bites and punctures, others life-threatening injuries, and a few have undoubtedly died after a fight. Although they live in water, an otter's bite is not clean, and bacterial infections are often the result. Sometimes the sepsis starts in the root of a tooth which gets fractured in the battle; otters have slender, sharp canines, and if the tooth breaks off too low, the resultant abscess can give rise to a general sepsis. Death from tooth-ache.

An increasing number of otters get kidney stones. This is now up to one in six, and rising steadily. Nobody is sure why this should be, but some of the stones are considerable in size. Equally mysterious are some of the abnormal uteri that have been found; and the malformations on the retina. Perhaps these are a result of the continuing absorption of various forms of the pollutant PCB. Whereas other forms of pollution have reduced, principally lead and the OC pesticides, PCBs are still prevalent. They suppress Vitamin A, so could be implicated in damage to the eyes and the reproductive system. A strong statistical balance between PCB burden and enlargement of the adrenal glands has been found. The reduction in the pesticides seems to have almost entirely eliminated the cases of white-eyed blindness.

Despite all this, we have a vigorous otter population. The only area of real concern is the recently imported Bile Fluke, which infects most of the lowland otters in our area, and which is spreading. It undoubtedly wrecks the livers of some animals completely, but not in every case, and we still have our otters. We do not yet know how damaging this parasite will be.

CHAPTER ELEVEN

GETTING CLOSER

All these activities and investigations were basically driven by a widespread anxiety over falling otter numbers. Its focus was on the underlying causes, and on the geographical spread of the species. There was a sort of unspoken assumption that an increase in range of the species would mean an increase in the total numbers, but nobody had really looked into this. It could be argued that if the habitat was degraded to a point bordering on the unsatisfactory, such otters that remained might have to roam far and wide just to make a living, and keep themselves alive.

The overnight surveys on the levels had demonstrated that a very few otters,

if unconstrained as to territory by lack of neighbours, would wander in a seemingly random way over a very large area. After all, why not, if one fish is as good as another?

So, while we made nice maps and charted progress of some sort, we had very little idea of what was actually happening out there on the ground. It was considered axiomatic that one could not count otters, not even with hounds. Their mobility and restlessness precluded identification. I remember having an unusually energetic conversation about this with my friend Penny Howells, who ran the Otter Conservancy consultancy business, over lunch one day. I wanted to try to set up some kind of counting system, or to attempt an estimation of some kind. Penny was adamant that it would be wrong even to try, as the results would be so wildly inaccurate, little better than guesses, and therefore potentially dangerously misleading. We should confine ourselves to phrases such as 'more' or 'fewer', and not even try to put a number to it.

Otters on the move

It is hard at this distance of time to remember how low the numbers would have been. I do not think we would have had to take our socks off to count our otters on the Tone system. In fact I still have a postcard from Penny herself, excitedly claiming that it looked as if there were four separate otters on the system.

Shortly before that, she had insisted that I take her out along my local bit of the Tone, and show her all the otter evidence I had been so enthusiastically claiming – I rather think she had been asked to check it, (or me), out, to make sure I was not letting my enthusiasm run away with me. I remember we started down at Hele, just above Taunton, and found the padding of a large otter, presumably a dog, travelling upstream.

We moved on a bit, and found his tracks again, an otter with a purpose, galloping hard across the sand banks on all the eroded bends above Bradford. And again below Wellington, and yet again above Wellington, at Harpford Bridge. He was still going at Wellisford. We quit there; it would have been harder to get padding higher up, as the river becomes very stony, and there is less mud or sand.

That was the sort of day I really enjoy, and it was especially exciting so soon after the return of the otters to the Tone, the pivotal event that I described at the beginning of this book. That otter had gone more than 10 kilometres in one night, apparently without intruding onto the patch of any opposition. It was a sparse population indeed.

I was intrigued about what had actually been happening, what was the individual reality behind the maps. For what motive did the pioneer otter, the one that first recolonised the Tone, suddenly one night leave its home range on the River Exe and venture upstream into an unknown area? How far did it travel at a time? How urgent was its need to push on, to bring about the salvation of the species from the very edge of extinction in England. Remember, only 170 sites had sprainted in the first English survey: how few bitches of breeding age did this represent?

What must have happened was that one animal set off one night into the otterless unknown. As it journeyed upstream along its tributary, up the Batherm perhaps, it found no trace of its own kind. The big holt at Hukely would be cold and scentless, totally uninviting after years of emptiness. If it holed up there, how long did it linger? That holt has been home to generations of otters from time immemorial, so why did it press on past it, and ignore the Bittescombe lakes, to cross the watershed, through the disused railway tunnel perhaps, and to drop by chance into the equally otterless Tone? Why did it then remain, and not return?

Mysterious life of otters makes them difficult to protect

We still know so little about the way of life of this species, and its requirements, that we are restricted in our conservation efforts to little more than supplying as clean a set of rivers as we can, and hoping that if their prey prospers, they will prosper too. They are impossibly difficult animals, mysterious almost to the point of myth. If you are seeking a species to study, my advice is not to choose a chocolate brown, nocturnal

Otter footprints in the sand — often the only evidence available to the patient otter researcher.

animal with no distinguishing features, which is notoriously nomadic, and which spends most of its time underwater anyway.

Otters are inconvenient, invisible and usually absent elsewhere. If some new epidemic were to beset them, we are still not in a position even to recognise its onset, and, like last time, we have no method nor mechanism by which to measure any decline until it is nearly complete. Supposing that 50% of the otters were taken out by a mystery illness or parasite, perhaps one of the new illnesses at present establishing themselves in our hitherto protected island by the recent practice of allowing the free movement of dogs backwards and forwards, protected only against rabies. Those of us who monitor spraining activity would initially notice little difference, as the survivors would take up the vacant space.

Assessing their density, or counting their numbers, is therefore very difficult. Such a census is essential if we are to be in a position to do anything in response to any possible future reversal in their fortunes. And even if we did suspect some kind of problem, there is no reporting system. Each county wildlife trust or

group of amateurs follows its own method, and does with its results what it will. There have been various clumsy attempts to standardise and centralise things, but nothing has come of them. One of the problems is that the insufficient information that our amateur methods give is often not worth centralising at great cost. And once you have centralised it all, what happens next?

Attempts to standardise otter research

About ten years ago, the prestigious mammal research outfit Wildcru, a part of the Zoology department of Oxford University, sent out a consultation letter as how best to design a consistent monitoring scheme.

I was less than enthusiastic. Population monitoring is a means only, towards the end of helping the otters by practical action. There is a strong danger that the challenge of devising and setting up an adequate system of counting them will become an end in itself, and thereby waste energies, resources and money which would be better used directly to help the otters. There were already too many examples of duff statistics being used as fact: the conflicting hare surveys, for instance, or the 10-year-old and oft-repeated figure which the Mammal Society gave for the annual destruction of badger setts by badger diggers (9000 a year, or 25 a day!) — which would have resulted in the total obliteration of every badger sett in under 5 years, if their other figure, for the total number of setts, is also to be believed. Or the calculation for barn owls in Somerset, 834.6, a figure more than ten times in excess of what appears from the records to be visible on the wing.

If it is hard to get a meaningful result for large, white, day-flying birds, it might almost be better not to attempt to count brown, underwater, nomadic, nocturnal mammals. After all, what use is to be made of such a figure? Supposing we create a system sufficiently sensitive to detect a 30% reduction over a short period, then what? What actions could or would result from such information? And why can those actions not take place now, without waiting for the elaborate and expensive setting up of the counting procedure?

Spraint recordings

The map square I live in has regular otters and I look at one spraiting stone every day, when I walk the dogs. This stone disclosed the presence

A tranquil section of the river Torridge in North Devon, the place of inspiration for Henry William-son's birth holt for Tarka.

of an otter, from the size of its padding probably a bitch, on 42 occasions to 25th July, but it then had a negative run of over 5 weeks.

There are two equally probable alternative explanations: either she is dead, or she is busy with cubs not very far away. Both are natural events in the life of the local otters, yet the difference in a count between one death and two cubs is a factor of 3 otters. In other words, although I live above the shop, I cannot detect numbers to any useful degree of accuracy.

Not surprisingly, nothing much seems to have come of all that. There is no agreed system that we should be following, nor is there a clearing house to receive our results, although the otter is a priority species under the BAP scheme that was put in place after the Rio Conference in 1992.

In the early days, when otters were still extremely scarce, I used to record negative

searches as well as positive ones. The ratio of positive to negative sites can give a good indication of a changing trend, but it cannot really be relied on mathematically. The difficulty is to define a negative site. If I find a spraint on a rock, that is a positive record. If I later find that rock has no spraint on it, is that a negative? Yes, if the water levels are the same, probably not, if the level has dropped a lot.

There is no point in an otter climbing up a high bank in summer to spraint on a winter level rock, as the scent will be blown well above the head of the next otter to pass that way, so it will put it lower down, where it will be found, which will make the original rock blank. If a friend sees an otter while fishing, that too is a positive. If he does not see one, is that a negative?

Eventually the otters came back in sufficient numbers to make my negative records merely records of the chance vagaries of the hazards of riverbank life. They had become a matter of luck, and ceased to tell me anything meaningful about the status of the river, so I saved space in my books by ceasing to record them, unless I was undertaking a prescribed survey to a preset pattern.

The Somerset Otter Group has been carrying out this sort of consistent effort survey for some decades now, and has built up an accretion of information, some 24,000 records, which is at last being analysed statistically. The members go to the same pre-selected sites every month, and fill out a form. There is consistency of effort. The basic skill is to find and recognise a spraint, even the very small ones. The big ones are obvious enough, unless mink are about as well, but the smallest ones are often overlooked in the grass, and of course there is so-called 'Anal Jelly'.

New or old spraints?

A more advanced skill is to be confident in distinguishing between fresh and older spraints. A new spraint, that is one from the previous night's otter activity, can be over twelve hours old by ten o'clock, when the more relaxed or civilised sort of surveyor takes to the riverbanks, and even experienced spraint addicts can call them wrongly under certain weather conditions: drying wind and direct sunlight can take the shine off a brand new spraint in a few hours.

The helpful 2003 procedure for monitoring British rivers that are SACs (Special Areas of Conservation) removes this element of subjective judgement by replacing it with a description of the spraint itself. Instead of 'fresh', 'recent', and 'old', the categories are now, 'wet intact', 'dry intact' and 'dry fragmented'. The object of this Natura 2000 EU initiative is to produce standardised reporting for the purpose of comparison between different rivers.

We pioneered its use in April 2004 on the river Axe, which forms the boundary of three counties, Devon, Somerset, and Dorset. Because of this administrative split, nobody was looking at this important river, so a small group of volunteers decided to use the new method to survey the entire catchment on one day. We established that otters were using pretty well every part of the catchment, including some quite small tributaries, but we had suspected that before. We have now repeated the exercise six times, and can be confident that there is a sustained presence of otters, so presumably a viable population. Incidental reports of cubs indicate that this is a population that is not dependent on immigrants from other rivers.

Slow re-colonisation on the River Axe

The method was intended to produce standardised comparisons, yet when comparisons from one Axe survey to the next are made, subjectivity has to rescue the maths from being misleading. In 2006 we found 88% of our sites positive, and in 2007 only 56%. However, the 'adjudicated scores' are very similar for both years, and fit well with previous years. The adjudication is that somebody looks at the distribution of the fresh spraints on a map, and estimates how many otters were present during that night. The need to rescue the varying raw percentages from being misleading has led to a sort of count.

It is not a count of otters, but of areas where otters were active. There may well be a bitch with cubs, but it still goes down as one, the minimum we can be certain of. I suppose it is a count of adults. The map this year disclosed 10 or 11 otters, with a maximum of 12, and a minimum of 9. This is consistent with what we appear to have found in previous years.

We are gradually building up a set of 'adjudicated scores' that ascertains the carrying capacity of the Axe, in its present, rather damaged state. Some people aver that the density of an otter population is prey related. If that were the sole factor, there would have been more otters in the healthier olden days, but the hunt diaries do not support this. The hunt had always to go a long way between finds, and it seems probable that these mobile animals have an inbuilt need for space, for roaming room. If you watch them in a zoo at feeding time, a meal is always followed by a period of moving about, backwards and forwards, or round and round the perimeter path. Of course, if the Axe had far fewer fish, it probably could not sustain its ten or so otters, but if it had more, they would not pack into the tributaries much more densely.

Any count of otters, therefore, is always going to end up with a low total, and the incidental hazards, like road deaths, or a major pollution, will have a considerable effect in such a small constituency. It is impossible to count every otter, but with numbers so low, every otter counts.

We have been encouraged by our results from the River Axe. It looks as if it is possible to assess the whole of a small river in such a way that a good estimation of its carrying capacity for otters can be made. Although their number is low, if my interpretation of the statistics is reliable, at least it is being maintained. Whatever population there is, seems to be sustainable. This is a relief, for the recent history of the river was far from encouraging.

A small population hung on until 1978, but then the Axe too went blank for ten years. There was a single otter made its way into the catchment in 1983, but it was run over as it arrived. At least, my arrogant self-confidence in my abilities as an otter surveyor led me to think that. The week before the dead animal was found I had spent a whole day checking the Axe, and had concluded that otters were still absent. It may be that an otter invading a new catchment is cautious at first about sprainting too vigorously, but there is plenty of good mud in that part of the river, and I found no padding either.

After this sad failure to re-colonise the Axe in 1983, there were three blank years until 1987, when I found otter work on 5 occasions. From this, things built up steadily, and a small population seemed to have got going again. Then we recorded 5 deaths in the year 2000, which must have been a colossal setback, especially as one of them was a lactating bitch, whose cubs must also have died, from cold or starvation.

Light oil pollution kills slowly

Everything seems more stable again now. Although we steadily get a small number of road casualties, this does not seem to affect the quantity nor the spread of the evidence that we find in our co-ordinated searches. But pollution does have an effect. The most recent contamination was comparatively minor, a light surface film of diesel oil for a few miles at the top end of the catchment. No fish seemed affected, and there was no reason to suppose that the invertebrates on which the whole ecosystem is built would be harmed by a floating surface film in the winter, with plenty of water in the river. At the time we thought that the only casualty was a sick otter cub, with oiled fur, which was taken into care.

Perhaps the name he was given, "Diesel", was inauspicious, but he seemed to thrive and grow on well at the sanctuary where he lived with another orphan cub from a different river. A good six months later the staff were worried to find Diesel's chum in distress and agitation one morning, which was because her playmate had suddenly died in the night.

The post-mortem investigation showed that his insides had been considerably damaged by the exposure to the oil; he would never have been able to cope with a stressed life as a wild otter. Yet it was a very minor dose of pollution. The Environment Agency staff traced it to some roadworks where the road surface had been repaired with tarmac for a short distance alongside a stream.

The trouble with tarmac in winter is that it can be stiff and unco-operative; to make life easier and to be sure of getting home on time on a cold, damp, winter's day, mix a few splashes of diesel into the bucket when you come to smooth off the top of the trench. As the tarmac sets and settles, the small amount of diesel will leach out into the ditch. And, as in this case, from there into the stream and thence into the river, where a little of the minute amount floating downstream as a rainbow sheen will be caught in the otter's coat as it surfaces. When the otter grooms itself, as they so regularly do, it will swallow enough to damage its insides.

We do not know what happened to the rest of Diesel's family; we did not even know that there was a bitch with small cubs in that part of the river. But at the next survey there was in that area a considerable stretch of main river and associated tributaries which were completely blank.

This shows three things: that it is possible to monitor otters to a degree of sensitivity that is useful, that otters are so sparsely spaced along a river that a damaging event like this leaves a gap, and that these apparently tough predatory animals are very vulnerable to even minor pollutions.

This was an impassable weir for otters until the baskets of stone were put in place along the edge.

Creating an 'otter loo'

This vulnerability showed up in other of my monitoring schemes. When we moved to this house, in 1987, one of the first improvements I made was to install an 'otter loo' on the stream that borders my garden. Where it flows under the road bridge outside my gate I placed a small heap of boulders, just at the upstream edge of the archway, so that I can peer over the parapet and check for otter spraint without having to go down into the water at all.

This I do every day, when I take the dogs for their morning walk. The score is recorded on a calendar, yes or no, an otter or not during the night, and the positives are worked out as a percentage of the total checkable days. Some days the stream is in spate, so the stones are submerged; at other times I am away. These days are simply omitted from the calculation.

As my stretch of this minor side stream is only a minute part of the lebensraum of any otter, the frequency of the visits is very varied, but the totals have recorded a pleasing increase as the otter population has gradually re-established. I am sure a small network of similar observations would yield invaluable information. I am keen to build up a network of daily recorders, as a method of looking at some of the detail of the population. With our widespread otter distribution, and with evidence that otters are now well-established residents rather than precarious frontier pioneers, we can learn little new from geographical exercises such as the National Surveys. But a team of daily recorders would soon start to build a picture more related to the scale of the catchment.

Cattle slurry drives the otters away

In 2002 an abominable peasant upstream from my house deliberately dumped a load of toxic cattle slurry into the stream at dusk on the Friday before the August Bank Holiday. Agricultural pollutions often occur just as the Environment Agency reduces to a skeleton staff for a long weekend. The hope is that the poison will be miles down river before the authorities notice.

In this case in late August the water was extremely low, and the rate of flow past our house was only half a kilometre an hour, so not only was it noticed, but the damage to the waterlife in the stream, vertebrate and invertebrate, was massive, and made worse because a

I put these stones under the bridge to make an 'otter loo'! As you can see they appreciate the facility.

selfish old lady got her son the schoolteacher to turn off the EA's aerating pumps at bedtime in case they disturbed her sleep.

I got up early on the Sunday morning to check on the state of things, and met a furious man from the EA staff who had conscientiously got up very early and made the journey from his home to refuel the pumps, so as to be sure to keep the remedial measures going. The tanks were of course full, as old ladies go to bed early, so the pumps had hardly run at all.

But had we been away, and had the farmer got lucky, so that his crime was not detected, the simple method of monitoring for otters by peering over the bridge for a minute every morning would eventually have disclosed that there had been on this stream a problem of some sort.

The Otter Loo score for 2000 was 17%, for 2001, 18%. In 2003 the first eight months returned 12%, a slightly lower score because of the low flows, a percentage which might have been expected to pick up before the year's end with the autumn rains and the annual boost to the figures from the spawning trout.

After the wipe-out over the August bank holiday, the final four months returned less than 6%, with no signs at all in September and early October. I do not think my otter had been killed, but it certainly ignored the depleted part of its range until wet weather and time had had some chance to repair the damage.

Annual 2-day survey

I am also looking into seeing whether a careful recording of bitches with cubs can give an insight into the size of a population. My thought is that for the immediate period of the birth and rearing of the small cubs the bitch otter is more fixed to one place and residential than normal.

Dog otters and dispersing juveniles are so consistently mobile that they confuse the whole picture. They form a sort of zoological kaleidoscope: every time you look, things are in a different pattern. But not the bitches. They are anchored to one place for a while, and this may give us a key into producing some valid numbers. One might be able to estimate the recruitment into the population over time.

Every spring I co-ordinate all the volunteers of the Somerset Otter Group to undertake a simultaneous Two-day Check on the whole county. Everybody looks at their patch on the same Saturday, and then again the following morning, on the Sunday. New evidence is registered on a map, as definite proof of the existence of an otter in that place during that night.

The disclosures can be fascinating: sometimes a string of fresh spraints shows how far an otter has moved in the course of the two nights; or an area which appeared well occupied, with lots of older spraints, may turn out to have been vacant for the whole weekend. And now that we have a sufficient number of surveyors, we create on our map a sort of snapshot of the entire otter population.

There have been problems with such a major exercise of course. It is hard to get enough volunteers, or to get volunteers in the right places, the places where the otters are, not where the most people live. It can almost become a sort of field sport, a virtual otter hunt, and the problem with that manifestation of over-enthusiasm is that the surveyors ignore their negative results. If the whole exercise is to be meaningful, we need to know the negatives as well as the positives, so that we can express the findings as percentages, and can compare one year with another, despite an unavoidable variation in cover and effort from one year to the next.

After 12 years of developing this exercise, we are in a fair way to have established a meaningful and consistent method, and can start to assess what all this pleasurable activity by so many people has discovered. It seems that we have a steady level of occupation in most areas. On most of our rivers it continues at a satisfactory density. I think we are establishing the normal carrying capacity of the local rivers, at least under the present state of the fish population.

Interpreting the results

There are two levels of interpretation of the results. The first is a straight numerical assessment and comparison of the scores. As long as the volunteers can be bullied into filling in the form correctly so that we get full details of where they went and what they found, this cannot be gainsaid. The other level is the conversion of the raw scores into numbers of otters, the adjudication. Some clusters of dots on the map are distinct, and interpretation is obvious and easy; other groups of dots tend to run into one another, so subjective and unsupported judgement is required.

Onto this considered verdict one then has to extrapolate dots at much the same sort of frequency across those areas for which we had no surveyor, and this will give a putative total for the number of otters in the county. The results are starting to come out over the years at a very consistent level. And by repeating this system annually, it appears that we are starting to define a stable, baseline level for the population.

There are purists who maintain that it is not a count at all, that otters cannot be counted like this. I tend to approve of this note of caution. The media always ask how many otters there are now. When you try to explain the difficulties involved, they glaze over impolitely, but if you utter a figure in any part of the explanation, that statistic will be the heart of an invented quote as an established fact in their report the very next day.

Although one can dismiss such passing media attention as just ephemeral and superficial entertainment, it is, or would be, helpful, to know the size of the population. Deer managers carry out annual counts, we regularly sit out at dusk in the summer to count the bats in our roof for the national census, fishery owners need to know the numbers that have been caught from their water.

As there are probably fewer otters in the whole of otter-rich Somerset than there are Red Deer in one wood on the Quantock Hills, or about the same number of otters in Somerset as there are bats in my roof in June, it seems to me that numbers are more important for our understanding of this fragile species than for many others.

I think that the numbers we already have are better supported than the doubters know. The results from the annual Two-day Events can be compared with two other sets of facts, the pattern that we discover on the same rivers throughout the rest of the year, and the results of a severely scientific exercise we took a vigorous part in a few years ago.

The regular monthly checks by the amateur volunteers of the Somerset Otter Group have not thrown up any major discrepancies between what we claimed from the Two-day Event, and what we have found on the river subsequently. An occasional grumble of disappointment from somebody who could not find his regular otter on the main weekend is about all the difference we have found. As we have confirmed on the River Axe, the system works.

DNA survey

It is also consistent with the scientific study we undertook using DNA to establish the size of the population. Sadly, this has now ceased, as being very much too expensive, but it lasted long enough to produce a strong basis for comparison.

I was approached in the late 1990s to see if I would help with the collection of spraints, for a feasibility study to see whether it is practical to investigate a group of otters by means of the DNA traces in their spraints. Although I am not a scientist, I readily agreed. The proposal was to compare three different types of otter population. The River Torridge in North Devon would be used as an example of an area where the otters had never completely died out. The River Brue, on the Somerset Levels, would represent a frontier population where re-colonisation and expansion were currently happening. The Itchen in Hampshire was considered to be a wholly artificial population resulting from deliberate releases of captive-bred stock.

I was to help with the Brue. I suggested that this would be a difficult and disappointing river, which might contribute very little. I had been looking at it for many years, and considered that it had very few otters still, and that these otters would be tricky to investigate, because of the nature of the habitat, and because the roads are perforce so far away from the river on such swampy and peaty ground. It therefore involves many miles of driving to cover even a short stretch of river.

By contrast, the Tone, where I lived, had stable otters and a system of roads which follow the watercourses more closely, so sampling is much more convenient and economical. This consideration was not just for the comfort of the 'sprint shoveler'. My task would be to obtain as many fresh samples of sprint as I could, and for this exercise, 'fresh' meant collected before 9.30am.

What was wanted by the scientists was a sample of otter DNA in readable form. To get it from the tissue of a dead otter is a simple technique: to get it from the foetid micro-environment of a newly produced piece of excrement is much more problematic. Most of the sprint is composed of partly digested fish tissue, well enriched with bacteria, on the surface of which are a few cells scratched from the stomach lining of the otter by the fish bones. The bacteria emerge at blood temperature into the oxygen rich air on a plentiful food supply, yell 'Christmas!!' to each other and get stuck in to an orgy of feasting and multiplying. This damages the otter material, and rapidly makes it unreadable.

So the collector needs to get there early, before the day warms up, and to bung the whole sprint into a test tube of industrial alcohol to spoil the bacteria's picnic. The Tone would, I recommended, yield a more steady supply of spraints, and they could be collected early more easily, so it was included as a fourth river.

The statistics show that this was a good idea. On the Itchen they identified 13 different animals over almost two years: 4 males and 9 females. The Brue turned up 11 animals in ten months, 8 of which were males, but 8 animals were found only once, including two of the females; this indicated a population in even more turmoil and instability than we had expected.

On the Torridge they collected far fewer samples; although they found ten different otters, they found only three of them more than once, so they did not really demonstrate anything more about the nature of their population than the presence of several otters. However, 20% of the sprint samples on the Tone gave a useful reading, and produced DNA profiles of 22 different otters in 13 months; 8 of them turned up sufficiently frequently to be considered resident. This was the beginning of the profiling of a population across a whole catchment.

I was more thrilled than I can say. For the very first time, we could positively talk about individual animals. My great friend, Dick Treleaven, studies peregrines in Cornwall; his birds are sufficiently recognisable to be given names, the great and charismatic "Kate", bigamous "Orangefoot", the tireless hunter, "Bloody Mary", and her useless mate, "Idle Angus." I could not go so far with my otters, but at least they now had numbers. However, this turned out to be a PR error, in that fishermen took it as evidence that we had released the same number of otters into their waters. This misconception is now too well established in their folk memory to be eradicable, but not to worry, it is a small price to pay for such a step forward in my understanding of what was going on.

The scale of activity revealed on my local river is entirely consistent with what our other methods of assessment have indicated, and is strong evidence in support of our present, less science-based efforts to continue to monitor things. Especially if one feels, as I did, that it is justifiable to go beyond the over-strict constraints imposed on the interpretation of results by the lab scientists. To be fair, the DNA study was set up to evaluate the possibilities of the method.

On one occasion we took John Dallas, the biochemical expert who processed all the spraints, out onto one of our rivers to show him what his work was in aid of, what his results meant. We could not get him at all interested. What he was focussed on was the intellectual and technological challenges presented by these test tubes of mess, and the extent to which he could obtain such a tricky reading from such unsatisfactory material.

So we sort of gave up on including him. He became a background part of the processing method, and we tried to incorporate his results into our interest, the animals themselves. Which we should not have done, strictly speaking. Strictly speaking, unless a sample gave a reading for 5 of the 6 pairs of numbers in its DNA code, we could not claim to identify

The front teeth are for holding and killing prey, the back teeth are for crunching. So otters eat at the back of the mouths, switching sides frequently.

the otter which had produced it; statistically, there would be a one in six thousand chance that two different otters might provide the same incomplete reading. Therefore it must be considered invalid.

Never mind the fact that there were fewer than 6,000 otters in the whole country; disregard any other sources of information we might have about the sample; the theory was that these samples should be able to stand on their own as incontrovertible evidence of the otters involved. The aim of the exercise was to validate the method, not to find out about otters. But I could not help seeing it as a part of a jigsaw of otters.

In the 13 months that they ran the study on the Tone, 49 of the spraints I submitted produced a reading of some sort, but only 35 to the standard considered reliable. From these, 22 different otters were profiled, 12 dogs and 10 bitches, but only 8 of the 22 were reliably identified more than once.

That was, however, enough to establish a pattern of distribution, and to measure the size of their ranges. Resident dog otters seemed to be claiming 10 to 12 km of water, bitches 6 to 9. No otter was recorded as swapping from one tributary to another. The puzzling factor was the number of otters we found only once. This may have been partly a result of the low interpretation rate, although 20% was better than in other areas. But the fact that we found a new otter every month indicates some sort of floating population of transients. Perhaps they were dispersing cubs from previous years or from other areas.

In March 1998 a fisherman friend watched a bitch and small cubs in the Tone near Wellisford. I went out early the very next morning, to try to find them. It was a lovely spring morning, bright with birdsong. I crept quietly down the riverside, hoping to get a glimpse of the family playing in the warming morning sunlight. I worked right down to the bridge below, but they were not to be seen.

So I turned about, and came even more slowly back up towards my car. Despite having failed to see them, it was still an absorbing morning for me. I found it exciting to be using all my accumulated knowledge of that stretch of river, and all my experience of otter habits, to try to locate their spraints and to take them away in my test tubes of alchohol as bizarre trophies from this esoteric but deeply satisfying form of safari.

Cubs as small as these produce very inconsiderable spraints, and have not got the hang of depositing them very accurately. They often have to omit the main sprainting rock, as too ambitiously big or steep for them, so they tend to aim for lesser stones on the shingle beds. However, as they are short of practice at this ottery art, they are poor shots, and often miss their target. (So do grandchildren, we find.) I spent a happy morning looking for pencil-lead-thin bits of spraint, to be found at a few places in the crack between two medium-sized stones on a rocky stretch of river, and had good success. I found that very satisfying, although I knew it would be some weeks before the interpretation of my tiny samples came back from the lab.

Over the following weeks I made every effort to collect as much spraint from that area as I could, in an effort to get all the small cubs onto the register at their place of birth. If we could have kept the scheme going for longer, we stood a good chance of finding out where they subsequently went, and how cubs disperse when the territories are all occupied. But the scheme had to close, so we never knew.

I still hoped that perhaps we might have found one of them as one of the corpses eventually handed in for post-mortem examination, but the two different schemes were never co-ordinated, so this opportunity was lost.

Tissues from several dead otters were sent

for analysis, to a different laboratory. Sadly the geneticist who processed them was not briefed, and treated them as just a set of laboratory specimens, and lost the labels which related them to a time and place, and through which we might have been able to identify old friends.

The Environment Agency was glad to close the DNA scheme while they were still ahead of the game. A lot had been learned from it, but the difficulties and drawbacks that emerged made it hard to justify the continuing costs, so they called a halt and wrote up the report.

The major stumbling block, apart from the cost of processing large numbers of samples which gave no viable reading, was the weird nature of the genetics of some of the Itchen otters. This river had been included in the study as a fully introduced, artificial population, and was thought to consist of either released otters, or their offspring.

Duplicate DNA

Consternation set in after the death on a road of a juvenile bitch otter from the Itchen. Her size and teeth indicated that she could have been no more than six months old; a DNA reading from her tissues claimed her to be a known otter, but one that had first been recorded from spraints found almost 9 months earlier. Of course, very small cubs do not emerge to take part in sprainting until they are over two months old, so according to the DNA, the 6 month cub should have been about a year old, full grown, not half grown.

The confusion increased when spraints with the same DNA signature continued to be found for another 3 months after the death. There had been two otters with the same pattern of numbers on the same stretch of river.

This was considered by those in the labs as an almost fatal blow to the success of the project. They had been partly expecting something similar. The otters of the south and west of England had been reduced to such low numbers in the 1960s and 70s that they must have gone through an extreme genetic bottleneck. Studies on cheetahs show that the effects of descent from very few ancestors persist for hundreds of years, and the English otters had undergone at most only three decades of recovery from their lowest population. I think we would be amazed if we knew just how few bitch otters of breeding age survived the bottleneck to contribute to the initial beginnings of the revival which is still continuing. Studies from the tissues of dead otters had prepared the experts for a lack of genetic variability in the English otters, but I do not think they had expected exact replicas.

The cause of this anomaly was almost certainly the limited number of captive-bred otters from which the released stock had to come.

The only source of captive bred otters was The Otter Trust, set up by Philip Wayre, the man who first found out how to get otters to breed in captivity. There is a hazy story that a Victorian vicar had a pair that bred, but on the whole zoos all over Europe accepted that otters were a species that would not mate in captivity. Part of the successful method is to keep the otters apart for most of the time. They are, after all, usually solitary in the wild. But that makes for a dull exhibit in a zoo, and can lead to deprivation in the animals.

Otters that know each other play intensely when they meet. They may be solitary, but they are also sociable and affectionate at times. Read the distressing episode in Gavin Maxwell's other book, *The Rocks Remain*, when he released from solitary confinement the otter that had been so aggressive and dangerous towards him, and his guilt-laden description of its pent-up need for contact and affection.

Philip Wayre had put his mind and his famous determination to cracking the problem

0

0

0

of getting zoo otters to breed because he saw that the otters were in such a marked decline that it might be necessary to use a captive breeding programme to save the species. English otters were in deep decline, but most industrial countries of Europe had lost them completely. Our diminishing stock was more precious than most people realised at the time. And obviously, to accomplish his aim of a captive rescue, he had a limited stock of otters to start from. The important thing at that time was to get the number up, not to worry about the fine tuning,

Otters may be solitary for long periods, but they are also sociable and affectionate at other times. Accommodating this has been a challenge to those looking after them in captivity.

such as pedigrees in a stud book.

So the otters that came onto the Itchen were more closely related than would have been ideal. There is a slide of the first group, and one of the bitches has a deformed foot, a tolerable and unhindering recessive deformity which has since turned up in other otters, its descendents.

The method of releasing otters is to put a group of two young bitches and a stranger dog otter into a release pen for two or three weeks, then open the door to the riverside and let them find their own way out at their own speed.

The idea is to choose young otters at an age when they will start to be looking for members of the other sex to mate for the first time. This incipient attraction should hold the trio as a group, and make them reluctant to wander too far from the area chosen as suitable for them. When the releases first started there was a strong belief that one of the main reasons the otters had vanished from some areas was that the habitat was no longer suitable to support otters. When the chemicals were being widely used as sprays, that was true, but latterly care had to be taken to find a release area with a good amount of cover for them to live in, and sufficiently quiet and secluded to enable them to settle down with confidence in the unfamiliar wild.

Less concern could be afforded as to the nature of the animals themselves. So the Itchen ones were perhaps too closely inbred, and the position was made worse when, as intended, they bred successfully together, and produced the same genetic signature.

This confusion of identity called into question the whole thing we were supposed to be looking at, whether the DNA method could be developed to investigate different individuals in an otter population. If this had been a natural happening, then the answer would be no. I felt that the artificial nature of this one instance meant that it was not a sufficient reason to call a halt, but only one of the other three areas had come up with as strong a set of results as the Itchen, so it would have been hard to get the Environment Agency to provide another three years of cash, and also hard to get a laboratory to undertake the processing of the spraints. John Dallas is an academic. He undertook the work as a research experiment, and published,

with Karen Coxon, a very comprehensive and technical report. He could not be expected to undertake routine contract work, and the commercial lab that was tried failed to produce consistent results for other reasons; the firm was taken over, the person concerned left for maternity leave, reasons quite unconnected with the nature of the work.

So my dream ground to a halt. Dreams always do, of course, but they also occasionally show what things could be like if only they were. By getting up early and going out to use my knowledge of the river to find a series of fresh spraints from probably different otters, in itself an enjoyable and satisfying form of safari or treasure hunt, especially for me who had for so long been unable to find a single spraint on my river, by doing in a more concentrated fashion what I so often do out of curiosity anyway, I had got close to having the state of things along the riverbank revealed to me, to getting an accurate count of the population. I nearly achieved in reality what I so often dream of doing.

And without a doubt I got close enough to see that the alternative methods we are using now to check on the otters are almost as good. The DNA study tends to support and validate our easier and less technical activities, rather than point out its limitations. We now know more about our otter mysteries than we did, and can be confident in what we have learned.

KNOWN UNKNOWNS ABOUT THE OTTER

It would be wrong if all the accumulated facts in this book were to give too strong an impression of firm knowledge about the otter. Here are some of the areas we do not understand fully.

- Opinions differ as to how to tell the age of an otter, but an increasing proportion of the dead otters we find are immatures or cubs. *Why?*

- Analysis of the post-mortems shows that there are seasonal trends in fight wounds, with different categories of otter beaten up at different times of year. Some social system must be driving these variations. There is more fighting in some parts of the country than others.

- Increased fighting presumably reduces the average age of the population, and this has the important effect of masking any inherent weaknesses, by killing the animal before medical defects have manifested themselves. So the otters may have more genetically transmitted problems than we realise. We have seen some instances of infanticide. How common or normal is this? Obviously our detection rate is always going to be low.

- In fact, is there such a concept as 'normal' or 'unusual' for so intelligent an animal? And would we see it if there were? Some otters have individual preferences, in diet for instance, but we also seem to find groups (families? clans?) with common behaviour not found in other otters nearby, so presumably these habits are taught or cultural.

- We know little about otter population structure and dynamics along typical rivers. We guess at the factors that control the size of their ranges, which are definitely different from those observed in coastal otters in northern Scotland.

- How much do otters prey on small invertebrates? Do all otters eat them from time to time? Do otters seek out seasonal concentrations of food, such as spawning frogs or migrating fish, or do they just eat them if they encounter them? How often do they resort to carrion? The problem is that when we find an instance of such behaviour, we cannot assume it is typical. Rather the reverse: perhaps we only see the failures, or those that are not exercising a choice, but doing the best they can in the circumstances into which the other otters have forced them. The recent, massive decline in eels must also be forcing an effect on them.

- What about eating plant matter? Do they eat it deliberately for scouring, like dogs, or do they get some incidentally, within their prey?

- How affected are they by pollutants? Are we even testing for the right pollutants? What about diclofenac, for instance? This is the veterinary medicine used in cattle which killed off millions of vultures in India. Cattle benefit from it: vultures are totally intolerant. 60% of hair samples from otters in the USA contain it, but as far as I know it is not tested for here. It is passed via the sewers into the rivers. Might it be behind the rapid increase in kidney stones, or the increased proportion of immatures in the post-mortems? Nobody knows.

One mystery seems recently to have been solved. It was proven that otters could detect dead prey under water, without visibility or vibration for the whiskers. How could an animal holding its breath scent the location of a dead fish so accurately? Film has shown that the otter can blow a small bubble from its nose, and then instantly sniff it back in again. They are indeed remarkable, and mysterious, creatures.

CHAPTER TWELVE

CAUSES OF DEATH

I began this book with a description of my discovery of the first otter to return to my river after a long absence. Yet when I had first visited Somerset, otters had been plentiful. What had happened to them? Did they die, or did they die out? The two are slightly different processes.

Obviously, every otter that is no longer with us has died, and death is a natural part of every life. Since we did not find a lot of dead otters at the time of the crisis, there is a sense in which the pollutants that caused their demise did not kill them, but merely caused them to die out. The agricultural application of the chemicals as seed dressing did kill pigeons. Dozens of pigeons were to be found lying in some fields. They are greedy eaters, and one cropful of dressed seed corn must have contained a massive dose of the dressing. Foxes too were killed; when an appeal went out for dead foxes to examine, hundreds were offered in the first week; there were scores of foxes lying about the countryside in the grain-growing areas of eastern England. They had been scavenging on the pigeons.

Yet other creatures with wider diets were not killed off in the same way. The peregrines, which eat a variety of bird species, were not killed outright. They did not die, but gradually died out, as did the otters, from an inability to reproduce and to replace those dying naturally. The natural death of a peregrine is presumably starvation; old age slows it down and it is unable to hunt in a period of difficult winter weather, so becomes weaker and declines rapidly once it has dropped below a certain level of fitness, and finally dies of cold on its roost in the night. I think very few otters die an entirely natural death, but we would find few of the bodies if they did.

Death would occur underground in a holt. When the Dumfriesshire Otterhounds had a good drag which ended with the hounds finding the body of the otter lying in a patch of wild rhubarb, it was considered most unusual, and was much talked about at the time. But before things got that extreme, a declining otter would more probably adopt risky methods to get easy prey, and would either be severely damaged in a fight with another otter, or attract the attention of a farmer, and be shot in a hen run or duck pond.

This was the case with two of the otters that took to lamb worrying. They were old, with damaged teeth. In an area without human influence, and no lambs to turn to, they would have been well on the way to a natural death, from debility and starvation. The farmers shot them: perhaps this shows that unnatural death is the norm, the natural way in modern Britain for an otter to end its days.

Ironically, we now know more about the deaths of our otters than we do about their lives. Or perhaps it would be more accurate to say we know a great deal about some of the modes of death of our otter population. The Environment Agency, and its predecessor body, The National Rivers Authority, have funded a programme of research through post-mortems, and more than 800 animals have been examined.

This work started in 1988, when otters were still very scarce. Just how scarce is shown by the small number of bodies submitted for examination in the beginning. The reason 1988 is the start date is that in the previous nine years

from 1979, no otters were sent in, although the Veterinary Laboratories Agency was handling many other forms of wild life.

There were no otters out there to provide the specimens needed. Again, there were none during 1989, but 6 in 1990, 3 in 1991, 12 in 1992, 11 in 1993, and 20 in 1994. This reflects the remarkable natural recovery of the species, but 20 dead otters on the lab. table must have been a stressful percentage of the total population at that time. And deaths known about are only part of the total mortality.

Causes of otter deaths

Road deaths provide between 80% and 90% of the carcasses found each year. However, we do not know what proportion of even the road deaths this represents. If one starts a conversation in the pub about running over a badger with the car, somebody is bound to come up with a tale of an animal hit, but not found; it was hurt, but could escape through the hedge into the darkness, to die later, and not feature in the statistics. Presumably this also happens to otters, and more are killed by cars than we know about. So most of our knowledge is based

A fleeting glimpse in the dark – all one usually sees.

173

only on those otters that are killed outright on the roads.

The next cause of death is bite wounds, many caused by other otters, but a few by dogs, and in one case the otter had died from a mink bite that had gone septic. We do not get to hear of those that are deliberately and illegally killed, or accidentally trapped in fyke nets, lobster pots and crayfish traps. Recent legislation has imposed a duty of care on people who set such permitted devices, so if they drown an otter they are now unlikely to own up to what could be construed as negligence. We assume that there is little natural mortality for adults, but we do not know the extent of natural mortality in cubs.

Otter cubs spend the first two months of their life in the holt; we have no idea what the wastage is, although clues from the examination of slightly older cubs killed above ground indicate factors that are likely to have caused a significant degree of loss in the nest. This is confirmed by finding bitch otters with placental scars in the uterus that show that she gave birth, but with no indication of having suckled a family.

There are several possible reasons why this might happen. The cubs may not have been viable, and may have had a defect from birth. There is some evidence for this in the study of abandoned orphan cubs, and also suggestions in the chemical analysis of various tissues at post-mortem as to what might cause defects in very small cubs. Or they may have been killed by another otter. There is evidence for this, too.

Two otters in Cornwall were so engrossed in their fight that both were killed by a car; one of them had the remains of otter cubs in its stomach. Or a sudden flood may have drowned them in their nest.

One unlucky little cub was killed on what was probably its first outing above ground by Charlie Martin's aggressive old brute of a gander. The goose was sitting on eggs in the corner of the orchard, and the cub was dead nearby, killed by one massive blow to its fragile little skull. But I know of no instance of them being predated by mink, which was widely suggested as a likely restricting factor in the early days of the otters' comeback, when mink were very plentiful. The few that are killed by dogwalkers' terriers are usually out and about, so are older, and the bitch has been suckling them for several weeks. But for the bad luck of the encounter, they would have been viable recruits to the population. So, although we seldom find the bodies of small cubs, we are aware that there is probably considerable loss at this stage.

Although it is deaths that we know about, births are far more important from a conservation point of view than deaths. I am trying to slant the emphasis of my current studies towards a more accurate assessment of the recruitment rate in the apparently stable population in this area of Somerset. We have no idea how much that stability depends on topping up with dispersing youngsters from outside the area, or whether we have a surplus to export to other areas.

Another major consideration is, that with such a mobile and difficult species, the best way to form an estimate of the ongoing strength of the population will be to concentrate on the breeding bitches, the most visible and the only static element in the otters' social set-up. However, this approach is more tricky than I thought it would be. At present, during the summer, our small rivers, especially the side-streams where the bitches go to breed, are obscured by tree leaves and big stands of riverside plants like nettles and balsam. Access is made difficult by standing crops. Yet as soon as the vegetation is reduced by harvest and the autumn floods, the hours of daylight reduce, and the activity I am hoping to record will be hidden by darkness.

So it is more practical to continue to concentrate on the deaths for a picture of our population and its problems.

Most of the evidence comes from skilful and detailed post-mortem examination of road casualties. There is debate as to how far this provides a representative and unbiased sampling of the otters. I remember our surprise at the first road casualty I saw.

In the early 1950s, when otters were plentiful and petrol rationing had stopped, so the roads were quite busy, we were driving down the Lune Valley towards Kirkby Lonsdale. As we passed Treasonfield, where the golf course now is, father exclaimed that he thought at first there had been a dead otter on the verge, but of course it could not have been, it must have been a cat; we were some distance from the river, and anyway, in the very unlikely event of one getting onto a road, no otter would ever be so dozy as to get caught by a car, with a noisy engine and bright headlights to give warning. Father was then over 60 years old, with a lifetime experience of otters, having whipped in to the Eastern Counties OH before the first World War, and had never heard of such an unlikely thing as an otter getting run over.

On our way home, we stopped out of curiosity to check on the cat. It was not a cat, but a largish dog otter, and to father's indignation, the hooligan that killed it had taken off both forepaws as trophies. The mystery was, what had it been doing there in the first place, so father asked about at the farms and checked out the lie of the local ditches and becks. He discovered that it had not been run over. It had been asleep in the haygrass on a hot day, and, on being woken suddenly by the presence of the two huge horses pulling the mowing machine, it had bolted without thought straight into the blades, which severed both front legs. So the farmer had had to kill it, and in order to stop his sheepdogs messing about with the body, he

had slung it over the hedge onto the road verge. Father was vindicated; "There, I told you so. I knew no normal otter would ever be knocked down by a car". He was usually right about country matters, and I revered his knowledge and skills.

The Environment Agency's report published in 2007 gives details of 561 otters killed on the roads in the 12 years to 2003. That is an average of 47 a year killed on the road. In the early Fifties, the time of that first, surprising casualty in the Lune Valley, when otters were considered so plentiful as to be disregarded as just a normal feature of the rural fauna, the annual total of those killed by all the hunts in Britain was about 200.

In 2003, according to the 4th National Survey, otters were present in only one third of the country. So, to make a rough comparison, multiply the annual average by three, which comes to 141. (That assumes that otters are as densely spread in all parts at present as they were in the fifties, which is obviously an overestimation.) But never mind that, what the rough sum shows is that we are killing our scarce otters on the roads at about 70% of the rate that the 13 packs of hounds achieved in the 1950s from a full population. Plus the ones that crawl away into the scrub to die uncounted. Father, who was the Master of one of the packs, would be surprised.

There are many more cars nowadays, and they go faster, but, on some of the rural roads, not that much faster. Some of the disturbing difference between none and 561 must be in the otters themselves. Why did the otter cross the road, or try to? Well, in many cases it was not crossing it, but using it. Especially in hilly country, the easiest and most convenient place for the road to be sited is along the valley floor, and in places the road and river run side by side. In such terrain the swollen rivers flow very strongly, and there is a big incentive for an otter to run up the wet road instead of trying to force its way upstream against the excessive current. Or at places where otters frequently cross the road, the cause is often an inadequate tunnel for the river beneath.

When the river is in spate, the effect at some bridges and culverts is similar to putting a finger across the end of a hose pipe: the force of the pent-up water makes it impossible for an otter to get past the bridge except by going up and over the road.

Yet rivers ran fast in father's time, when this did not seem to happen. Post-mortems have shown that the need for economy of effort is increased in about half of our modern otters, by their having been in a recent fight. In 2003 52% of the dead otters had recent wounds, and 7% of the deaths were directly caused by them.

In many cases the bites were so severe that they must have greatly increased the likelihood of the victim being on the road, and of it being slow in evading danger. Even if the loser in a fight did limp through the traffic, there is still a considerable likelihood of sepsis, which reduces the fitness level of the otter or even kills it directly.

Another cause of debilitating, even fatal, sepsis, comes from fractured teeth, where the broken stump forms an abscess that leads to septicaemia, and death from pleurisy and pneumonia. The incidence of this dental damage has been increasing throughout the period of the post-mortem study, and is almost certainly a product of the increasing amount of fighting.

Fighting otters

Otters have always fought, of course, but there were no records I know of from historical times of this degree of damage, nor of this amount of aggression. Two dog otters might have a dispute over a bitch, and one presumes that range boundaries were sometimes discussed rather vigorously, but the whole point of the system of spraint marking is to reduce the need for that sort of proprietorial action.

Going for a cheek hold – in this instance only in play.

The preventative system seems to be working rather less well nowadays, if half the otters at any one time have recently been in a serious fight, so severe that 41% of the dogs and 35% of the bitches have broken a tooth. To postulate that half the otters have been in a recent fight is to assume that the roads are sampling the population indiscriminately, that the proportion of dogs to bitches and adults to cubs lying dead on the tarmac is the same as the proportion in the population as a whole.

There are seasonal variations in the sampling which indicate that the selection by car is not entirely random. There must be some reason in the social life of the otters that causes more males to be killed in early autumn and spring, and the majority of bitches to be found in the winter. High summer is a slack time for mortality generally, possibly because the sun sets after the peak of motor traffic, whereas in winter otters start their night's activity at rush hour.

However, the extent and ferocity of the fighting revealed by the post-mortems is very worrying. Any otter is liable to attack, bitches and cubs as well as adult males, and the nature of the fight is extreme.

Many species take a long time before a fight to wind up to the point of actual attack, with lots of display and posturing and noise, all designed to settle the argument without actual physical risk to either combatant. It is much better to scare off a lesser animal and save your energy if you can, or, if you are the lesser animal, it is better to cut and run before the larger one confirms your suspicion that you are bound to lose.

One would think that this would be more the case for an active predator like an otter, which needs its fitness not just to dominate rivals, but for the basic daily business of eating, than it is for a stag which is equipped with a special fighting apparatus designed to take most of the force of the aggression without actual physical hurt. Yet it is the stags that snort and roar and bash the vegetation to prevent it coming to a clash of antlers, while the soft-skinned otters attack silently, without even raising their hackles as a dog does.

The explanation is in the circumstances of their habitat. An otter following its river in the dark has no method of detecting the approach of a rival from the opposite direction, until they have both rounded a bend and are silently and suddenly at close quarters in the darkness. There may be a slight advantage to be gained by attacking as soon as you are aware of the presence of the other, in the hope that the direction of the wind has perhaps masked your approach from him, and you can get in the first bite undetected.

And the objective of a fighting otter is different from that of a stag. It is sufficient for a stag to drive away his rival just for a short while, until all the hinds have been mated for this year. After that the other stag is of no consequence in his life: ten days deterrence is enough.

Not so for the otter. Every rival is a liability on his territorial assets, a potential drain on his fish resources, and a possible danger to his health at any time. Perhaps it is the rival that may have the advantage of surprise the next time, which could enable him to inflict a wound that leads to death. So the fight is for real, with no element of warning or "let this be a lesson to you, my boy." There is little point to try to bite the skull and shoulders of a muscular dog otter in a head-on charge; that will barely scar the skin of so powerful a creature.

No, in the water it is best to try to get beneath your opponent and to direct your teeth towards the softer underbelly and the genital area, or failing that the feet. I always check the webbing between the toes of any dead otter for puncture wounds, to see if it has been fighting. The damage inflicted to the belly region is not always visible to an external glance: bites can be masked by the dense fur. But in other instances the damage is all too frightfully apparent, with great rips in the skin, or parts of the genitals bitten off.

Dog otters not infrequently (8%) have fractured penis bones, having been bitten through the skin. This is not always fatal, as in several cases the bone has healed, often at an awkward angle. I do not know how much this renders the otter incapable of siring cubs, but it must impair things in many cases. That would mean that there are dog otters holding territory and guarding bitch otters that cannot produce cubs. Otters breed at a low rate anyway, so this by-effect of all the fighting could have a seriously depressing effect on the population's ability to recover.

The other area to look for bite wounds is on the face. I think this is a defensive hold; if you have him by the cheek, he cannot get at your nether regions. Cubs gnaw at each other's cheeks when they are play fighting. This phase of a fight is presumably when teeth get broken. Face bites are often neat punctures through the skin, and these can be measured.

The canine teeth of an otter are about 20mm apart, and this is one way of identifying the aggressor. Dogs have wider bites, mink much smaller, at about 10mm. Strangely, mink bites are not unknown, and in at least one case, they had led to fatal infection. They were more common in the early years of this decade, but fewer are seen recently. They were nearly always on the face, and represented the dying effort of a mink to get back at the otter which had caught it. It is confirmed that the main reason that mink have declined so much is that otters have dealt with them.

A few otters that have been fighting have died of a lung infection, caused by inhaling plant material. I suppose that the involuntary gasp of pain when the opponent's needle-sharp teeth penetrate some particularly sensitive organ near the tail is sufficient to draw down all kinds of duckweed and floating bits into the lung itself, where it starts to rot and fester.

Why the fighting has increased

All this gory detail serves to emphasise the extent of the fighting that goes on nowadays, but it does not explain why there should be so much more destructive aggression than there was. I cannot believe that the species has evolved a system of juvenile dispersal which involves every young recruit to the population having to run the gauntlet of all the neighbours seriously trying to kill it. We do not know how otters are in theory supposed to disperse along a linear river past all the other established residents, but it would not make ecological sense for them all to be killed off as juveniles. In some instances it seems that they are chased vigorously out of the catchment.

This may explain why we find dead otters on the roads that run along the top of high ridges. The North Devon Link road is an

Otters seem to be fighting more frequently and aggressively nowadays and the reason for this is not clear to scientists.

example; several otters have died crossing it high on the Rackenford moors. They must be going from the Taw system to the Exe, or vice versa. I think flight also explains why a young male otter got onto the raised portion of the M5 that overlooks Taunton Rugger Ground. The canal bridge there can take a barge and horse, so the water level can have had no influence in driving a fit young animal up a steep and high incline to reach nothing of any interest to it.

Fear of a larger rival was probably the impulsion. As it was for the young dog otter found not very far from the Wellington Monument, which sits so proud on the very summit of the Blackdowns escarpment that I can see it now, as I type, from a distance of about six miles. Flight may be an evolved component of the process of leaving the natal patch, but is death?

The post-mortems may throw some light on this conundrum. It seems that the question is not, 'Why did the otter cross the road?" but, "Why did it need to?" Because it was too lame or too frightened to swim is a primary answer, but why then was it in such a state? Histology and chemical analysis of the bodies sent for post-mortem reveal another layer of problems.

Before I plunge into another dismal catalogue of things that are wrong with our otters, I must sound a note of caution. All these gloomy findings come from the bodies of the failures, the dead ones, and what they indicate may not be valid for the more successful

survivors. There are those who will say that the car is an unselective tool, and that as it kills a random sample, these results will be broadly applicable to all otters. I do not agree; I hope I have already shown that there are reasons why some otters are more likely than others to end up under a car.

There is also the point that every otter has got to die of something, and that it is probable that a 21st century otter will meet a 21st century type of death. Not many otters were run over by chariots in the Middle Ages, but perhaps the bears or wolves clobbered the old and frail instead. It was probably not bears and wolves, in fact, that culled the otters, but monks, who were just as bad, from the otter's point of view. Monks were the botheration factor in the days when every religious house had to keep a stew pond to supply fish for the days and seasons when meat was forbidden and fish was obligatory. Later, fur wearers exerted a similar pressure, then the main cause of death became the gin trap, and now it is the car, aided by the badly designed road culvert. While I recognise that some otters will of course die on the roads, I do not agree with those shallow thinkers among my acquaintance who try to reassure my anxieties about the large numbers being found. They tell me that it is a sign that the otters are there in sufficient numbers for the roads to take a toll, and that this tip of casualties indicates an encouragingly large unseen iceberg of live otters.

Admittedly, when we had no otters, none got run over, but I always ask these shallow optimists to select between schoolboys or vicars. If, driving home on a dark night, you knock down somebody in dark

Adult otters enjoy rowdy play as much as juveniles.

clothing, you will get out to see whom you have killed. If it turns out to be a schoolboy in a dark blazer and school trousers, not to worry at all: the badge on the blazer is a sign that there are three or four hundred identical other ones in a playground nearby, and the educational system can carry on.

However, if the dark clothing should be the black cassock of a vicar hurrying home from evensong with his mind on higher things than the road, you have a problem indeed: there will be nobody to confess this terrible deed to for several miles around.

Whatever my friends say, the car has replaced the gin trap at a rate that is alarming in view of the restricted population of the species. Even if the process were just mechanical, in that some of the otters that crossed a road from time to time got unlucky and were killed, the accidental attrition rate is too high.

But if it is too high because of hidden causes which make it more probable that otters meet cars, then I am right to be worried, especially if those causes are ones that are not restricted to otters, or to similar wildlife forms.

Poison in the tissue

The microscopic and chemical aspects of the post-mortems point to several such factors. So far all that has happened is that these things have been demonstrated to exist. Nobody has looked at how serious or significant they are, nor is there any procedure in place for alleviation of anything worrying that might come out of this and similar studies. Under the Thatcher government, certain areas of wildlife research were forbidden to the labs so that they would not find out anything that would need actions that might be unpopular or expensive.

The chemical analysis of otter tissues has recently been given a priority status under European Union health procedures, as an indicator of the state of the aquatic environment; by accumulating contaminants over time, the top predator acts as a magnifying glass on what is in the system. But I know of no procedure to be followed if the results of the analysis should be alarming, as it is probable they may be, or else the authorities would not bother to undertake the investigation in the first place.

There is a precedent for this inaction. At the time when dieldrin and similarly useful chemicals were banned, the NRA set up monitoring of the water in the Bristol Channel below the three main Welsh rivers, the Usk, Wye and Severn, to check on the extent that sheep farmers were using up stocks of now illegal poisons. The tests were done and the results logged. It was many years before somebody by chance glanced through the results and saw that the harmful stuff was still plentiful. Nobody had instructed the testers what to do with the results. I fear that the analysis of the otter tissues is similarly disregarded, and written up merely as interesting wildlife research, just as the information from the peregrines was missed in the early days of the decline.

No major diseases

Some of the results are encouraging. It is reassuring that there is no evidence of infectious diseases. No otter has been found to have TB, the current scourge of the countryside.

Otters can develop many of the diseases that it is necessary to innoculate cats and dogs against, and it was feared that feral mink might be a vector for carrying these problems to the otter population. Despite two suspected instances some time ago of Aleutian disease, a virus found in many mink farms, there seems to be no epidemic.

It is encouraging too that the amount of lead in their bones started to fall off as soon as it was withdrawn from petrol, and is now levelling off at a background level. This is a prime example of how the otter can throw light on things of importance to other species, such as ourselves. Heavy metals are generally not a problem, although some areas have a natural, unavoidable, geological input. Organochlorines, such as dieldrin, have dropped considerably, and the amounts still present are presumed to come from residues in river silts, and perhaps from accumulations in long-lived eels.

We did not use these poisons for long, but their effects will linger for ages where accumulations have been deposited. These chemicals have a very long half-life. But the situation is much better than it was.

The scientists have to make comparisons over time very carefully. There is definite evidence that the otters are generally smaller than they were before the decline, an average reduction of 2kgs (20%) for males and 1kg, (14%) for females, and some indication that the average age of the population has dropped during the period of the post-mortem study, that is, a measurable drop over the last twenty years. Both these developments are factors which could skew a comparison of the levels of substances that accumulate over time, in that the younger animals have had less time to accumulate a burden, and the burden is greater if measured as a proportion of a reduced body size. Some of the scientists see the reduced average age as a good sign, indicative of an expanding population. I am not so sure that it is good. It is the vicars or schoolboy conundrum again. If the older otters are not showing up in the sampling, to keep the average age high, where are they?

The implication is that they are dying young. Otters breed slowly, and start late. One post-mortem report found that "48% of females had reproduced at least once". That means that 52% had not. It is known that maternal skills increase with experience, that otters rear more cubs in their second and third litters. It does not

augur well for the future if a disproportionate amount of the population is below reproductive age.

Ageing an otter

The ageing of a dead otter is interesting, and important. The main method is by cutting through a tooth and counting the rings of deposition, as one does for a tree. This seems to work well in the otters from Shetland, which undergo a lean period of low prey availability every spring. It has been shown to work well in Scottish badgers, for the same sort of reason, but badgers from Kent do not exhibit the same consistency of annual deposition of a layer, probably because they suffer much less from the seasons.

I have long doubted some of the findings from the use of this method on otters from southern England, where seasonal deprivation is unknown: one table has one year old otters of 18 and 20lbs in weight. They would need steroids to grow at that rate. A subsequent report gives details of two experiments to judge the validity of the tooth method. In both, the results were judged unreliable: "the recorded dental age was clearly not compatible with the animal's physical characteristics." The trend now is to use a combination of factors, such as body length, skull development, size of penis bone in males, and the size or weight of various internal organs, such as the thymus gland.

It has always been possible to sort otters into four rough categories by the state of development of their teeth. Cubs have deciduous teeth still in place, immatures are not full sized and not fully developed sexually, sub-adults are full sized, but have unworn teeth and their canine teeth are still slender, and adults show some wear and tear to their teeth.

The importance of guesstimating the age with some confidence comes in the consider-

A good set of sharp teeth – an indication of youth.

ation of some of the chemicals that have not declined much recently. Of these the most concerning are the PCBs. There are lots of different varieties, or congeners, of PCB, but together they are still worryingly common in the samples in the labs (98%). They accumulate steadily with age, so the age of the otter is needed to assess the extent of the exposure. These nasty substances show no decline in the environment yet, although we have been aware of their worrying presence for a long time. The amount in each individual varies, of course, especially between different regions of the country. The levels are consistently higher in the industrial areas such as the North-west and North-east of England. But the averages show that dog otters carry a significantly higher burden of PCBs than bitches of the same age, which at first seems bizarre, considering that their exposure through their diets must be the same.

The highest burden of all, however, is found in little cubs. What happens is that the mother offloads a major portion of her accumulated pollutants via her milk, especially in the first few days after birth, when the milk contains fat-rich colostrums. Otters' milk is very fatty, (24%), much richer than cows' milk at 3% or 4%, so the cubs receive a massive dose of the fat-soluble PCBs in the first few days of life, when they are tiny.

We do not know how many die in the nest because of this. We do not really know how damaging PCBs are to otters generally; they are too rare an animal to submit them to lethal experiments. But research on farmed mink in the USA has shown that moderate levels can be lethal, and that lesser burdens can affect apparently healthy animals' metabolisms, by closing down their ability to reproduce, for instance.

High PCBs are associated with low levels of Vitamin A; the messenger platelets that distribute the vitamin to the areas of the body that need it become clogged with PCB, which has the same molecular shape, so the infant otter is starved of the vitamin, even though it is available in its diet.

This vitamin is especially important for those organs which continue to develop after birth, including the eyes, (otters, like kittens, are born with sealed eyes), and the reproductive mechanisms. The eyes of 66 otters were examined, and 30% of them had major abnormalities, mainly retinal dysplasia. It is not thought that these otters were blind, but their sight must have been affected, and one suggestion is that they would probably be 'night blind'. This occurs sometimes in certain breeds of dog, which can live happy daytime lives, but become fearful and hesitant after dark. We know that totally blind otters can manage to feed themselves very adequately by using their vibrissae (whiskers), but these only detect vibration at close range in the water. They are of no help in navigating across country, nor in detecting the approach of danger such as a car. Thus it is very possible that these persistent chemicals are contributing indirectly to the large number of road deaths.

An even more indirect factor may be the influence of an infectious disease, toxoplasmosis. It too can cause blindness. 30% of dog otters, and 60% of bitches, are carriers of *toxoplasma gondi,* spread either through cat droppings, or across the placenta to the foetus. Most carriers are little affected in their health, but it can cause serious disease if the immune system is weakened or unaccustomed to it. This has been the case in the sea otters off the coast of California. Much of the progress of the conservationists' recovery programme for this nearly extirpated population has been undone by a recent fashion for smart cats in and around Hollywood.

A vogue for designer moggies of exotic breeds, led by the film stars and the famous, has resulted in masses of cat litter being flushed down the posh toilets into the Pacific Ocean, where anchovies and sea urchins filter it out of the water, and pass it on to the sea otters, which lack immunity, resulting in a major drop-off in their population.

Our otters have their immune systems to some extent compromised by the cocktail of chemicals in their livers, but there is no record of anything similar occurring. However it is known that this organism, besides having various clinical effects as a disease, also affects the behaviour of the carriers. It affects judgement, by increasing risk taking, and at the same time slows down reaction rates. So the otter crossing the busy road at night may be night blind, and reckless, and lethargic, all for unseen and unseeable reasons.

That is perhaps expressing it rather more strongly than circumstances probably warrant, but it underlines that the problems our wildlife face are more than just speedy drivers on busy roads, and it shows the value of the detail that is slowly emerging from the post-mortems.

Consider yourself for a moment a member of a coroner's jury, and, in the light of all this morbid information you have just read, consider a verdict as to cause of death in this recent case, as written up in *Newslotter 22* of the Somerset Otter Group:

The sad case of a Tone otter

In mid-February an otter was reported from a very small stream at West Monkton, near Taunton. By the time I got there it had had 9 out of 10 tame ducks from a smallish pond, and had been seen eating one of them while being watched by the baffled dogs, which were obviously unsure what to do. It seemed very small and thin, and probably unwell, so the RSPCA were called. They were unable to extract it from a small culvert where it had taken refuge, so they put out some mackerel for it and left.

Ungratefully, it left the fish and moved on. It was then seen near Ruishton and noticed to be lame. On 1st March it was eating an eel in Firepool, by Taunton Market, in broad daylight. It was so lame that an EA worker nearly caught it. (I wonder if they are insured against bites.) In mid-April it was seen limping past the windows of AC Mole's new offices at Blackbrook, from where it made its way up the little stream into Lisieux Way. Here the RSPCA finally cornered it in a garden, and took it to their hospital at West Hatch. It had a bad ulcer on a leg. The vets made excellent progress in promoting the healing of this wound, and the poor, thin, little creature soon began to put on weight.

Ungrateful again, it started to devote all its newfound energies into breaking out, so much so that it was damaging its muzzle and its pads to an extent that was worrying to the vets. So it was moved into an outside pen, with grass rather than hard flooring – from which it escaped on the first night.

About a week later Dennis Pavey picked up a small bitch otter dead on the A378, which went fresh to Vic Simpson for post-mortem. Vic rang me to say that it had been a most unusual and interesting case. In additions to lung lesions and a fluke-infested gall bladder, it had weird lack of coat, a bitten eye, ruined feet, and no whiskers left on its muzzle. It was run over 6.5km from the RSPCA hospital.

Although still only an immature in size, internal examination revealed that she had given birth to no fewer than 6 cubs, although there was no sign of her having suckled them successfully. For one so young, it had been an exciting and eventful life.

In my summing up to you as the jury, I must mention aggression and wounds, poor eyesight, stress from child birth, and from being taken captive, reduced health generally, hunger, recklessness in the face of dogs, and the busy traffic on the A378. It was the car that administered the coup de grace, but what was to blame for this untimely death, so far from any water? Things were much less complex in the days of the monks. The otters knew where they were with the monks.

Increase in kidney stones

The only thing that this otter did not have wrong was kidney stones. There has been a recent surge in cases of this disease. The average incidence is that 10% of all otters have some renal calculi of some size but the incidence varies from region to region. As none were found in wild otters in the earlier years of the post-mortem programme there is speculation as to what might be the cause of this recent increase of what in people is a very painful condition. In 2003 33% of the adult otters in South and South-west England suffered from this problem, some with very large lumps of stone which must impair the function of the kidney, besides possibly being acutely painful.

One possible explanation is that bacteria get into the otter's system through a bite wound, and cause a small lesion, which acts as the focus

for deposition of the stone, as a bit of grit in an oyster starts the growth of a pearl. Calculi were frequently found in otters with wounds or sepsis. The bites could be the cause of the kidney problem, or the result. An otter with a major and painful problem might be the one that loses in a conflict, and the stones could result in the carrier getting more bites. Or both could happen. Any defect in a carnivore can be the start of a rapid downward spiral in ability to cope, with resultant loss of condition and further inability to function properly as a predator. Few active hunters can remain at 90% efficiency for long, especially in a very competitive species such as this; if they do not recover full function rapidly, they will start to decline below 90%, a process that is very difficult to reverse.

The bile fluke

This is what was so worrying when we discovered the bile fluke in the otters of Somerset.

The poor little bitch otter that you readers sat as a jury on, had this disease, or infestation. *Psuedamphistomum truncatum* is a parasite previously unknown in Britain. Its scientific name translates as Dwarfish False Two-faces, a fair reflection of its lack of loveliness, but not a designation I would otherwise wish onto any creature, except perhaps an MP. The first recorded case came from Stoke St Gregory, a village very near where the little bitch from the RSPCA had all her misadventures. In March 2004 Mr Guernsey was walking his dog when it discovered an otter in a hedge not far from the river Tone, alive, but too sick or injured to run away. I used to take his daughter out to the rivers with my school's otter group, so he knew of my interest.

He rang the RSPCA, and told me. The RSPCA caught the poor animal quite easily, but the vets decided, correctly, to put it down. It was a large adult dog otter, but it was so thin it weighed only 5 kg. It had septic bite wounds, and associated damage to its liver, lungs and a kidney. But its bile duct and gall bladder were severely affected in a way that Vic Simpson could not identify.

He had previously commented to me that he had noticed a problem in a couple of otters from our area that he could not categorise, one that he had not seen before. So with this extreme case he made a major effort and spent a long time investigating the bile system of the sick otter. One method revealed a lot of eggs, so he persisted with other approaches until, finally, he was able to see the microscopic flukes.

They are much smaller than the similar and frequently encountered liver fluke. 'Pseud trunc' is about 1 mm long, but despite this it can cause considerable damage to the bile system of an otter, or of any similar animal. In Russia and Eastern Europe it is found in a wide range of wildlife species, seals, foxes, raccoon dogs, mink and otters. It has also been found in dogs and in a majority of the dockside cats in fishing villages along the Volga, where it has also caused debilitating ill health in the people. No wonder the boatmen sing such lugubrious songs.

So its sudden advent into England was both worrying and surprising. It has been very little investigated, probably because it is comparatively uncommon in Eastern Europe still; it was introduced there from further east, and I believe its natural home is the Amur basin in China. The only published literature merely mentions its distribution, in studies of mammal parasites generally, and gives it as an incidental and unusual occasional addition to the normal range of worms etc.

So the authorities can only assume that its life cycle is similar to that of other flukes, in that a snail consumes the egg, which develops into further stages, until a fish eats it, when the fluke forms a cyst under the skin of the fish, and waits to be eaten by a fish-eating mammal. Then it seeks out the gall bladder, where it anchors itself

into the flesh and proceeds to lay its eggs, in order to start the complicated process all over again. The gall bladder reacts at being hooked into, and if sufficient parasites have been ingested, the wall of the bladder thickens and hardens, and even cracks.

Two more cases were identified that spring, from the same area. Vic Simpson reviewed the records of the previous 445 otters he had handled, many of them from the same part of Somerset. Although the flatworm had not been identified previously, 7 of them showed the same sort of damage, and six of these came from the same area within the previous two years.

It seems probable that the new fluke was introduced in a consignment of fish that contained some sunbleak, an unassuming, minnow-like, little fish, popular in aquariums for its lively behaviour. The Somerset anglers have christened it the "Motherless Minnow", because it suddenly turns up in consider-able shoals in water where previously it was unknown. It probably came into this country in a smuggled consignment of coarse fish.

I got into conversation with a long distance lorry driver last year. He had contacted me to report seeing three dead otters on a road, which had concerned him greatly, as a country lover. He was a most interesting man; one of the things he told me was that he and some mates were discussing jobs that had paid unusually well. The winner by far was the driver who had twice been to Russia to collect carp for a fish dealer, a cash-only, don't mention it about, sort of job. I had not thought of international fish smuggling as a career, but apparently it pays well.

Sunbleak are vigorous breeders, and their liveliness enables them to outcompete other more usual and more sedate forms of fish fry, so they do well, at the expense of the locals, and have colonised many different parts of the water systems on the Somerset Levels. The fluke they

brought with them can colonise other species of cyprinid fish, so its spread is no longer dependent on the Motherless Minnows. Which is why now, only four years later, the parasite is to be found in several other areas of England. Fish movements by anglers have carried it with them.

However, the wide and artificial geographic spread does not make it a common species anywhere. With such a bizarre life history any one individual parasite needs to be very lucky to reach maturity, and as is the case for any newly invasive species, it is a struggle to get established in sufficient numbers to be sure of maintaining a viable population. So, many of the fish available to the otters are likely to be free of parasites, or to carry only a low number after so few breeding cycles for the fluke.

Some of the infected otters have carried only a small number of the parasites, and there have been signs that some mildly infected gall bladders have thrown off the burden and partially recovered, by a process of self heal. They are still thickened in places, but the investigators have been able to find no actual invaders on board, and the otter has seemed to be healthy. Whether this gives an immunity or defence against any parasites that may be ingested in future is not known. Nor is it known how long an adult flatworm lives and lays eggs before dying and dropping off the bladder wall naturally.

This is encouraging, in that it appears to suggest that this newly imported health hazard is not going to be as greatly harmful as the state of the first otter, and several subsequent ones, suggested. When we saw the debilitated and damaged bodies of the worst early cases we thought that this might be the start of another massive decline, and so we tried, in vain, to get the government's conservation organisations interested.

They all declined to look into it in any way. They would not even send any scientists to a conference to pool knowledge, which Somerset County Council proposed to host. As the problem was totally unforeseen, there was no budget for it; as there was no budget, they could not send anybody. And two members of English Nature's staff, who should have known better, contributed only by saying that, as Russian otters co-existed well with the parasite, there was no reason to expect it to harm our population. They knew nothing about the health of Russia's otters, nor the status of their populations in the areas, equally unknown to them, where the fluke now existed over there. They did not even know for how long it had been introduced to Russia. It was an assertion based on a wishful thought, to get rid of a problem from their intrays.

I am a little encouraged by the cases of apparent self heal. But not as totally confident as our wildlife officials. Many of the infected otters have carried a massive burden of scores of parasites, and have been sick unto death. It may be that any otter which preys on a school of smaller fish runs a risk of eating a lot of flukes, and we know that otters often concentrate on concentrations of tiddlers: sticklebacks, fry, or minnows, motherless or legitimate. As the parasite consolidates its populations, (a different process from spreading its geographical range), it is increasingly likely that any otter will be more infected.

We may start to see less self heal, and more infestations. This will depend on which other animals can provide the final definite host for the fluke. Otters are self-spacing, and mink are in decline, so the fluke must be short of egg distributors in many areas. A lot of the fish that carry the penultimate stage must be wasted to herons and cormorants. However, the fluke is now so widely distributed, and is found in sick otters and mink in sufficient numbers sufficiently often, for us to be sure that it has established successfully. By reducing the

numbers of its limited supply of definite hosts it may regulate its own numbers somewhat, but I fear that may be the best we can now hope for, that it will kill sufficient otters not to be able to kill them all.

That it is a significant influence on the otters of Somerset is exemplified by a post-mortem report that has just arrived. It concludes, "Cause of death – drowning following severe fighting injuries; also infection around head injuries." That seems, Oh members of my coroner's jury, a pretty well cut-and-dried statement.

But consider some of the details. This was a small, sub-adult bitch, only 750 mm in length, and weighing only 6lbs; "had never reproduced". The poor youngster had multiple puncture wounds around vulva, anus and lower abdomen, too many to measure; bruising, septic bites and swelling to both sides of the head and neck. Why had an apparently fit, "not emaciated", young otter, not so young as to be totally inexperienced, come off so badly? "Gall bladder thickened – on dissection 132 flukes found". "Cause of death" is not in this case the same as "reason for death before producing any young".

Disgracefully, the statutory bodies charged with protecting our environment and natural resources are doing no research into this problem. Cardiff University, which now handles all the post-mortems, is looking into the genetics of the fluke to see how it has spread. One of its scientists has recently been awarded funding for a three year study of the parasite and its effects. Their map showing the places where dead otters have been found with and without it appears to confirm what was an incidental finding in the only serious piece of research that I know of. Simone Gentner did a dissertation at Nottingham University.

She looked into the feasibility of detecting fluke eggs in otter spraint, as a method of establishing its presence other than by post-mortem, which is the only method currently in use. Her work was a little hampered by a lack of fluke in some places; she did not find as many as she had hoped to enable a good comparison between her three study areas. But it seemed to me that she demonstrated by this lack of specimens that the pest does not inhabit faster-flowing waters. This may be something to do with the environmental preferences of the water snails, or it may be, as some have suggested, that the fluke cannot infect salmonids. If this turns out to be really the case, then the problem will remain localised to certain habitats, and it will not damage all otters.

Another parasite has recently given us cause for anxiety. Sue Farrington, an enthusiastic member of the Somerset Otter Group, found some large white creatures alive in the spraints on her survey area, Clatworthy Reservoir. They almost resembled the segments of tapeworm sometimes passed by dogs, but on examination they proved to be entire invertebrates, with a head and a gut faintly visible through the creamy-white body; the body, which is about the size of the nail on my little finger, seemed to change shape, rather like an amoeba, but it did have a front and a back. As there were several of these in some spraints, we were at first worried, until we identified it as a fish parasite which specialises in living in the gut of sticklebacks. They are bad news for the sticklebacks, but no problem for the otter.

And they enable me to finish this morbid chapter about all the ghastly forms of death facing our otters on a positive note. This parasite makes life easier for the otters, in that it affects the behaviour of the sticklebacks and makes them easier prey. Not that otters need their tiddlers slowing down. They are competent predators, and despite all the adversities I have listed here, we must remember that in the western parts of England they have come back from the brink, and that we have a viable population again. There is bound to be a turnover through death, and if we had no otters we would be finding no corpses.

CHAPTER THIRTEEN

OTTERS AND MAN

The otter, unlike many other types of major wildlife in these crowded islands, finds that it has perforce to live alongside us. Rats, and some foxes, choose to join our communities because they scrounge our leavings, but otters have to tolerate our inconvenient proximity because we have chosen to place our towns and settlements alongside their rivers.

We are all familiar with the provision of reserves and sanctuaries for the benefit of rare forms of wildlife; plants are fenced off from harm, swards are managed for orchids and butterflies, colonies of terns are wardened and protected from competitors. But the lifestyle of the otters means that we cannot do this sort of thing for them. The concept of the "Otter Haven", areas exclusively for the otters which would be closed to people, was tried at the stage when otters were so scarce as to be in imminent danger of disappearing totally. They had little effect, and the idea has been abandoned as impractical for the increased population of otters we need to accommodate nowadays.

They need too much room and mobility, so they find themselves sharing our space, which means that the ways we use or abuse the rivers must affect them, will we or nill we. The most obvious of these influences is our manipulation of the habitat. Engineers do it obviously, by dredging, building and exploiting rivers.

I often wonder what the effect on the otters was of some of the more extreme hydro-electricity schemes in Scotland; the bedraggled stone bed that is all that is left of the Garry beside the A9 near Blair Atholl must be as disappointing to the otters as it is unsightly to the tourists. The river near Rannoch goes up and down as the demand for power fluctuates; it must be hard for a mustelid to appreciate that its ease of feeding or even the safety of its cubs is affected by the time of the final whistle of a big televised football match. Otters are presumably as indifferent to football as I am.

Rubbish in rivers

Our influence on the habitat ranges from the macro to the micro. The understandable and "harmless" bit of fun that so many small boys have a go at from time to time, of putting a bottle on a rock and seeing who can first smash it into the river with a stone, results in cut pads for many otters.

The lads mean no harm, and I can assure you from my skilled stone-throwing experience that the result of a successful shot is similarly satisfying to dusting a clay pigeon. But the broken glass will endure as a danger for ages, and the cuts must be a considerable disadvantage to a nomadic predator. Thoughtless boys are not the only people who dump harm into the otters' living space. Many riverside gardeners are just as bad, chucking their debris in for the floods to give to somebody else. The trouble is that grass cuttings are not neutral; the bottom of the lawn-mowings heap is a festering place. Rotting

vegetation makes a huge demand for oxygen, which harms fish. There is a village near Yeovil, Stoford, which keenly enters 'Best-kept Village' competitions. All the grass verges are beautifully mown, (and devoid of wild flowers), but the grass cuttings are all tipped down the bank beside the bridge into the river. There is a sort of septic glacier of rotting plants continually leaching into the stream. Why is the state of the village stream not included in the judging of the competition? If I were the judge, it would carry the most marks. I have mentioned this abomination to the Environment Agency, but, when last I looked, they had not stopped it.

They did very little about another occasion that I contacted them. I took my dogs for a walk one summer's evening, and met a boy fishing, who asked me if I knew anything about fish, as the ones he was after were behaving strangely. He showed me shoal after shoal of fish, all beached on the shallows with their faces out of the water. While he had been quietly watching his float, a tractor had reversed down to the water's edge and dumped a back rake of what he called hay into the river.

Almost immediately the fish had started to rise and rise, and then had voluntarily beached

An artificial man-made river with nowhere for an otter to hide.

themselves to try to obtain some oxygen from the air. The load had not been hay, but the sweepings of old silage from the bottom of the silage pit, which was being cleaned out prior to the next crop coming in. It had at once started to grab all the available oxygen in the slow-moving pool where the lad was fishing, and it continued to affect all the fish for a considerable distance, as it progressed down river. Although the EA found that there was a complete kill-off of invertebrates starting at the fresh tractor tracks, and a healthy population under the stones immediately upstream, and although hundreds of fish were dead, they felt they could do nothing.

Of course the river more or less repaired itself in time; it gets a lot of practice at doing that. The EA records each separate incident originating from a 'point source' as it meets it, but cannot consider the overall accumulative effect of all these little incidents over the years, nor the steady deleterious effect of the ongoing diffuse infusions of slurry and contaminated silts, such as the constant run-off from open-cast pig farms. However, the fishing fraternity is starting to work towards improving the health of the river habitats, and the EA is supporting them as much as their ridiculous finances will permit. All politicians are banging on about the environment, ecology, sustainability, and other generalised and all-embracing concepts, while the reality is that the budget for practical environment-enhancing actions has been slashed to pay the European fine incurred by the incompetence of another department.

Habitat management

In my youth, the fishermen managed the rivers principally for the benefit of the fishermen. Work parties in the spring would cut out overhanging branches and trim back the skirt of vegetation trailing in the water's edge, in order to open things up for their casting.

The aim was to make the pools accessible, but there were incidental benefits for the fish and for other forms of aquatic life. All the trimming let in the light which is the basis of the food chain: without photosynthesis a river becomes a drain. But the tidying of the lower banksides left the fish without a home; like any other creature fish have needs and preferences for where they live, and one of their main requirements is security. They feed avidly when there is an abundant hatch of fly, but at other times they like to lie doggo, out of harm's way from the likes of herons or cormorants.

Every fisherman will testify to blank periods when the fish were doing nothing, and then bursts of activity when it became possible to catch several fish. During the quiet times they need a refuge, and this should be under the overhanging plants at the water's edge, the ones that the fishermen used to trim out of their way. Happily, this attitude has now changed; a consultant advised our club recently that the best investment we could make would be bankside fencing. This would keep the stock back from the water's edge, and allow the banks to stabilise, so that there would be no silt trodden in, and a fringe of plants would establish naturally, to shelter the fish and to encourage the insects.

But before we put the fences up, we should thin the alder trees. After the phase when it was the custom to open up the river for casting, there was a reaction in favour of tree preservation, not just along rivers, but everywhere. Tree preservation orders were introduced, and all trees except commercially useful conifers were to be considered a good thing. This led to farmers and riparian owners leaving the self-seeding alders to their own devices along the banks. It even became part of the received wisdom that the alders held the banks against the winter floods. In fact you can see that the opposite is the case.

The alder is not naturally a riverbank plant. It prefers braided swamps and marshes, with slower and shallower water, and it has evolved to out-compete other plants in such a situation. Very few plants can grow beneath an alder; the bare ground means that the alder gets all the nutrients, and grows vigorously. Along a river such as the Tone, the alders used to be cut as useful timber, and from the stump, other shoots would sprout to replace the tree. So, when it became the norm to leave them alone, there were 7 or more saplings growing vigorously from every root, and, as they prospered, they increasingly killed all other vegetation beneath them.

The final result is a dense wall of light-obscuring trees that prevent water plants from growing in the stream, which severely reduces the insect life. And rather than holding the banks, the bare and unprotected ground at their base is prone to erosion by the power of the winter spates, so, gradually, the trees isolate themselves, until they lose stability and fall into the river. This is ideal from the alder's point of view; that is the way to recreate the lowland swamps that our Iron Age ancestors tamed, the ideal habitat for such trees.

Many fishing clubs are now working hard towards the better concept of a well-fenced and fringed river, shaded by a few trees, but with plenty of light to encourage in-stream plant life, and thence insects, and thence insect-eating fish. There is a colossal spin-off of incidentals such as dragonflies, kingfishers, even otters. If the demise of most of the alders allows the growth of otter-friendly trees with good root systems such as ash and sycamore, so much the better. There was among environmental graduates an indoctrinated prejudice against sycamore, as a non-native species. But they have been here for a very long time, and those who use their eyes for themselves in the north of England will see that their tentacle root systems hold the banks extremely well, and provide excellent otter holts.

I am glad to say that an enlightened environmental consultant persuaded the authorities to allow the deliberate planting of sycamore at a new sewage treatment plant near Watchet recently. The otters will benefit directly from that, but the point of all this explanation about fishery management is to emphasise that whatever we choose to do to our rivers affects the otters in some way or other, even if they are far from our thoughts when we do it, and the benefit is indirect and incidental.

Misusing otters for 'nimby' purposes

This unavoidable involvement of the otters in all our waterside actions can be a source of conflict, of course. People propose what to them seems a reasonable waterside scheme, only to have it opposed on environmental grounds. In some cases this is necessary. The development of a chalet park on the Lune had recently to be modified to protect a breeding holt. In other cases people over-react.

Otters are not so fragile that they cannot live alongside us. The Kendal and District hunt used regularly to leave otters in the gasworks at Milnthorpe, or in the drain under a bustling caravan park on the Wyre. I get quite cross when people try to recruit me in some NIMBY battle, very often people who should know better. I have recently been asked to oppose a pop music evening on behalf of the otters, but I declined to support the killjoys. The worst that the racket could do would be to get the otters to shift to another part of their extensive territory, always assuming they were not there already on the evening in question.

The selfish inhabitants of another village wanted to use otters to block a proposal to develop the yard of a derelict hide tannery as a children's go-cart track, on the grounds that the river ran alongside the site, and the otters would be disturbed. They used to use a holt very close to the tannery when it was in full operation, so a few kids on go-carts would really not faze them much.

I declined to support their objection: firstly, the yard was back from the river bank, secondly, the focus of the activity onto the track would ensure neglect of the banks, and permit a good fringe of natural vegetation, and thirdly the karts would go quiet at tea-time, and the otters would then have the place to themselves. As the site was a good kilometre from the village, it seemed to me an ideal place to put an activity that might benefit the bored and underemployed youth of the area, something the village worthies are concerned about, but for which they have few practical proposals.

However, that was not my concern; my point was that the scheme as proposed could only benefit the otters, and that it is immoral to oppose something just because otters are sometimes present on a river.

The worst case of this misuse of the presence of otters was when an official of the Environment Agency rang me to enquire whether otters had returned to a river on the edge of Exmoor yet. I told him that they recently had. "Oh good," he exclaimed, "Now we can oppose that bungalow." I disapprove of this so strongly that I am tempted to name him, although he is a nice bloke and his heart is in the right place on these sorts of issues.

Otters are not weapons. Because they are affected by everything we do on the rivers, we ought to consider the effect on them of what we intend to do before we do it, so that we mess them about as little as possible, but we should

Plenty of good cover for otters along this river.

never use their presence to protect our own quiet and selfish solitude.

The villagers did not know that there were otters on the stretch by the tannery; they rang me in the hope that there would be. That is in the same league of dishonesty as the importation of otter spraint to the site of the Newbury bypass, so that it might be "discovered" and the supposed otters used to hold up the road the objectors wanted to stop. Suppose there really had been otters there; would it have been a legitimate move for the beleaguered people of Newbury who desperately wanted a by-pass to go out and remove or eliminate them? Or can only those on the moral high ground employ deceit?

Other manipulations of the habitat are designed to affect the otters directly. The current vogue seems to be for the installation of otter holts. Farmers can get points towards the agri-environment schemes for things which benefit wildlife, such as beetle banks, new ponds or home-made otter holts. Whereas a beetle bank will increase the number of beetles, and a new pond will soon develop a whole range of aquatic plants and insects that could not manage without the water, the provision of the otter holt does not benefit the otters in quite the same direct way.

Very few of the many holts recently built will have resulted in an increase in the number of otters; most of them are inadequate or unnecessary. From time to time pictures appear in the local papers of the Brownies beaming beside an "otter holt" they have made with the help of a "wildlife ranger". Logs were arranged on a riverbank to form a series of tunnels and chambers, and it was then roofed over with brushwood to make it snug. The intentions are good but most of them are far too small for a large animal to feel secure in.

The sleeping otter needs to be well away from the outside world, and its possible dangers,

so a bigger and more complex heap is what they prefer. The spoil heap from a bulldozed hedge would be ideal.

Artificial holts

There was such a pile in our parish. When the three riverside fields changed hands, the new farmer made it into one, larger field, and at the same time tidied up the much-neglected tangle of fallen branches and logs along the riverbank. There was strenuous objection from some in the village, who called in the tree warden, who made him stop, because the trees were black poplars. The owner's insistence that they were willows carried no weight. It was winter, there were no leaves to clinch the identification, and she had the clout, so he had to stop two thirds of the way down the field. In the spring he was proved right, but by then the improvement had stopped.

However, there were two benefits: the village loves the cleared bit, with its increased birds and dragonflies, and easy access into the water for all their dogs, and the cleared logs

A view of Marie White's excellent artificial otter holt on the otherwise featureless Huntspill river.

and stumps made a large pile of debris the size of a bus, or bigger, which the farmer carefully stacked on the inside of a big bend. More fuss from the amenity brigade about that, of course, but the otters, and foxes, and nesting birds, all approved. The river ran down one side of the pile, the footpath was tight to the other side, but the whole thing was so large that an animal could sleep sufficiently deep within it to be undetectable by all the damp dogs on the outside. Such a heap could not have been made without the use of farm machinery.

It was a convenience to the otters, but it would not by itself have increased their number. Each otter has many resting places along its territory; one more may be nicer, but it is a luxury not an essential. When people consult me about building a holt, I always use the analogy of opening a new bar in the town. People will undoubtedly go to it for a drink, but it does not follow that they would have died of thirst without it.

Holts, like bars, are usually built for the benefit of the proprietor, not the customer. Certainly my artificial holt was. We had lived here for many years, and shared our stream with an increasingly stable otter population, but when we had a digger in for something else it seem a good chance to put in a drain across the corner of the paddock, a drain with two ends and no purpose. It has one exit onto the stream, and the other into the deep channel which takes the overflow from our pond, but it does not convey any water. The idea was that it would be nice for me if the otters occasionally dwelt on our patch rather than always passing through.

That the otters did not really need it was shown by their lack of interest. I felt a bit like an estate agent with a poor property on his books. They found it soon enough, explored it and sprainted nearby, but it was a long time before they used it, and even now it is occupied only

occasionally, by a passing dosser, not a resident.

I do not think this is because it is badly designed. The basic layout was used in many hunt artificials in former years, and many of those were very successful in holding otters. The idea was that the hunt created a simpler holt which would encourage the otters to rest in a place that the terrier could evict them from.

There would be fewer days on which the drag led to the location of their quarry in an impregnable natural feature. Some of them were very sure finds, others were less popular with the otters, as mine is. But I do get a little proprietorial glow on the occasions that they do deign to visit me.

Marie White had better success with her two holts. The Huntspill river runs dead straight for eight engineered and featureless kilometres near Bridgwater. It was part of the water system for the ammunition works at Puriton, a completely artificial, canal-like channel. Otters could not use it, as there was absolutely no cover, so Marie, who worked for the Environment Agency, got two holts put in.

The artificial holt in close-up, showing the pipe (arrowed) and the thorny protective shrubs.

A short length of pipe, a manhole liner for the chamber, some thorny plants as protection, and a bit of fencing to keep the stock off until the prickly plants established themselves, was all it took. There was instant benefit for very little cost, thanks to the imagination and energy of one enthusiastic woman. Not only can otters now reside on that length, but it forms a link in a circuit, and strengthens a whole area of territories.

The provision of artificial otter holts is to some extent a chicken and egg conundrum. The hunts put them in, for their own benefit, in the days when there were plenty of otters. When the otters disappeared nobody bothered for a while to put new ones, or to maintain the old ones. Then the Otter Havens Project put in a large number, on rivers without otters, to try to tempt them back: it was the main opinion of that time that it was lack of cover that had extirpated the otters. Of course, on very bare and over-engineered rivers, an artificial holt may make a big difference. But otters had collapsed pretty well everywhere, so much so that some of us thought building holts was akin to putting out bait for the dinosaurs.

It would be lovely if it worked, but, without some dinosaurs to start with, it never will. But if you have got some dinosaurs, that shows that they can manage without the bait. If they could not, you would not have any to bait for. That we have such a good set of otters shows that we do not really need any more artificial holts hereabouts. With a territorial animal, it is not the same as nest boxes to increase the density of blue tits. But it may well be the case that the 40-year-old holts dug by the Otter Havens people are now being used gratefully by the otters that subsequently returned, and it could well be that their return to some areas was hastened by this provision of refuges. As far as I know, nobody is still aware of just where or how many holts were put in.

The Otter Trust breeding programme

More recently still, provision of holts was part of the release programme of the Otter Trust. This organisation was founded as long ago as 1971 by Philip and Jeanne Wayre, as a logical extension of their successful wildlife collection in Norfolk. The Wayres cracked the supposedly intractable problem of breeding otters in captivity. Many others had tried, including several prestigious zoos, but the only previous success was rumoured to be a Victorian vicar whose otters reared young.

However, the Wayres discovered how to do it regularly, and set about building up a collection of otters as an educational facility, and for possible release. This was more difficult than it now sounds. Otter were in short supply in those days, and the few stock animals that they were able to collect, otters rescued from various predicaments, matured and bred as slowly as they do in the wild.

Gradually, numbers increased, and in 1983 the first three otters were released into the wild, on the Blackbourne, in East Anglia. East Anglia was the focus for all the initial releases. It was the Wayre's own area, and, because it is such a highly developed grain-growing area, it had suffered a massive infusion of the harmful chemicals, and its previously plentiful otters had been almost totally wiped out in the decline.

The procedure the Otter Trust devised was to wait until the otters were almost fully mature, at over a year old, and then to install a group, consisting of a young dog otter with one, or sometimes two, nubile females, in a pen on the banks of the chosen river. The river had to be suitable, in that it had cover and fish; it needed to be as secluded from disturbance as possible, and the locals should be otter friendly.

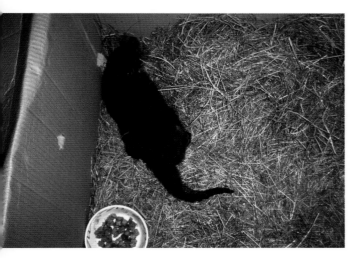

An orphaned cub on its way to the orphanage.

The easiest condition was that it should not already have resident otters.

Once the group had settled down in their new surroundings, the riverside gate would be opened, and they would be allowed to make their own tentative forays into the world outside, until eventually they ceased to come back for the food, and thus declared their independence. The idea is that, being proto-adults, they will form a sexual group, and stick loosely together in the chosen area, and mate and breed. This worked well in many places. However, like all theories, it went better on paper than on the ground.

Especially in the early days, there was understandable concern about the suitability of the sites. After all, if the rivers had been otter-benign, they would not have lost their otters. The chemicals involved are known to be persistent, and cumulative; their toxicity lasts for decades in the river silts, and in the flesh of the eels. Further, East Anglia is a highly developed place, and the waterways are subject to considerable agricultural and recreational pressures.

It is impossible to find a remote and secluded stretch with good habitat over all of the large

distance that an otter normally occupies. The selected conditions could only obtain over a short distance, so wherever an otter is put, some of its territory will be considerably less than optimal. The project was criticised from the very start by those who felt that the otters were being released into places that had shown that they could not sustain otters, and that this was at the least futile, and possibly even cruel, to consign them to an inevitable, lingering death.

By the end of 1987, 14 otters had been put out in 6 releases, 6 dogs and 8 bitches, one of them a replacement for a dog otter run over in the Minsmere bird reserve. The Trust claimed that in the first four years 13 litters were bred by released bitches from three of these groups, and, in addition, two second-generation bitches had bred: there were grandchildren to both of the first two releases. That means that a bitch released in 1984 bred a bitch cub, which bred a litter in 1987. Such rapid success showed that the anxieties of the critics were wrong; the area could support otters again.

This should have told us all that it was not the area that had been the cause of the decline. It was not the removal of physical features in the otters' habitat that had done for them, but the introduction of poisons. Now that they had been withdrawn, the otters could start their recovery.

The Trust expanded the programme, and by the end of 1999, 17 years later, it reported that 117 otters had been let out in 38 releases, and that they had registered 69 known litters of cubs from 18 of these releases. The report concludes, "Breeding is now so commonplace that it will be difficult to keep track of it the future." The project was undoubtedly a success, and was responsible for the restoration of the otter to the east of England.

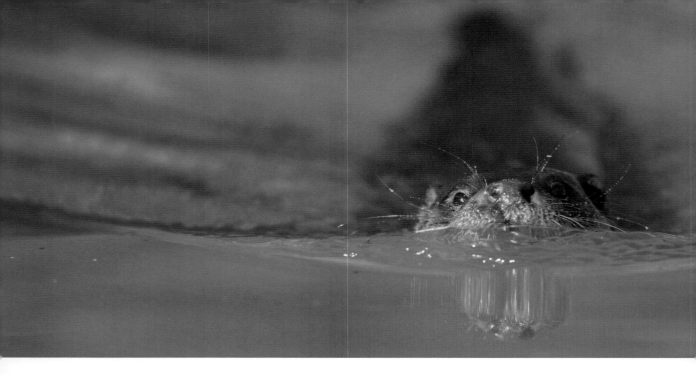

Problems with releasing

It was not just as straightforward as this simple statistical outline suggests. The breeding programme became very successful, and a considerable number of cubs were being produced regularly. Their cuddly attractiveness added to the appeal of the three "Wildlife Parks" to the general public, and the money from the entrance tickets was increasingly necessary to support the considerable cost of rearing so many youngsters.

Otter cubs destined for release need a lot of secluded space, and have to be fed on expensive food for about 15 months. Without regular litters of cubs for the zoo-going public, the scheme would have been too costly. But the regular production of young otters meant there was a bit of a queue for release, and great pressure to find more sites. In 1989 there were three releases, of 6 otters, 2 of them far to the west in Wessex. By May 1991 9 otters had been exported to the Dorset/Wiltshire borders. There was concern about this, as it was in contravention of the agreement that otter releases would only take place in the barren east of the country.

It was felt that otters bred in a zoo, in close proximity to other animals, including dogs and cats, but especially foreign species of otter, might be carriers of some infection to which the precarious, remnant, indigenous otter population would have no immunity. In order not to endanger the tentative recovery of these few western otters it had been agreed that no otters should be introduced west of a north-south line going roughly through Manchester and Portland Bill. These Wessex release otters were not welcome to those of us in the area.

But the Otter Trust had otters to find rivers for, so they carried on unabashed. There were 4 releases in 1991, 1992 and 1993, five in each of 1994 and 1995: 62 otters in 5 years. That the trust was under pressure from overproduction is shown by the change in the pattern of these releases: initially they followed the original recipe of one dog and two bitches, but in six of the later releases they put out two dogs and two bitches.

As the idea was that the dog would establish a territory and mate with the two females, this could well have been a recipe for severe fighting between the dog otters, and one of them being

Otters swim low in the water giving the observer little to see apart from a powerful bow-wave and flat head.

Itchen in Hampshire in 1993 were very closely related.

A photograph taken at the time shows that one of them had a deformity of the foot. In my opinion it should not have been released, nor bred from. But this genetic peculiarity turns up in DNA studies, and has proved useful in tracing the spread of the progeny of that otter, and mapping the spread onto other rivers.

It was this close relatedness of the Itchen otters which nearly scuppered the trial of DNA identification in spraints. An adult otter and an immature bitch gave the same genetic finger-print. The most probable explanation is that the dog was released with his own daughter, and the cub of that incestuous mating carried the same six genetic codes.

Cross-bred otters?

There are some indications that a mating took place between an European otter and an Indian smooth-coated otter, during the early period when the zoo was less specialised to the Eurasian otter breeding programme, when it had otters of other species on display. This might well have happened; otters are skilled escapers, and at mating time would exploit any weakness in their cage fencing. It was alleged at the time, and bluntly denied, but otter keepers still have two lists in their stud book. That we do not know the full story of what went on can be deduced by maths. During the breeding programme the Trust's newsletters recorded the successful births each year. It also subsequently published the number of otters released. There is a larger number of cubs unaccounted for than

driven away, to be 'wasted', in conservation terms, on his own. The urgent need for more sites meant that the parameters of suitability had to be relaxed, and the trust incurred further criticism over the unsuitability of some of the sites.

There was a row over this at the Homerton Otter conference. This criticism was aired openly, with slides of some of the allegedly unsuitable sites. But instead of this issue being debated, the following morning Philip Wayre made a brief and terse statement dismissing it all, and left the conference. He was a practical man who liked to get on with facilitating actions. All the criticism of the scheme that he believed in so passionately had the effect of making him less communicative and of stifling consultation. So there is no full record of what went on in this important restoration project. From a small beginning with orphan otters from Scotland, he had built up a considerable breeding stock.

Other orphans had been added from time to time, but some of the progeny was definitely too inbred. The pedigrees of his breeding programme have not been recorded, but there is no doubt that the otters released onto the can be explained by recruitment to the breeding stock.

It is a pity that secrecy and lack of transparency so affected the excellent work that the Otter Trust did. As the achievement was due to the effort and skill of one man, or of one man and his wife, it was in a sense no business of anybody else what they did or how they chose to do it. And some discretion was necessary to protect the released animals from interference.

But secrecy was inappropriate for the release of so many so large animals which perforce would turn up in the lives of so many people along the rivers, and rumours arose, which persist to this day. I have no method of judging their validity, but merely record that many people believe that the Trust released otters into the toe of Cornwall after the derogation permitting the use of the banned chemical Aldrin was removed.

The otter distribution maps of the time show a persistent lack of otters in the areas where the spring bulb fields are, a gap that was rapidly and suddenly filled. Other people were suspicious of the location of the Trust's third collection of otters at a remote farm high on the ridge of the Pennines, on the grouse moors above Bowes. They considered it an unlikely site for a tourism and educational facility, and that it had been chosen as convenient to the headwaters of three huge river systems, the Eden, the Lune and the Tees, to take surplus animals. Such stories engendered criticism.

Thames otter releases

The Trust could have done with supporters and allies, rather than critics, after its last major release venture. It released otters into the top of the Thames. Nothing wrong with that, as the Thames was the last major catchment without an established otter presence, but the method caused a lot of problems. The Thames is a very inhabited and much-used river, so remote and people-free sites were obviously hard to find.

The one they chose, not far from Stroud, was in itself suitable, but very close to the trout farm of my former pupil, the one I tried to discourage from a career in fish farming. It was also close to a major carp fishery, Horseshoe Lake, which is the carp man's equivalent of Twickenham or Lords.

Pressure on fisheries

To compound the problem this caused, they used the same release site repeatedly, and let a total of 17 otters go in a succession of releases. Not a good idea: the first lot had got nicely territorial and established when out came the next ones, and then again.

Inevitably, this caused fighting, and some degree of dispersal, but at least some of the otters reacted by regressing socially, and reverting to a less aggressive stage, so that they could operate as a gang of juveniles without stress. Several were to be seen fishing together, which upset the trout farmer, and sent the carp men ballistic.

There had already been sore mutterings in the carp magazines about the damage done by otters, and exaggerated and baseless claims that the return of all the otters was entirely due to conservationists releasing them in droves all over the place. You can still be assured that all the otters on the Somerset Levels are releases, and they will give you exact numbers. It is incontrovertible folklore, and I don't bother to argue anymore. They "know" that the scheme when we surveyed the population by means of their DNA in the spraints was a release scheme: how else would we know the DNA of the individuals?

So the high profile appearance of numbers of otters which were in fact the product of the overdone Thames releases was petrol on the flames, and the cause of a major and protracted

Otters are adaptable creatures and can find food in small ponds just as they can in fast-flowing rivers.

anti-otter campaign in the fishing magazines. This hostility was not confined to the upper Thames, but spread generally to other parts, another wedge between the conservation movement and the country dwellers and users. And in the end it is the otters that suffer from people who feel justifiably aggrieved.

Otter groups and fishermen

However, some degree of tact and understanding has recently helped calm the conflict. As Somerset is a major coarse fishing area, we see several cases of conflict every year, and I have taken part in conferences run to help fishery owners solve the problem of otter predation. Devon Wildlife Trust was ahead of most

others in this, and held several field meetings at fisheries where the redoubtable Mary-Rose Lane had been successful in installing preventative fencing.

In Somerset we produced an informative pamphlet which we sent to all fishery owners; not only did this ease matters, in that it showed the fish owners that we were aware of and sympathetic to their point of view, but the pamphlet gave the web address of the advice about fencing to be found on the Specialist Anglers Alliance site. There is now a booklet giving practical help, published by the Environment Agency, so perhaps this winter we will have fewer conflicts.

It is in winter that the bigger, specimen fish are taken. Carp are not native to Britain, and we are at the northern limit of the temperature range they can tolerate; in times of cold weather, when the water temperature drops, carp become dormant, and burrow into the mud on the bottom of the pond, where they lie in a torpid state. I watched a bitch otter hunting for them one afternoon.

At a meet of the harriers, Ron Greenway asked me to come and see the otter in his pond; so at teatime the next day I went to his farm. To my surprise, the pond was the one in front of his house in the farmyard, slap bang in the middle of all the activity of a busy working farm. The otter had already been active before I got there, so I thought it worth waiting to see if it reappeared. I leant on a wall, with my face towards the evening light, and waited a short while.

A bitch otter reappeared and started to patrol the pond, which was about the size of a tennis court. Three of us were plainly visible, and the otter undoubtedly had noticed us. The water was muddy, but she caught an occasional small roach, although that did not seem to be what she was mainly seeking in her underwater quests.

Suddenly the surface wave convulsed: she speeded up and chased something rapidly across the pond. When she emerged she had a medium-sized carp by the snout. I had never seen that before. She had been ploughing through the mud layer to bump up a torpid fish; that was why the water was so dirty. When she hit one, it fled, and she chased it, but as an otter's mouth is so small compared to the size of the animal, being designed for holding eels and small fish, she could not take hold across its back, but had to catch it by the face. Ron was thrilled, but then he had no commercial interest to protect. In summer she would have been very lucky to catch so strong a fish; it would have been too speedy for her.

Welfare releases

The Otter Trust has wound down its activities, and the only releases taking place nowadays are by other organisations for welfare reasons. There are comparatively few of these, so they cause less aggravation, but they are still the subject of controversy. I try not to get involved in this aspect of things, and to confine my activity to the monitoring and welfare of the wild population as a whole. I do not know quite where I stand on the question of individual releases of rehabilitated otters.

I am totally against the release into the countryside of hand-reared fox cubs: it serves no conservation purpose, as foxes are common and widespread animals, in no need of conservation assistance to maintain their population; it is also unkind to the individual fox, in that it has to try to fend for itself without a proper basic training in hunting skills, and it has to learn the hard way that many people are hostile to foxes, especially to half-baked ones that have to turn to domestic prey to be able to cope; it also upsets the farmers, pheasant rearers and guinea-pig owners who have the orphans dumped out on them without permission, another unnecessary wedge between "conservation" and country management.

By contrast, otters are not so numerous that I would advocate the humane putting down of all orphans, as I would for foxes. There is, or there was, a conservation argument for trying to rear them and restore them to the population. Otters were amazingly scarce. On the other hand, the welfare of the individual animal has to be considered, and it is increasingly for welfare reasons that orphaned or abandoned cubs are taken into care.

I have considerable doubts about the kindness of releasing them to fend for themselves, particularly as the authorities, principally the RSPCA, have not moved on from the policy they adopted in the early days of the recovery of the otters, that an orphan ought to be returned eventually to the catchment it came from, on the grounds that each individual animal was a scarce and valuable part of a fragile and small population. Every possible breeder was needed back in its population, to ensure the continuing future of that group in that area.

Now, with many more otters on many more rivers, the chances are increased that a cub will come from a numerically strong population. When, after a year or so in the orphanage, it is returned to its place of birth, even if it can learn to feed itself, it will be sure of a hostile reception. To me, this negates the welfare purpose of the exercise, so much so that I think such a release is possibly actionable in law as cruelty, or certainly negligence, as would be the release of a naïve kitten near some terriers.

There is a case that it could be released into an unpopulated area, to start a population off, but there are three snags to that; such areas are more difficult to find as the population expands; it is increasingly probable that any area still devoid of otters is for some reason unsuitable for them; and the fishery owners of that area would have a genuine gripe that they had been given a problem, which is harder to accept than one that occurs by natural regeneration.

The half-tame, released otters are most likely to venture into domestic situations for their food, and to make a nuisance of themselves.

Orphaned otters

An instance of this arose in Somerset recently when a wildlife rescue organisation, 'Secret World' released 3 cubs. Splish, Splosh and Splash had quite rightly been picked up not far from Secret World. A farmer had heard them calling and complaining in the small hours of the night, but had sensibly left them until the afternoon to see if the bitch rescued them. They were still crying at teatime, so knowing that they would not survive another cold night in the open without food, they were taken into care. Lucky little things, they went into the skilled and dedicated care of Ellie West, who reared them well until the time came to make

them more independent, and to start feeding them by remote means, and weaning them of human attention.

Months later, they went out into the wild. As far as we know, two of them took to it well, but the third, a young dog, grew too familiar and took to hanging around houses and gardens, the back of the pub even, so he was caught up again, for his own good. What to do next? He is an expensive gurt animal to keep, he could go somewhere more remote, but the problem is that he, having lived wild in our rivers for some months, is almost certainly a carrier of the bile fluke, and so he cannot really go to another area. Infection was the reason that there was supposed to be an agreement that otters would not be released west of the line through Dorset.

According to our spring survey, we have a full house of otters, and cannot really offer him a secure and vacant patch. Luckily he is not my problem, but I do sympathise with the tender and caring staff of the rescue centre, whose aim is only to do the best they can for the welfare of the individual animal. Lord knows I have spent long hours looking along the riverbanks after the death of lactating bitches, searching for bereft cubs. Quite what I wanted to do with them if I found them I do not know.

I think that the few genuine orphans ought to be used where possible for educational purposes, and be retained in captivity in some sort of wildlife park or well-run collection. I am not thrilled at the conditions in some of the tourist attractions I have visited, but others seemed to have contented and prosperous otters, which were well looked after and serving a useful purpose for education and conservation. Only the genuine orphans should be taken.

There are some cubs which are rescued because their mother was absent; she cannot carry more than one at a time. Others have been deliberately abandoned by the parent as being defective; although they seem to do well at first, with plenty of devoted care, they fail at the onset of adulthood, and would probably have died earlier under the rigours of life in the wild. Nor do all the reared cubs survive. There is a stress from being captured and reared which can cause them to die before being fully grown.

On one occasion I was involved in an attempted release. Two cubs had been found wandering about a busy trading estate, so to stop them being run over they were taken to the RSPCA, where a sensible member of staff realised they might still be able to be reunited with their mother. The idea was to take them back to the lake in a cardboard box, and to let them squeak on the shore, until the bitch heard them; she would then come across, put her paws up on the box, which would then fall over and release her family.

Sadly, other people in the RSPCA animal centre prevented this happening. They ensured that the cubs had an enormous meal before we collected them to take them out. My wife and I spent several fruitless hours looking through the car windows at a distant and totally silent box containing the sleeping cubs. So we had to return them to the centre, where they became frequent stars of a animal TV show, and gained lots of publicity for the rescue centre. What a pity. I wonder what became of them.

The most interesting part of the night was when the cubs were to have their DNA taken. They were offered a spatula with cotton wool on it, to collect saliva. The ferocity with which they attacked and savaged it was a revelation to me; even at that tender age they had all the aggression and instincts of a truly wild predator. Perhaps such animals are better to be released than kept in captivity. It is too difficult a problem for me to think through.

Avoiding road-deaths

Most orphans are the result of the bitch getting run over when she has to leave the cubs to fish. It seems to happen when the natal holt is up a sidestream, or back from the main river. The mother leaves the cubs and follows the tributary down to the river to feed. This process drifts her some distance downstream from her entry point, so, when she stops feeding and wants to return rapidly and anxiously to her abandoned and vulnerable little ones, the quickest route is to cut directly across the corner rather than to follow the way she came.

This short-cut means she misses out the river bridge under which she could pass in safety, and tries to nick across the road above, as being more direct and quicker. This explains why we sometimes find dead bitch otters some distance along a road from where one would expect an aquatic animal to be. These instances are hard to prevent, as we cannot predict the secluded corner the bitch will chose for the birth holt. However, we can and do try to do something about more regular sites of road accidents.

By carefully logging all the places where otters have been run over, we have identified problem sites, and in many cases we have been able to install mitigation. One such place is near East Lyng, on the edge of the Somerset Moors. The main road comes down a slight slope from the ridge on which the village perches above swampy land, and at the first rhyne (stream) crossing we had a succession of casualties.

It was hard to see why; it was an unassuming little ditch, going from nowhere to nowhere, and the levels are a chequerboard of such ditches. What was the attraction of this ditch? Somebody noticed that this ditch was bendy and had meanders, unlike all the others, which ran more or less straight, as one would expect a field boundary to. This clue revealed that in the middle ages it had been the course of the main river Tone.

In those days there was fierce and possibly unchristian rivalry between the monks of Wells and the monks of Glastonbury, two vast ecclesiastical centres on the edge of the wetlands, situated only about 5 miles apart. The wealth of these religious powerhouses was based on agriculture. The river Tone was the boundary between one lot and the other, so one dry summer the cunning abbot got the workforce, who regularly did drainage and land reclamation, to built the Baltmoor wall, and thus divert the river to its present course, thereby draining and grabbing the whole of Northmoor from the other lot of neighbour-loving brothers.

As a taxpayer you may be interested to know that you have just forked out some £4 million to repair this wall and protect the town of Bridgwater from the inundation that would follow its breach.

Deduct it from the collection plate next Sunday, and rejoice that the wise otters rose above such sly dishonesties by taking no notice of the difference and continuing to follow the former, much reduced, river course.

Prism-reflectors help crossing otters

Once we cottoned on to what was happening we were able to install prism reflectors on low posts, so that the lights of an oncoming car would be turned into the face of an otter trying to cross the road. We have proof that they worked, in that the death rate reduced, and the only otter to be killed was much farther down the road, at a place where no otter had crossed before, just beyond the last reflector post. Such posts were tried in Germany for the protection of deer, but they resulted in some places in an increased mortality; the deer would not face the lights, so they were waiting until daylight, when the lights ceased.

This meant that more deer were trying to cross after dawn, at the beginning of the rush

hour, and meeting more cars. But we have found them successful for otters, although their installation is not as simple as it sounds. They have to be on slight and shallowly-planted posts, which would not damage a car in the event of an accident. These posts are sited on the verge where they impede the mechanical mowers; the mower drivers soon learn that they knock down quite easily, so we lose them steadily.

It is against health and safety for us to undertake the hazard of mowing them ourselves. The present state is that we have got the council to replace all the posts, but there is a monastic-style dispute between the council and the Environment Agency as to who pays for the replacement reflectors, so there aren't any yet, and the tractor drivers have to mow round some useless stumps. They say that most of the people from the Levels are descended from the (celibate) monks anyway. Certainly little changes in these parts; like the otters we keep to the old ways.

Weirs and sluices

In other places we have been more permanently successful. Marie White, who also installed two refuges on the bare shores of the Huntspill, was responsible for putting gabions of stone up the vertical sheet steel weir at Ilminster. What poor awareness of where he is and what goes on around him must the man have had who could erect as a weir a four foot high wall of steel pilings at right angles to the flow, and put it so that the walls of a bridge turn it into a box with impassable sides, so that no animal or fish can progress upstream.

It was this unimaginative monstrosity that forced the last bitch otter on the Isle out onto the main A303, to die in the May bank holiday traffic. She was pregnant with three big cubs, almost ready to be born. With their death all otter activity on the river ceased for more than

207

10 years. Then padding of two otters was found. Marie moved swiftly, and had the gabions in place within a week. The otters sprainted on them at once, and later that year cubs were born and raised. However she could do nothing much about the A39 at Minehead, where some idiot flood-prevention engineer has forced an entire Exmoor river through a steel strainer and then down a slanting pipe with a top sluice to make sure the pipe is always full.

The Environment Agency has installed a high level ledge on the relief channel, but it was a problem to get the otters to deviate so far out of their way as to find it. We tried fencing, to force them away from the sluice towards the ledge, but the local badgers resisted diversion and dug under it. Marie had the fence strengthened; the badgers dug deeper. We had to admit defeat when the badgers started to lift the tarmac on the footway at the edge of the road. Inflexible brutes.

At Beer Wall there is another engineering monster. The trouble is that it is easier, and presumably cheaper to incorporate the walls of the road and the bridge into the flood regulation structure you are constructing, rather than build a freestanding gadget some distance upstream in the field, so that an otter can safely come out round it without going near the road. At Beer Wall two rivers, or rather drainage channels, come together just above the bridge, and go under a straight bit of a busy road only some 20 yards apart.

Every otter in the two catchments is funnelled towards those two bridges, which are blocked by the flood relief structure, so they have to go over the fast road. Martin Jacoby and I investigated the problem and submitted a plan which would involve a high level drainpipe as an animal underpass. It must have been expensive, but to their credit, the Environment Agency dug up the A372, and installed it. It works well, except that the fishermen, tidy minded but confused, use it to stuff their picnic rubbish in. It saves them having to climb over a stile to the litter bin in the layby. Inflexible brutes.

The golf course otters in Spain

Martin has had other successes with otters. He now lives in southern Spain, and was for a while the naturalist to the prestigious Valderrama golf course. Under the enlightened guidance of the owner of the course, Martin was able to develop the considerable wildlife potential of the land surrounding the playing areas, including looking after the otters which turned up in the water features.

These features are very economical of water, an especially precious resource down there; it is all pumped round and recycled, so it keeps a good level despite the heat, and it attracted otters. They were leaving fish remains very conspicuously on the short grass of the course itself, so one of the groundsmen offered to get rid of them. Mr Patino, the owner, was outraged, and ordered extra fish. He has been an enthusiastic supporter of the movement for golf courses to be ecologically friendly, and when his course was awarded the honour of hosting the Ryder Cup, he got Martin to erect display boards explaining the wildlife richness of different features, and to draw the attention of the press and TV people to them.

Our otters enjoy the hospitality of sensibly managed golf courses, too. Vivary Park is a small municipal course in Taunton. It does not look ideal wildlife habitat, but the otters use it just as much as they do the more rural setting of Oake Manor, with its extensive lakes. They are adaptable creatures, and all they need is a little thoughtful care from us people, with whom they have to share the rivers.

Toleration of disturbance

In Taunton again, the council men used every summer to strim the river banks down to the cobbles, to remove any plants which might catch debris and decrease the flood carrying capacity of the river between its flood walls. When this happened, the otters used to quit the town; they were totally exposed under the street lights. As soon as this was explained to Mr Viv Verrier, the parks superintendent, he changed the system. The men now do alternate banks on alternate years, and the otters, having a slight protective fringe of vegetation, continue as they want.

It will be interesting to see the effect on the otters of the extensive works to regenerate and improve the whole of the river corridor through Taunton. Emma Daniel and her friends are surveying the otter presence before, during and after the work. This will be the Somerset Otter group's third such survey of the effect of our activities on these alleged fragile and nervous creatures.

We recorded the presence of otters regularly during the frantic, all night and all day efforts to re-open the main railway after a tanker train crashed and caught fire. For over a week there were lights, men and machines continuously at work in a quiet country field, with the Tone running past.

The otters sprainted as usual. Some years later, Russell and Sara Gomm monitored the effect on the otters of extensive repairs to the M5 bridge over the Tone. The engineers accepted a few sensible precautions, such as not storing plant at night too close to the water, and the otters carried on as normal. As they did when Jodey Peyton and Emma Kobliseck monitored the construction of a flyover and a Park and Ride facility beside a favourite stream junction.

The centre of Taunton is busy and noisy. Valderrama golf course is much manicured and managed, a far from natural area. Yet otters can dwell in such places. Some of the influences of Man are unwelcome to the otters, but many are not, and some are beneficial, either directly or incidentally. It is wrong for the conservationists to oppose developments as often as they do on behalf of the otters.

All it does is to devalue conservation. The daftest instance was the East Devon council planner who stopped a proposed short link between two bridleways at Five Fords, on the Culm, "because it might disturb otters." Such disproportionate lack of sense served only to alienate the riding fraternity, and to increase the widespread perception of conservation as an inconvenience and a nuisance.

CHAPTER FOURTEEN

PRESENT POPULATION

At the start of this book I tried to convey to you my excitement at finding the otter footprints on the bank of the river Tone on that pivotal February morning 21 years ago. Because some people might not find a few paw prints in the mud as electrifying an experience as I did, I have tried to explain the origins of my obsession with the otter.

Who knows into what degenerate directions my interests might have led me, had the otters not returned from the brink of extinction?

Certainly it would have freed up a lot of time. But those imprints were of more significance than just to me personally.

Until that otter crossed the watershed from the Exe onto the Tone, the depleted otter population had been confined to the rivers of moorland origin in the far south-west of England. Forty percent of the otters found in the whole of England in 1977 were living on rivers rising on Dartmoor. This was the first individual to move towards the east, the tentative start of an

211

amazing revival of the keystone top predator of our aquatic life systems. It was fortunate that the revival started when it did: things were pretty desperate, and any more delay would have reduced the numbers too low for them to breed back up again.

Most of the earlier effort after the turn-around went into locating the remnant populations, and into trying to make sure they continued to prosper, or, more accurately, just to continue to exist. I have related what went on, and my involvement in it, because I feel very strongly that we must continue to be vigilant. There is no reason to suppose that new circumstances could not arise which would have a similarly lethal effect.

It now begins to look as if the new bile fluke may not be quite as devastating as we at first feared, when we discovered it in 2003, but it is early days yet: much research is needed, and I know of several dead otters who would disagree with that assessment. The slowness and inadequacy of the authorities' reaction to the arrival of this new parasite shows that we do not have any better system in place to protect the otter population as a whole than we had the last time.

However, there is now a programme of post-mortem examination of dead otters. That is a great improvement on the situation before: at the onset of the first crisis, the wildlife pathologist working in the government's labs was forbidden to examine dead otters. But as far as I know we do not have in place any system for evaluating the results or for taking any action should the results show up a problem.

In terms of otter research, most of the present energy and cash is still directed towards assessing the spread of the population. This is the sort of thing I did for many years, and still do, via the Somerset Otter Group's two surveys. 2009 is the year of the 5th National Otter Survey, and if it shows as it almost certainly will, according to the anecdotal word along the riverbanks, that the increase has continued, and that otters have both spread to new areas, and filled in at increased density on areas newly-colonised at the time of the last survey in 2000, then the general supposition that all is basically well now with our otter population will be vindicated. But if it does not register a continuing revival, what then? Who would do what? When we had questions asked in the House of Commons about the potential effects of the bile fluke, the ministry men blocked them all with a straight bat, and nothing came of it, although the parasite is known in other countries to be a serious problem for domestic animals and, in places, people.

This is not merely a theoretical anxiety, a personal hang-up perhaps from my involvement at the time of the big collapse: it is borne out by two recent developments here in Somerset. Let me put them into context.

I have related how I investigated the otters on the borders of Somerset and Devon during the years following the start of their spread. That was the obvious place to concentrate at the time, the area immediately to the east of the rivers of Dartmoor and Exmoor. That is where the otters were.

At about the same time, Libby Lenton started her series of checks in the Brue valley, farther east, where a small relict population had hung on in the wet peatlands of the Somerset Levels. Gradually, the otters spread eastwards, until the two groups joined up. At about this time Libby became ill, and had to give up her meticulous and invaluable surveys. So a small band of enthusiasts got together to carry on her work, and from this the Somerset Otter Group developed, and also its present set of surveys.

All the active members have a patch, a stretch of river which they monitor once a month. The presence or absence of otters is recorded, and the results go to the Somerset Environmental Records Centre. This provides on a smaller

A relaxed and healthy otter, oblivious to how close her species came to extinction in England in the 1980s.

scale and at a greater frequency, the same sort of information that the National Surveys give: the extent of our population. However, we go one stage further. Our regular surveys had confirmed, some time ago, that Somerset held a widespread population, and that the activity we were now recording was evidence of a settled population of resident animals, and no longer the sporadic result of the random and unconstrained wanderings of a few frustrated pioneers, the sort of result that our early surveys of the Levels had revealed.

So it was time to try to do more than look for just presence or absence. By organising our now quite large team of surveyors to undertake a two-day survey on co-ordinated dates, we should be able to evaluate the strength of the population to some degree. All the members do their patches on the same Saturday and Sunday; the fresh evidence found on the Sunday is plotted onto a map and gives a snapshot of the position of these restless creatures, arrested all on the same night.

Something bad happened to our otters in 2006. We did nothing about it, and we do not know what it was that went wrong. But all our accumulated evidence points clearly to a severe reversal in the fortunes of the otters. As far as we can tell, things have since picked up again, but supposing that they had not: to whom should we have gone with our findings? If that considerable and sudden decline had continued, what would be the appropriate response?

It was discovered (although recognised far too slowly) by a bunch of enthusiastic amateurs using equipment no more scientific or sophisticated than a pair of wellies. In that we produced some figures, percentages and a map or two, we were slightly less anecdotal than the wise old otter hunters who first stirred the rumours of the last disaster. But little else has changed; certainly not the speed of reaction.

The second reason I am anxious that we remain vigilant towards our precious otters is this: I fear that the 5th National Survey may also find that little improvement has taken place in part of our area. The indications from our recent surveys are that the eastern side of our county still holds a rather poor number of otters. I have already told that the portion of the Brue Valley that is included came in at only 27% and 29% in the last two surveys. Our recent results from that area point to a continuing disappointment, and I shall not be surprised if the National Survey again finds little improvement at a time when otters will have seemed to prosper.

Nobody knows why this may be, but my point is that even though they have expanded their range and generally prospered, we still have amazingly few individual otters in the whole of England, spread very thinly across any one area. Had the local downward graph of 2006 continued for the subsequent years, Somerset by now would have very few otters indeed.

There are those who will say that it is understandable that I am making a fuss, 'he is known to be besottered, so take no notice, there are plenty of otters.' Or, if it is a carp fisher: 'there are too many d… otters.' When I disagree, it is not because I am partisan, one for whom there could never be too many otters.

It is because I think that after all these years of following their fortunes and recording their activities in my notebooks, I believe I know two things relevant to the refuting of that dismissive point of view. Firstly I think I can show that the otters are self-regulating, and so, while they may

The Torridge, a perfect location for otters, and the setting for both book and film of Tarka the Otter.

be seen to have increased in the period since the last big survey, they cannot have increased in all areas. Some places, including most of Somerset except the easternmost two valleys, are already full. There is no room for any more otters; they themselves will police that, territorially. I think I can demonstrate that they already do so.

And secondly, I think I now have a reasoned estimation of the sort of numbers that involves. Philip Wayre was widely quoted as defending the success of his reintroduction scheme in East Anglia, by claiming that there were now 'hundreds' of otters in that region. He was of course, I assume, using the phrase as a figure of speech, a synonym for "lots, but not exactly sure how many." I think we would all be surprised at how few hundred otters there are in all of England: each one takes up a lot of space.

If anybody were to make such a claim for Somerset, even for just one hundred, I would ask where he thought he could fit in so large a number. I suppose that in a fruitful breeding year, the bitches with cubs might push the total to about that figure. But our surveys suggest that there seems to be space for many fewer than that, counting adults only. We have now done 15 annual two-day surveys. The early ones were incomplete, because we had too few people to cover everywhere. And as they were done before the otters had fully settled in to all the areas they now occupy, the totals from them are not fully comparable to more recent results.

They do however show the pattern of occupation on some rivers, and serve to show the sort of spacing we might expect in other places. Since the turn of the century we have had enough people to consider the situation across the whole county to the west of Mendip. The small eastern segment, where the rivers flow the other way, towards the Bristol Avon, got its otters back much later, and we have not had such a good depth of coverage from there.

As it is still obvious to most people that otters are too invisible, too indistinguishable and too mobile to count, or even for us to estimate their numbers, I must proceed cautiously, and, first, attempt to justify my claim that we have made some progress towards quantifying the animals we never see. That way, at least those who dismiss what we claim will have reasons for doing so based on what we have done, and not just on their sensible preconception that the attempt itself is futile. I have already gone into the maths and the thinking behind our annual surveys of the River Axe, on which we base a claim that the catchment regularly holds about 10 adult otters.

As it is just a one-day survey, it does depend on quite a lot of subjective judgement and interpretation. Each surveyor has to decide on the freshness of the otter spraints, and then the adjudicators have to assess the distribution of the dots on the map. The main thing in support of this system is the consistency of the results with themselves. If our method was haphazard, our results would probably be more erratic from one year to the next.

In our minds, if not in scientific logic, another reason to have confidence in what we say we have found on the Axe is the similarity of our results from this river to those from the Tone. Two important factors make the results from the Tone more robust: they are the result of two-day surveys, and there is an objective scientific yardstick to compare them with.

The freshness of the evidence is beyond dispute, and the interpretation of it fits with the results obtained by the DNA feasibility study. The fieldwork for that pioneering research was done in 1997/98, probably before the otters had fully re-established themselves. Although the very top and the lower end of the river were not included as sampling points, the DNA scheme revealed 7 resident animals, positively identified and located by the DNA found in their spraints. Subsequently, our Otter Group has done a comprehensive survey of the catchment on 8 occasions. The layout of the river and its tributaries make the adjudication of the results definite in most cases; we found in the DNA scheme that the otters did not swap from one tributary to another, and this seems to still be the case. So the element of subjective guesstimating is minimal on this catchment.

The findings are remarkably consistent from one year to the next. The average of the maximum possible interpretations is 9.6 otters, ranging between 8 and 11. The minimums come out at 8, between 7 and 10. This population size, and its distribution along the streams, fits well with what the DNA evidence showed. It also fits with what one might in theory expect. There are some 50 kms of main river; that should be space enough for 5 otters. The three main tributaries should hold one each, bringing the total up to 8. There is room on the Halse Water for one more, as there may be in the complex of streams around the Back Stream, or up the Blackbrook below Taunton. That makes 11. I cannot really see where you might find space and food enough for many more. There are strong grounds for thinking that this survey method gives a meaningful result for this catchment.

So it is with some confidence that I dare to expand it to cover the whole of the county, and to be so unconventional as to try to estimate our otter numbers. The same sort of evidence, and similar reasoning about it, gives a total of about 65 otter ranges for the county. We have never found quite as many as that. Every year we have a few unavoidable gaps in our coverage, and need to extrapolate as sensibly and cautiously as may be, to work out a putative total, and every year recently that has been between 60 and 65. There are obviously more animals than that alive at any one time. There are bitches with cubs, some of which we know about, others we have not discovered. The method we adopt

counts only one otter for each set of sprainting places; that total is irrefutable, and by sticking to the rule we get a consistency for comparing one year with another. There may also be dispersing juveniles and transients lurking in odd corners. I suppose we are not really counting animals, but locating territory-holding otters; many of the lesser members of the population are surplus, and will be wasted, either by cars, or by the bile fluke, or by aggression.

Although this is a strong population, and although the distribution map shows a pleasing spread of otters into almost all parts of our water systems, it is also a worryingly small number of animals to ride out any kind of reversal. Had whatever went wrong in 2006 continued to kill otters at the increased rate, a very few years would have been enough to register attrition. Happily, the problem did not continue, and the reduction was made good almost at once, presumably by recruitment from the normal breeding in previous years. On the Tone, the cub production in 2007, following the disaster, dropped to one litter, against an average of 4 a year, but the overall population indicators seemed healthy.

That points to the way forward for me and the other enthusiasts. If we could expand our knowledge of the breeding that occurs in our area, we would have reassurance that the otters are sufficiently healthy to continue to prosper. And we might make some tentative progress to discovering more about the otters themselves. Ian Coghill wisely cautioned an audience of otter studiers that we would know little about our deer if all we went on was their droppings. But it is almost true that that is what we have been studying: the natural history of the spraint and not the sprainters. I feel we ought to move on, and that here in Somerset we have enough otters for us to make a start.

Breeding bitches are the way in to the secrets, I think. An accurate assessment of

Charismatic but not to be trifled with. A big male will defend his patch aggressively.

their numbers and location would be a start to discovering the structure of the population. For instance, we have just completed a big survey of spotting, and have located between 23 and 26 otters on or around Exmoor. The distribution shows that there are several otters resident on the high moor. I had half expected the survey to confirm my suspicion that otters visited the small moorland streams, but that they also dropped down to bigger and more productive stretches of water, to find enough food.

The results show otherwise. The moorland otters on several rivers have other otters below them, presumably blocking off the lowland stretches. I would very much like to know more about the hillbillys: are they outcasts, immatures which cannot get a better territory; is their life fully viable, or are they struggling to make ends meet? One answer to that would be the discovery of cubs up in the headwaters.

That would point to a viable social structure among the Exmoor otters, and show that it was more than just a refuge for surplus animals.

Not only do we have very little idea about what goes on in the world of the otters, about the age range, about where juveniles disperse to, about the relationship between a dog and his bitch, or bitches. They seem to greet other otters they know playfully, affectionately even, but aggression is widespread, and the wounds are found on both sexes.

To what extent does the bitch have to hide the cubs from the dog? Three otters allowed themselves to be watched, and photographed while browsing on sticklebacks in a roadside ditch. The group was a big dog, a bitch, and her nearly full-grown cub. They fed together for over an hour, apparently peacefully. Yet the cub kept the bitch between it and the dog all the time, or perhaps the bitch guarded the cub; either way, the cub was protected by the body of its mother, and exhibited some nervousness, in that it kept physically in touch with its mother for much of the time.

I observed a bitch taking a cub for a swim. She put it into the water, to overcome its bankside nerves. It seemed to enjoy its swim, but mother kept her body between it and the open water the whole time, and when she hauled it out, the now-enthusiastic cub found its way back in blocked by the presence of mama. Another mother quelled the demands for milk of a full-grown cub larger than herself by "pin down". She got on top of his neck and shoulders, and stayed there. The cub had to decide either to submit or to fight; it submitted.

These are tantalising glimpses into the way of life of an intelligent higher animal, a species whose behaviour rises above the level of mere instinct. Yet so difficult are they to see, that we have only hazy ideas even about the sprainting on which we rely so much for our "understanding". It is known from zoos that otters have a very rapid digestive system, yet we do not really understand how much of an otter's output is necessary excretion, and how much a territorial statement.

We think that some otters are at pains to hide their presence by not displaying spraint, but do not know which otters, nor how frequent this is. In those otters that are not insecure, and which do spraint mark, how many of their spraints are deliberate statements, and how many just necessary voidings? I have seen otters spraint on the bank where they had gone after feeding, without seeking a sprainting rock.

My son observed an otter below him in a large reservoir. It swam along the shoreline, and landed at intervals to spraint; it did not fish or forage at all. He had the impression that it

was engaged in a marking patrol. In the case of anal jelly, we know little about it, except that it is misnamed. Originally it was supposed to be a scent mark of pure product of the anal glands which give the mustelidae their name, the secretion that is coated onto each spraint to convey social or territorial information. It is the mucous that protects the gut from the sharp bones and scales that come through the rapid digestive system, and which needs renewing frequently to retain its effectiveness. But it appears to be used demonstratively.

Can an otter produce it deliberately? Does every class of animal produce it equally, or use it equally, or is it more frequent in some sorts of animal or at some times of their cycles? We just do not know. Although we have studied the natural history of otter dung for years, all we know is that sometimes you find AJ, and often you don't.

There is so much that would be fascinating to know about. Some of it would also be useful in understanding what is necessary for their conservation. The post-mortems pose several interesting conundrums. They reveal that different types of otter are more likely to be killed at different seasons: immatures in summer, dog otters in late autumn, and a peak of bitches in late winter/early spring. Why should this be? Most of the rivers we monitor have exhibited a pattern whereby there is a sudden peak in otter deaths. There were 9 on the Exe in 2000, against a ten year average of 3.6; there were 17 on the Parrett in 2006, against an average of 9. The Avill lost 9 in 2000/01, against an annual average of 2.6. We have no idea why this happens.

To what extent does drought affect them? It has been suggested that a severely dry summer may prevent bitches achieving the weight to enable them to breed. Certainly we had a poor otter year following the last dry summer, but against that otters seem to hang on in Spain

and even Morocco. I have recorded them in the water features on Valderrama golf course, in southern Spain, and even in the Draa river on the edges of the Sahara desert, in Morocco.

This confirms that otters as a species must be highly adaptable. It would be interesting to find out how much they vary in their habits and behaviour in England. It seems that small groups have learned behaviours, and prey preferences, habits which are transmitted to subsequent generations in a restricted area, such as raiding fishing boats for food, or concentrating on waterfowl as prey.

My ongoing interest in otters has been rather like walking across the moors towards a succession of horizons. In front of you can see the skyline of the ridge you are slogging up, but as you think you are about to attain the horizon the outlook changes and the skyline of the next ridge is there in the distance.

When I started, there were too many otters to discern any patterns. Next I was recording the decline, presiding at their wake. I tried to help examine the possible causes, and looked into diseases, especially the incidence of blindness. After the pivotal, and chance, discovery of the first returning wanderer, I was busily engaged in mapping their recovery.

The optimism of the DNA scheme was short-lived, and followed by the anxiety of the discovery of the bile fluke. But the DNA opened the way to progressing from mapping the extent of their recovery towards quantifying it. From that important summit I can see a very steep and imposing hill ahead of me, the top of which is lost in the mist and clouds. That is to discover more about them as individual animals, starting with the observation of family life.

It was one returning otter which led me back to the Tone, away from enjoying the dramatic and highly visible certainties of peregrines and birds of prey, to worrying about the mysterious possibilities of our enigmatic, nocturnal top predatory mammal. Perhaps I can now get to know one individual better. I had high hopes of this last December. A bitch had her cubs in the drain I installed on our stream. We gave her supplementary fish, to try to prevent her going across the main road to feed. She accepted it well, until she stopped. She had moved the family. But, just as the February footprints got my enthusiasms going again, so that bitch's brief sojourn has revived the attraction of these fascinating and enigmatic creatures.

All the adjectives that fit what we observe of these charismatic creatures are ones that we associate with health and wholesomeness; qualities such as being lithe, sleek, athletic, muscular, graceful, playful, even resourceful, independent, and intelligent. Darkness hides much, so we seldom see the downside to the otter, ruthless aggression, or rapidity of attack. We can omit those from our mental picture.

I am not alone in being in some way mesmerised by the unique quality of an otter every time I see one. On each occasion, be it a fleeting glimpse or a prolonged period of observation of behaviour, something about the presence of the creature absorbs me entirely, so that it is only afterwards that I can digest what was going on and make some reflective notes. Every otter seems so much more completely good at being an otter than lesser species are at their given metier.

Each otter is as totally absorbed in being an otter as I am at watching it. It is for me in some way an ultimate animal, and to see one is an ultimate experience.

Luckily, I know that there are others for whom this happens, and it is my pleasure to dedicate this summary of a lifetime's absorption to two younger enthusiasts, who will, I am sure, long continue to carry a torch for these wonderful animals that we are so privileged to find still in our crowded, industrial island.

INDEX

PHOTOGRAPHIC ACKNOWLEDGEMENTS

I am indebted to the following photographers who have generously allowed me to include their fine photos in this book (numerals indicate pages on which the photos are placed):

Ian Anderson 6, 22, 130
John Crispin 173
The Environment Agency (Sharon Robinson) 131
Charlie Hamilton-James 1,7, 11,18, 21, 22, 25, 35, 37, 43, 44, 48, 51, 54, 57, 61, 65, 66, 85, 89, 91, 100, 103, 104, 108, 110, 113, 125, 129, 135, 139, 144, 146, 149, 150, 155, 158, 166, 169, 172, 177, 183, 186, 187, 191, 195, 200, 211, 214, 219
Alison Hickman 13, 14, 28, 38, 39, 49, 53, 60, 69, 71, 72, 77, 82, 90, 92, 94, 97, 106, 116, 179, 180
Karen Jack 52
Mary-Rose Lane 67
David Mason 5, 8, 15, 19, 47, 81, 83, 87, 121, 203, 208, 213, 217
John McMinn 50, 56, 80
Arthur Richards 114, 117, 119
Anne Roslin-Williams 17, 74
Peter Stronach 68